SCM RESEAR

Broken Bodies

Broken Bodies

*The Eucharist, Mary and the Body
in Trauma Theology*

Karen O'Donnell

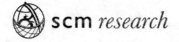

scm *research*

© Karen O'Donnell 2018

Published in 2019 by SCM Press
Editorial office
3rd Floor, Invicta House,
108–114 Golden Lane,
London EC1Y 0TG, UK
www.scmpress.co.uk

SCM Press is an imprint of Hymns Ancient & Modern Ltd
(a registered charity)

Hymns Ancient & Modern® is a registered trademark of
Hymns Ancient & Modern Ltd
13A Hellesdon Park Road, Norwich, Norfolk NR6 5DR, UK

All rights reserved. No part of this publication may be reproduced,
stored in a retrieval system, or transmitted,
in any form or by any means, electronic, mechanical,
photocopying or otherwise, without the prior permission of
the publisher, SCM Press.

The Author has asserted her right under the Copyright,
Designs and Patents Act 1988
to be identified as the Author of this Work

Scripture quotations are from the New Revised Standard Version
of the Bible, Anglicized Edition, copyright © 1989, 1995 by the
Division of Christian Education of the National Council of the
Churches of Christ in the USA. Used by permission.
All rights reserved.

British Library Cataloguing in Publication data

A catalogue record for this book is available
from the British Library

978-0-334-05837-3

Typeset by Manila Typesetting Company
Printed and bound by 4edge Ltd

Contents

For my Mum and for James

Acknowledgements

This book is a version of my doctoral thesis. My thanks, therefore, first and foremost, must go to my two supervisors – Siobhán Garrigan and Morwenna Ludlow. You have inspired and supported me as you have walked this work with me. I am forever grateful that you trusted me to go my own way and offered me signposts where I needed them. I am also grateful to Susannah Cornwall and Rachel Muers for their extraordinarily helpful comments on this work and to David Shervington at SCM Press who has been incredibly patient and supportive throughout this project.

I thank the Department of Theology and Religion at the University of Exeter for being such a welcoming, inspirational and collegial place to undertake this research. I've relished every opportunity you have thrown my way. I am grateful to the Arts and Humanities Research Council for a generous scholarship, without which I would not have been able to pursue this research. Various portions of this work have been presented at conferences around the world in the last few years. I am grateful to all those who asked good questions, made interesting suggestions and encouraged me.

My final thanks go to my family. To Lisa, Lydia and Georgie for brightening the tough days. To my Dad and Wendy for some diligent proof-reading. I thank my wonderful Mum for encouraging me every step of the way, celebrating every success with me, and making me believe that I could do this. Thanks, Mum. Lastly, but by no means least, I thank James for his patience, support and love throughout this work. My work and my life are better because you are in them.

I

Trauma in Bodies,
in Memories, and in Theology

Christianity's earliest and most persistent doctrines focus on embodiment. From the Incarnation (*the Word made flesh*) and Christology (*Christ was fully human*) to the Eucharist (*this is my body, this is my blood*), the resurrection of the body, and the church (*the body of Christ who is its head*), Christianity has been a religion *of the body*. We relate to God as corporeal bodies, and in our relations with other human bodies, we experience God. It is the recognition of these experiences of God in our bodies (our own and those of others), and the *critical* reflection on these experiences, that leads us into embodiment theology.[1]

Hope Deferred

Birthed in the wake of the embodied experiences of the crucifixion and resurrection of Christ, Christianity has always been a religion of the body. While attitudes towards the body over the last two millennia have not always been positive, bodily experiences of baptism, communion and community have remained at the core of the Christian faith. When one takes such embodied experience seriously – and, particularly, in the case of this book, the bodily experience of trauma – one not only engages

---

1 Deborah Creamer, 'Toward a Theology That Includes the Human Experience of Disability', *Journal of Religion, Disability and Health* 7, no. 3 (2008), 57–67, at 63. Italics Creamer's own.

in theology that is deeply meaningful and practical, but one also engages in a practice that opens up new and insightful perspectives into both theology and human experience. Simply put, taking trauma seriously has powerful implications for both the theological method and theology.

My own interest in trauma theology and its potential for a positive contribution to constructive doctrine came through a recommendation made by a colleague. She referred to the work being done by Serene Jones on miscarriage and trauma. I had experienced multiple reproductive losses and curiously sought out a copy of the book my colleague had mentioned, *Hope Deferred*,[2] and devoured it in the space of a couple of hours. It was the only piece of pastoral theology about miscarriage and infertility I had read that didn't make me angry (and I had been given many such books to read while I was trying to get and stay pregnant). The writers of this book, all women, knew how I felt; they took my experience seriously, and they used the experiences I shared with them to look to theology. This was not to offer me glib assurances of all things working together for the good, or to suggest that I needed to have more faith, but rather to say that these experiences, that are common to so many women, mean we need to read scripture and doctrine through the lens of this trauma.

Immersing myself in Jones' account of reproductive loss – the miscarriage of her friend, her own miscarriage and the feeling of leaving pieces of herself in various bathrooms, the sheer volumes of blood that seem to accompany this loss of life – allowed me to begin to process my own experience. But it was her reflection on the womb as a grave site and the experience of death within the Trinity that both comforted me and kindled my theological exploration of trauma. Her work demonstrated the enormous potential that trauma had to offer to theology.

Drawing on the psychoanalytical study of trauma, trauma theology is concerned with bodies and memories, and with

---

2 *Hope Deferred: Heart-Healing Reflections on Reproductive Loss*, ed. Nadine Pence Frantz and Mary T. Stimming (Eugene, OR: Resources Publications, 2005).

bodily memories. It is easy to see how the experience of miscarriage is intimately connected to both bodies and memories, but I will present here a vision of Christianity that is profoundly entwined with bodies and memories. As I noted in the opening quotation, Christianity is a religion of the body. It is with these early and persistently body-focused doctrines that I will be concerned. Taking this opportunity to present an embodied theology of trauma will reveal the interconnectedness of what I will show to be the fundamentally embodied beliefs of the Christian Church: the doctrine of the Annunciation-Incarnation event, the Christological discourse, the doctrine of the Eucharist, and the doctrine of the Church.

I found my faith again somewhere in between my contemplation of my own uterus, trauma theology and the Eucharist. I returned to the liturgical tradition of my childhood and found there the beauty of sacramental theology. I discovered that, while trauma theology is a very young field of constructive theology, the principles of trauma and trauma recovery were well understood by the ancient liturgists. While they did not have the language to describe trauma, these ancient liturgies were infused with the scent of trauma and trauma recovery. Christian liturgy holds within it an unclaimed memory and experience of trauma, and an unacknowledged instinct for trauma recovery.

The Emergence of Trauma

Before demonstrating the scope of the field of trauma theology, it is helpful to consider the ways in which trauma has been studied over the last 150 years given that the development of trauma theology is but one avenue in the evolution of this field. Suffering is 'the state of undergoing pain, distress, or hardship'.[3] This is not, as I will demonstrate, the same as trauma. The category of trauma is a relatively new distinction and its

---

3 'Suffering', in *Oxford English Dictionary* (Oxford: Oxford University Press, 2015).

application beyond the fields of medicine and clinical psychology is even more recent.

There is no universally accepted definition of trauma in any of the fields that have concerned themselves with the study of trauma, its victims and its symptoms. Judith Herman defined trauma with reference to power structures.

> Psychological trauma is an affliction of the powerless. At the moment of trauma, the victim is rendered helpless by overwhelming force. When the force is that of nature, we speak of disasters. When the force is that of other human beings we speak of atrocities. Traumatic events overwhelm the ordinary systems of care that give people a sense of control, connection, and meaning.[4]

This sense of being overwhelmed is a helpful one when considering trauma. In the experience of trauma, almost all victims experience severe emotional distress, and most experience frequent flashbacks or nightmares – the intrusion of past memory into the present. When exploring why some people seem to emerge from this 'overwhelming' more readily than others, Dutch psychiatrist Bessel van der Kolk, who has spent the last five decades working with victims of trauma, suggested that the inability to integrate the traumatic event into one's understanding of reality results in a 'repetitive replaying of the trauma in images, behaviors, feelings, physiological states, and interpersonal relationships'.[5]

One's understanding of reality is, for the Christian, one's theology. Any event that cannot be integrated into this understanding of reality thus poses a problem for one's theology. Some trauma victims seem to come by this ability to integrate memories more readily than others. Historically, this has led to the

---

4 Judith Herman, *Trauma and Recovery: From Domestic Abuse to Political Terror* (London: Pandora, 2001), 33.

5 Bessel van der Kolk and Alexander McFarlane, 'The Black Hole of Trauma', in *Traumatic Stress*, ed. Bessel van der Kolk, Alexander McFarlane and Lars Weisaeth (New York: Guilford Press, 1996), 3–23, at 7.

blaming of victims for the states in which they find themselves. Women suffering from hysteria in the nineteenth century were often considered to be malingerers or simply insane. Men suffering from 'shell shock' in the First and Second World Wars were branded cowards and accused of moral weakness.

In both these cases, existing theology helped to support the blaming of victims. Women had been presented by the Church as being crazy, subhuman, the bearers of sin, and the gateway to death; therefore, it is no surprise that there was little sympathy for these 'hysterical' women. Similarly, some portions of the Church of England regarded the First World War as a Holy War. How could any man not fight such a battle? As these two examples, and others, show, theology is not removed from the issue of trauma.

It was not until 1980 with the publication of the third volume of the American Psychiatric Association's (APA) Diagnostic and Statistical Manual of Psychiatric Disorders (DSM-III) – the benchmark of psychiatric diagnosis and treatment – that post-traumatic stress disorder (PTSD) was recognized as a psychiatric illness. At this point, the APA felt it necessary to point out that traumatic events were 'outside the range of usual human experience'.[6] Herman challenged this definition, explaining that rape, sexual and domestic violence, alongside military trauma, are so common now that they can hardly be described as outside the range of ordinary experience. She concluded that such events 'are extraordinary, not because they occur rarely, but rather because they overwhelm the ordinary human adaptations to life'.[7]

It is difficult to account for the absence of trauma awareness prior to the long twentieth century. Trauma was certainly present in society – women have always been raped, men have always been sent to fight wars, as but two examples. However,

---

6 American Psychiatric Association, *Diagnostic and Statistical Manual of Psychiatric Disorders*, vol. 3 (Washington, DC: American Psychiatric Association, 1980), 236.

7 Herman, *Trauma and Recovery: From Domestic Abuse to Political Terror*, 33.

modernity has altered perspectives on trauma. Life expect-
ancies have increased and, for some, life is not as brutal as it
once was. The industrial revolution and the concomitant rise
of modern technology has fundamentally altered patterns of
human existence. A brush with death has become less common,
and thus when one does experience trauma it overwhelms 'the
ordinary human adaptations to life'[8] precisely because in the
modern world, adaptation to trauma is no longer ordinary. As
modern humans, we experience trauma differently from our
ancestors.

In the mid-1990s, there was a literary turn towards trauma
led by scholar Cathy Caruth. In her monograph, *Unclaimed
Experience: Trauma, Narrative, and History*, Caruth draws
heavily on the work of both Sigmund Freud and Jacques Lacan
as she seeks to explore the complexity of knowledge and language of trauma in the literature of a century marked by traumatic experience.[9] Caruth's work in literary scholarship draws
our attention to the somewhat surprising impact of trauma –
the telling of a reality or truth not otherwise readily available.
Reading through the lens of trauma unsettles us. It forces us to
rethink that which has previously been taken for granted and
ruptures traditional narratives.

As I noted earlier, there is no universally accepted definition of trauma. Trauma has many different definitions drawn
from the variety of different perspectives from which it has
been considered. A synthetic view of these varieties of definitions reveals that trauma is primarily concerned with *rupture*.
I conceptualize trauma, drawing both on analysis done in early
works and on the experience of the individual trauma survivor,
as being concerned with three ruptures that take place within
the trauma survivor. First, the trauma survivor experiences
a rupture in bodily integrity. This may be a feeling of being
unsafe, or an experience of injury or invasion of the body.
Second, the trauma survivor experiences a rupture in time.

---

8 Ibid., 33.

9 Cathy Caruth, *Unclaimed Experience: Trauma, Narrative, and History*
(Baltimore, MD: The Johns Hopkins University Press, 1996).

This may be a blocking of the memory of the traumatic event, leading to a gap in their memory timeline. Or it may be the repeated incursion of that past traumatic event into the present through flashbacks or nightmares. Third, the trauma survivor will experience a rupture in cognition and language. This may be due to the fact that they simply do not remember the traumatic event in its specificity and thus they cannot access it in order to be able to understand it. Or it may be that the traumatic event is beyond cognition and that the trauma survivor has no language with which to express what happened to them and how they felt about it.

Similarly, the process of trauma recovery encompasses three identifiable stages. First, the trauma survivor will need to establish their bodily integrity – they will need to know that they are safe. Second, the key to recovering from trauma is connected to remembering and to narrative. The trauma survivor must construct a trauma narrative that makes sense of what has happened to them. This is both a narrative of remembering and a narrative that can carry the trauma survivor in the future. Crucially, this, and indeed trauma recovery in general, cannot be done in a vacuum; it must take place within a community of witnesses who will hear and validate the narrative of the survivor. The final stage of trauma recovery, then, is connected to the third rupture – of cognition and language. This rupture serves to alienate those who experience trauma from the world around them. The trauma survivor must reconnect with society beyond the community of witnesses. Some trauma survivors reconnect by choosing to make their trauma a gift to the world through campaigning and advocating for other trauma survivors or by being open to the possibility of post-traumatic growth. This stage of trauma recovery has practical and pastoral implications.

These two accounts – of the experience of trauma and the recovery from trauma – are simplistic in their outline of the processes at work. I do not wish to suggest that these are straightforward, linear processes that will always take place in this order and subsequent to the accomplishment of the previous stage. This is because trauma is complex and individual. Each person's experience of trauma is unique. However, these accounts can be helpful in attempting to draw some conclusions about the nature of trauma and recovery from trauma.

Central to the understanding of trauma is the concept of somatic memory. Bessel van der Kolk noted: '[T]he imprint of trauma doesn't "sit" in the verbal, understanding part of the brain, but in much deeper regions – amygdala, hippocampus, hypothalamus, brain stem – which are only marginally affected by thinking and cognition.'[10] Rather, argued van der Kolk, the core of trauma lies in somatic memory, not in semantic memory.[11] Bodies and remembering lie at the heart of trauma and trauma recovery.

Trauma Theology

Theologians have always been interested in suffering, even before the theories and theologies of trauma became prevalent. The human experience and its seeming incompatibility with a God who is omnipotent, omniscient and loving has offered plenty of opportunity for reflection on the category of suffering and its relationship with theology. For example, in the second century, Irenaeus, Bishop of Lugdunum, posited an epistemic distance between humanity and God. Irenaeus argued that 'God made man a free [agent] from the beginning, possessing his own power, even as he does his own soul, to obey the behests of God voluntarily, and not by compulsion of God.'[12]

---

10 Mary Sykes Wylie, 'The Limits of Talk: Bessel van der Kolk Wants to Transform the Treatment of Trauma', *Psychotherapy Networker* 28, no. 1 (2004), 1–11, n. 22.

11 Bessel van der Kolk, 'The Body Keeps the Score: Memory and the Evolving Psychobiology of Post Traumatic Stress', *Harvard Review of Psychiatry* 1, no. 5 (1994), 253–65. Accessed online at www.trauma-pages.com/a/vanderk4.php on 11/08/15.

12 Irenaeus, 'Against Heresies', trans. Alexander Roberts and William Rambaut in *Ante-Nicene Fathers*, Vol. 1, ed. Alexander Roberts, James Donaldson and A. Cleveland Coxe (Buffalo, NY: Christian Literature Publishing Co., 1885), Book IV, Chapter 37.1. Accessed online at www.newadvent.org/fathers/0103437.htm on 01/03/16.

This distance in knowledge allowed for humans to exercise free will and to reach spiritual maturity through their decisions.

Suffering was part of this experience and enabled humans to become spiritually mature. This is the purpose of suffering according to Irenaeus.

> This, therefore, was the [object of the] long-suffering of God, that man, passing through all things, and acquiring the knowledge of moral discipline, then attaining to the resurrection of the dead, and learning by experience what is the source of his deliverance, may always live in a state of gratitude to the Lord . . . that he might love Him the more.[13]

The experience of suffering was taken seriously by Irenaeus, even as he sought to explain its purpose. Taking as his example the experience of Jonah, Irenaeus demonstrated the way in which he perceived suffering, and God's deliverance from such experience, to be for the good. Jonah's suffering allowed Jonah to glorify God all the more since he did not expect to be saved from it. Jonah's experience subsequently brought 'the Ninevites to a lasting repentance'.[14] While one may disagree with Irenaeus' view of suffering and whether suffering can have any purpose, it is significant that even in the second century Irenaeus felt it necessary to offer some sort of explanation for the embodied experience of suffering.

In the twentieth century, in the aftermath of the horrors of the Second World War and the events of the Holocaust, theologians such as Jürgen Moltmann visited the issue of suffering again. This time, the gap between humanity and divinity was not widened, but rather reduced. Moltmann offered a vision of God that does not allow suffering for our own good, nor is this God unmoved by our suffering. Rather, Moltmann offered us the Crucified God.[15] This God experiences the suffering of

---

13 Ibid., Book III, Chapter 20.2.

14 Ibid., Book III, Chapter 20.1.

15 Jürgen Moltmann, *The Crucified God: The Cross of Christ as the Foundation and Criticism of Christian Theology* (London: SCM Press, 1974).

the Passion deep within his being. He is a God that suffers alongside us. Irenaeus and Moltmann were both writing before the development of anything that could clearly be identified as trauma theory. Furthermore, they were, among many other Christian thinkers, concerning themselves with suffering and not with trauma.

In the post-9/11 period, theologians have become interested in trauma as distinct from suffering. Dominated by female theologians, particularly (although not exclusively) white, western, women, the field of trauma theology has endeavoured to take the embodied experience of trauma seriously. Theologians such as Serene Jones and Shelly Rambo have explored the impact of trauma on Christian doctrine and faith and examined how one might 'do' theology in the light of trauma.

These female-written theologies of trauma hold a number of features in common, with regard to both their methodologies and their results. First, all of them take embodied experience, as a category for 'doing' theology, seriously. Rather than seeking to mould experiences of trauma to fit with existing doctrines and theologies, these theologians begin with the experience of trauma as the 'real' and allow that experience to inform and challenge doctrine.

This is the second common feature of these trauma theologies: trauma becomes a lens through which theology can be viewed. Such a perspective causes a rupture in traditional narratives. This rupture allows space for the construction of new theology. Scripture and doctrine, when read through this trauma lens, are critiqued and challenged. Using trauma in this way reveals the extent to which traditional narratives do not respond to the traumatic experiences of those who would be reasonably expected to believe them. The lens of trauma reveals inconsistencies and inaccuracies, it highlights holes and tears in both logic and doctrine. This lens unsettles the words on the page and places the body of the trauma survivor next to the theory to ask if what is said is true. Trauma destabilizes narratives.

Third, these trauma theologians highlight the significance of witness in trauma theology. In the case of psychoanalytic approaches to trauma, the significance of speaking out one's experience of trauma and having it recognized within a community is often acknowledged. In responding theologically to trauma, the Church must be a listening community. As such, the Church must find ways of witnessing trauma that validate the narrative of the trauma survivor and offer, if required, a theology of trauma that is not lacking in respect for the body, the experience, or the ongoing nature of trauma.

Bearing this in mind, the fourth common feature of these trauma theologies is a return to the body. The body and bodily experience forms the foundation of this type of constructive theology. Trauma is, itself, a bodily event that cannot be understood except in a holistic manner. The memory at the heart of trauma is a somatic one. It is unsurprising, therefore, that the outworking of this type of trauma theology is embodied, material and concrete.

Trauma and Christian Doctrine

The Body of Christ as an ecclesial body is formed of the individual bodies that are members of it. Some of these bodies are traumatized bodies. And, like a blunt force trauma to a lower limb, the impact of trauma is felt throughout the body – accelerated heart rate, inarticulate cries of pain, unconsciousness, shock. If individual bodies of this body are traumatized, then the whole Body of Christ experiences trauma. Furthermore, this ecclesial Christian body bears the hallmarks of having experienced trauma. If we consider the symptoms of trauma then we find the ruptured sense of self in the very use of the term 'Body of Christ' – the meaning of which is unstable. We find that time is ruptured in this body – ancient events press into present day and make their presence felt. One can see this very simply in the liturgical year. Repeated activities such as confession, celebrating the Eucharist, praying familiar prayers, all bear the marks of trauma. And this body has a mysterious faith. While we attempt to put it into words, language always fails to fully capture the Divine or what it means to have faith and be part of this community. Given, then, that this body bears the symptoms of PTSD, what was the trauma? What is it that is being repeated and repeatedly making itself known? It is this somatic memory, the memory held in the Body of Christ, with which we must begin.

Understanding that the Body of Christ is a traumatized body also reveals ruptures that are significant for theological endeavour. In the first place, there is a rupture between the Divine and the human. One could, if one wished, refer to this as sin, but I prefer to regard this rupture as a gulf between natures. In the second instance, the rupture is the rupture caused by the theological abstraction of the body. One cannot 'do' theology without taking the embodied nature of such 'doing' into account. Theology comes from bodies in material contexts. Such an exploration reveals the need for a holistic approach to theology – one in which bodies of theology, the Trinitarian Body, the Body of Christ, and human bodies, are not separated out in an atomistic fashion, but rather are interconnected and informed by one another.

Somatic memory teaches us that memories and ways of remembering cannot be removed from bodily experience. Trauma is not a rare occurrence limited to those unfortunate enough to be in the wrong place at the wrong time. Rather, trauma is part of the common experience of men, women and children. Their bodies, necessarily then, hold the memory of trauma and it is through the body that one can be healed. Trauma theologians are seeking new language to explore this theology and this new language comes through the destabilizing of old stories and the reading of these revealed narratives with fresh eyes. Allowing the hermeneutical lens of trauma to bring theology into a new focus brings with it the opportunity to take these traumatized bodies – that belong to so many of us – seriously. This lens enables us to see past the traumatized body of Christ on the Cross to the other traumatized bodies in scripture. This lens allows us to find the somatic memory of theology not in suffering, torture and death, but in the Incarnate Body of Christ – ruptured, along with the body of His mother, Mary – in the Annunciation-Incarnation event.

The Hermeneutical Lens of Trauma

This book is about trauma and trauma recovery even as it is a process of trauma recovery in itself. While allowing the content of this research to shape its form, I will also allow trauma to constitute a hermeneutical lens. Trauma provides theologians with a tool to consider theology by and through allowing trauma to constitute the hermeneutical lens. I am not concerned with constructing a response to traumatic suffering. Rather, in probing the relationship between bodies and memory in connection with the embodied experiences of what I will term the Annunciation-Incarnation event and the Eucharist, I demonstrate that allowing the hermeneutical lens of trauma to destabilize narratives and challenge assumptions ultimately allows the construction of a theology informed by trauma that takes somatic memory seriously.

Jones demonstrated a method of theological mapping that also helps to both underpin and describe the work of my own project. She wrote of Christian doctrines as 'imaginative lenses' for viewing the world as well as being conceptual spaces which we inhabit.[16] If doctrines are conceptual spaces, then this project seeks to layer trauma over the landscape of Christian doctrine in order to expose the contours of theology. Focusing on the relationship between body and memory and taking the embodied experience of trauma seriously, this layering of trauma over the landscape of doctrine can help us to read traditional narratives in a new and helpful light.

If trauma is primarily concerned with rupture(s), then so too am I. This method of approaching theology intentionally allows trauma to cause a rupture in texts, doctrines and theologies. It is only when these have experienced rupture, and thus been destabilized, that there is a space for the construction of something new and fresh. For example, allowing trauma to rupture our understanding of the Eucharist opens up space for the construction of a eucharistic theology that not only

---

16 Serene Jones, *Feminist Theory and Christian Theology: Cartographies of Grace* (Minneapolis, MN: Augsburg Fortress Press, 2000), 16–17.

adequately responds to the experience of trauma, but also addresses the implications for (all) the body/ies in the eucharistic experience. As a therapist gently probes the trauma survivor in order to aid their recovery so too will I confront the ruptures in Christian doctrine in order to construct a theology that is holistic and takes account of the body.

A Journey into Trauma

It is my contention that trauma theory offers a rich vein of exploration for theologians that has only just begun to be explored. Drawing on the methodology of the trauma theologians I have examined above and identifying the gaps in the work already done in the field of trauma theology, this book is primarily concerned with two interconnected questions.

The core of trauma lies in somatic memory. While other trauma theologians have taken the body seriously, and have considered the place of memory, no trauma theologian has, yet, drawn these together. I will begin by investigating this concept of somatic memory in the context of Christian theology in asking: 'Where and/or what is the somatic memory in Christianity?' This is a question that has been overlooked in trauma theology. If the core of trauma is to be found in somatic memory, then, the somatic memory of the Christian faith must be explored.

If bodies are key to understanding trauma then it is with bodies that one must begin. The place in which body and memory come together, for Christians, is in the celebration of the Eucharist. I will interrogate these ideas further in the chapter on the Eucharist as non-identical repetition (Chapter 2) and in exploring the work of an ancient theologian – Cyril of Alexandria (Chapter 3). These two chapters are both concerned with bodily integrity (material, eucharistic and incarnational) and as such they correspond to the first stage of trauma recovery.

It is surprising, perhaps, that when searching for the somatic memory at the heart of trauma theology, one does not arrive at the Cross (the site of Jesus' traumatic passion and death), nor at the Resurrection (the site of the triumph of the body), but rather at the Annunciation-Incarnation event. This leads to my second question: 'What are the consequences of considering the Annunciation-Incarnation event to be at the core of Christian somatic memory?' Crucially, I will demonstrate that when one allows the Annunciation-Incarnation event to rupture the traditional narratives of Christian theology, one is left with a theological space in which to construct new narratives.

When the somatic memory of the Annunciation-Incarnation event is recognized as the traumatic event at the heart of the Christian faith, this fundamentally disrupts traditional theological narratives. Having already established that somatic memory, connected as it is to both bodies and memories, is profoundly demonstrated, for Christians, in eucharistic celebrations, I examine the ways in which narratives, so integral to eucharistic theology, of priesthood (Chapter 4), sacrifice (Chapter 5), and Real Presence (Chapter 6) are disrupted by this somatic memory. I construct fresh narratives in the theological space cleared by such ruptures. Neither priesthood, sacrifice, nor Real Presence can be understood when they are abstracted from bodies. In particular, I propose a Trinitarian understanding of priesthood, sacrifice and Real Presence informed by the concept of *perichorēsis*, that takes bodily experience – especially Mary's body – seriously.

Having considered my second question in terms of the foundational theological narratives of the Eucharist (priesthood, sacrifice and Presence), I will then examine the impact of trauma theology on the Eucharist in a narrower focus. I examine, in the following chapter, the corporate, ecclesial experience of the Eucharist. In Chapter 7, I demonstrate that reading the Eucharist through the traumatic lens of somatic memory locates Mary's body in a place of significance in Christian Theology, particularly in the Eucharist. In the final chapter, 'Body: A Love Story', I will draw these findings together using the motif of loving the body and identify that the result of this project is a call to love the body in all its guises.

2

The Eucharist as Non-Identical Repetition: What is Being Re-Membered at the Altar?

'Do this in remembrance of me.' (Luke 22.19)

The sacrament of the Eucharist is the place in which bodies and memory come together. Jesus, in his celebration of the Passover meal with his disciples – taken as the model for subsequent celebrations of the Eucharist – refers to the bread as his body, the wine as his blood, and instructs a repetition of *something* as a way of remembering him. In searching for the somatic memory at the heart of Christianity we find the Eucharist to be a helpful starting place, precisely because it deals with bodies and memories. The celebration of the sacrament is repeated as a traumatic memory replays in the mind of a trauma survivor – intensely real and yet extraordinarily personal. In this chapter I will examine *what* is being remembered as bodies and memories come together in the celebration of the Eucharist. Having established that the Christian understanding of the celebration of the Eucharist lies in somatic memory, I will probe more deeply the nature of that memory.

In the contemporary understanding of the Eucharist, the dominant interpretation of the meaning of the sacrament, across Christian denominations, is largely couched in references to the Paschal suffering, death and resurrection of Christ. The Eucharist is primarily viewed as a sacrament in which the death of Christ is remembered. The Protestant reformers of the sixteenth century might have unanimously rejected the theology of the Eucharist as a sacrifice, but they retained an understanding of the Eucharist as connected to the final days of Jesus' life, and the Last Supper in particular.

In the twentieth century, Catholic theologian Louis-Marie Chauvet, in his work *Symbol and Sacrament: A Sacramental Reinterpretation of Christian Existence*, argued that the Pasch of Christ is the essential event from which theological discourse can begin. For Chauvet, the ancient cores of liturgical tradition are passion-focused.[1] Similarly, in his work on the Eucharist as a rite of initiation, Nathan Mitchell also drew a clear and strong connection between the Eucharist and the death of Christ. For example, he noted that the death of Christ became ritually embodied in the broken bread and the poured-out wine and that because the Eucharist celebrates the death of Jesus, 'the table welcomes all human beings as equal partners in the Mystery of God'.[2]

I do not wish to suggest that either Chauvet or Mitchell, nor indeed the great Protestant reformers, are incorrect in their interpretation of the significance of the Eucharist. However, close analysis of the writings of Christians regarding the meaning of the Eucharist from the early Church until the medieval period reveals that, certainly in antiquity and late antiquity (and arguably later still), understanding the Eucharist in sacrificial terms was only one among many legitimate interpretations of the sacrament. Something is clearly being repeated and remembered in the ritual actions of the priest at the altar. This chapter will offer some suggestions as to what is being non-identically repeated, in order to understand what is at the core of Christian somatic memory.

To briefly indicate the argument I will pursue: I will explore the concept of non-identical repetition with regard to interpretations of the Eucharist and its sacramental meaning. Then,

---

1 Louis-Marie Chauvet, *Symbol and Sacrament: A Sacramental Reinterpretation of Christian Existence*, trans. Patrick Madigan and Madeleine Beaumont (Collegeville, MN: A Pueblo Book published by The Liturgical Press, 1995), 486.

2 Nathan D. Mitchell, *Eucharist as Sacrament of Initiation* (Chicago: Liturgy Training Publications, 1994), 40.

beginning by offering the Annunciation-Incarnation event as a model for thinking about the Eucharist, I will explore two images used by early Christian theologians in conjunction with the Eucharist: first, the metaphor of 'dough' and its connection with both the Eucharist and the Nativity, and second, the imagery of the Eucharist as breast milk. The consideration of both the linguistic and the theological implications of these metaphors will allow analysis of the parallels between the Annunciation-Incarnation event and the consecratory epiclesis during the Mass. A subsequent exploration of the role of the Spirit in these non-identical repetitions of the Eucharist then serves to highlight the relationship between Mary and the flesh and blood of Christ. This critical relationship will be further developed in an analysis of the narrative of the Kollyridian eucharistic celebrations. Finally, the concept of non-identical repetition will be considered within the traditional interpretation of the Eucharist as a remembrance of the Last Supper. Understanding Jesus' commandment to 'do this in remembrance of me' is a command to non-identical repetition that defies a single, homogenized interpretation and opens up multiple opportunities for the exploration of somatic memory.

The Annunciation-Incarnation Event

Throughout this book, I will use the term Annunciation-Incarnation event. When doing so I am not referring to the temporal moment of the Incarnation, whether we consider that to be at the Annunciation – the moment at which Mary becomes pregnant – or the 'quickening' of Christ at some later date, or indeed the actual birth of Christ. Rather, the term Annunciation-Incarnation event is used in order to remind us that the Incarnation stretches beyond one moment in time and instead encompasses the whole of Christ's life from the moment of conception, his birth, his childhood, his adulthood, his ministry, his death, and his resurrection. The Incarnation of Christ is a holistic moment that draws all of these aspects together. Furthermore, it cannot be separated from his mother,

Mary. The Incarnation, at its very beginning, is dependent upon, and inseparable from, her.

Non-Identical Repetition

> Then he took a loaf of bread, and when he had given thanks, he broke it and gave it to them, saying, 'This is my body, which is given for you. Do this in remembrance of me.' And he did the same with the cup after supper. (Luke 22.19–20a)

In these Words of Institution, Jesus instructs his disciples to 'Do this in remembrance of me.' What is it he is instructing them to remember? Contemporary Christian liturgies primarily focus on the death of Christ and the Last Supper as the events Jesus is instructing his followers to remember, but it is possible to offer alternative understandings of Jesus' instructions. And such alternatives are necessary, not least when one considers that Jesus is unlikely to be asking the disciples to remember his death on the cross – an event that has not yet taken place! When one takes a holistic perspective on the Annunciation-Incarnation of Christ, the moment that is being repeated and remembered – the event at the core of Christian somatic memory – has an even wider variety of interpretations.

Whatever the answer to the question of remembering is, this remembering takes the form, to use Catherine Pickstock's term, of 'non-identical repetition'.[3] Non-identical repetition is a form of analogous repetition in which history and novelty are combined. All repetition is, inevitably, non-identical because it differs in location, intent, action and/or outcome. James Heaney argued, with relation to the Eucharist, that 'it must be recognized that the celebration is a self-identical, unique event that, even though itself a repetition, cannot be

---

3 Catherine Pickstock, *Repetition and Identity* (Oxford: Oxford University Press, 2013), 177.

repeated historically'.[4] But this specific type of acknowledged non-identical repetition is, for Pickstock, intimately connected to the Eucharist. Pickstock noted that '[T]he words of Consecration "This is my body" therefore, far from being problematic in their meaning, *are the only words which certainly have meaning, and lend this meaning to all other words.*'[5] The eucharistic transubstantiation becomes the condition of possibility for all meaning and, therefore, the distinction between thing and sign becomes unsustainable. For Pickstock, the words of Jesus at the Last Supper become intrinsic to everything else. The Eucharist is essential as the basis for all non-identical repetition, but furthermore, it is itself a non-identical repetition of a prior event. Thus, it is possible to perceive of the *Logos* as the gift of God to the world in which the *Logos* becomes, himself, a personal gift to the individual in their participation in the Eucharist.

This concept of non-identical repetition is a helpful way of exploring what is taking place on the altar in the celebration of the Eucharist. It allows a broadening of interpretative perspective that will reveal a variety of eucharistic referents in this chapter. However, Pickstock used this notion of non-identical repetition to claim that the Words of Consecration are words that are paradigmatic of all meaning. Pickstock is an advocate of the Roman Rite which 'provides a model for genuine consummation of language and subjectivity in and through a radical transformation of space and time'.[6] I disagree with such an emphasis on the Words of Consecration (and indeed with such a positive view of the Roman Rite). The Roman Rite, performed entirely in Latin, makes the congregation passive observers of the sacramental celebration and gives space only for the body and voice of the priest. A focus on the Words of

---

4 James Heaney, *Beyond the Body: An Antitheology of the Eucharist* (Eugene, OR: Pickwick Publications, 2014), 70.

5 Catherine Pickstock, *After Writing: On the Liturgical Consummation of Philosophy* (Oxford: Blackwell, 1998), 263. Italics Pickstock's own.

6 Ibid., 169.

Consecration alone gives a distorted picture of what is taking place on the altar during the celebration of the Eucharist.

Ambrose of Milan: The Varying Forms of Non-Identical Repetition

The early Church theologians employed the concept of non-identical repetition in their eucharistic theology in a variety of forms. Ambrose of Milan is a particularly helpful example to consider in this regard. His writings demonstrate so many of the varieties of non-identical repetition quite typical in early eucharistic theology. Furthermore, writing towards the end of the fourth century, Ambrose is one of the most important ecclesiastical figures of his time and had a significant influence on Augustine (who himself laid the foundation for sacramental theology). As Raymond Moloney noted: '[I]n Ambrose and Augustine we meet two writers whose works contain within themselves in embryo not only the teachings but the controversies which are to mark the history of the Western Eucharist.'[7]

Ambrose dealt with the sacrament of the Eucharist explicitly in a number of areas of both his catechetical and commentarial writings. It is clear from even a cursory analysis of his understanding of the Eucharist that Ambrose saw this sacrament as a non-identical repetition of many other events and moments. For Ambrose the sacrament of the Eucharist, and in particular the moments of consecration and consumption, are the supra-fulfilment of all these precursory events.

Ambrose explored the power of human language through the examples of Moses and Elisha the Prophet. Having established the power of the words of the human being, Ambrose asked how much more powerful is 'the divine consecration itself, in which the very words of our Lord and Saviour

---

7 Raymond Moloney, *The Eucharist* (Collegeville, MN: The Liturgical Press, 1995), 102.

function?'[8] Drawing on the powerful words of God in creating the world, Ambrose demonstrated that human language finds its fulfilment in the words of the Lord, repeated in the sacrament of the Eucharist at the moment of consecration, an idea developed further by Pickstock. No other words spoken by a human will ever have more power than these. Ambrose noted:

> [F]or that sacrament, which you receive is effected by the words of Christ. But if the words of Elias (Elijah) had such power to call down fire from heaven, will not the words of Christ have power enough to change the nature of the elements.[9]

Furthermore, when seeking to explain what is happening in the Eucharist at the moment of consecration, Ambrose turned to the mystery of the Incarnation and uses the one mystery to explain the other. Here Ambrose illustrated how Christ was conceived against the course of nature. This being the case, Ambrose presented the sacrament of the Eucharist, and in particular the moment of consecration, as a non-identical repetition of the Incarnation. Why would we expect the consecration of the Eucharist and the Christ-focused change in the eucharistic elements to conform to the course of nature, when Christ himself did not? The Annunciation-Incarnation event is one that defies and supersedes nature, therefore the eucharistic event does too. Ambrose asked, '[W]hy do you seek here [in the Eucharist] the course of nature in the body of Christ, when the Lord Jesus himself was born of the Virgin contrary to nature?'[10]

Ambrose drew on this non-identical repetition connection again in his work *On The Sacraments*. Here he posited the

---

8 Ambrose of Milan, 'The Mysteries', trans. Roy J. Deferrari in *Saint Ambrose: Theological and Dogmatic Works*, ed. Roy J. Deferrari, (Washington, DC: The Catholic University of America Press, 1963), Chapter 9, 52. All quotations from Ambrose of Milan are taken from this translation unless otherwise stated.

9 Ibid., 52.

10 Ibid., 53.

change in the eucharistic elements at the moment of consecration as a non-identical repetition of the creation of the world, the Incarnation, and our own regeneration through baptism. For example, Ambrose first noted that:

> [T]he Lord ordered, the heaven was made; the Lord ordered, the earth was made; the Lord ordered, the seas were made; the Lord ordered, every creature was generated. You see then how the creating expression of Christ is. If then there is so great a force in the expression of the Lord Jesus, that those things might begin to be which were not, how much more creating, that those things be which were, and be changed to something else.[11]

It is this 'expression of Christ' by which all things were made and by which the designs of nature were changed when he wished. Thus, Christ's own generation defies the course of nature in the same way the mystery of the Eucharist does. Furthermore, Ambrose forged an explicit connection between the Eucharist and Baptism. He wrote:

> there was no body of Christ before consecration, but after the consecration I say to you that now there is the body of Christ. He Himself spoke and it was made; He Himself commanded and it was created. You yourself were, but you were an old creature; after you were consecrated, you began to be a new creature.[12]

There is, clearly, a unity with regard to the Incarnation and the Eucharist mirrored in the historical and sacramental bodies of Christ. This unity gives, to those that receive the sacrament, a unity with Christ himself. For example, Ambrose used the Song of Songs to illustrate the relationship between the Lord and the Church. The Lord, having fed the Church with the sacrament in an image redolent of breastfeeding, delights in her fertility and

---

11 Ambrose, 'The Sacraments', Chapter 4, 15.
12 Ibid., 16.

is one with her. Ambrose noted that 'in us He himself eats and drinks, just as in us you read that He says that He is in prison'.[13]

Although it is in his catechetical texts that Ambrose offers his most concise reflections on the nature of the sacrament of the Eucharist, his commentaries on the Psalms also allow a glimpse into his Incarnation-centred reflections on the Eucharist. Again, Ambrose is drawing out the various events, particularly in the Old Testament, that are fulfilled in the sacrament of the Eucharist. Here the notion of non-identical repetition works alongside the established understanding of typology and typological fulfilment. For example, in his commentary on twelve of the Psalms, Ambrose indicated his understanding of the consumption of the Jewish Passover as a typological pre-figuration of 'the passion of the Lord Jesus on whom we daily feed in the sacrament'.[14] Thus, for Ambrose and many subsequent Christian writers, the sacrament of the Eucharist can be understood as a non-identical repetition of the Passover.

Furthermore, the sacrament of the Eucharist finds its origin in the gushing forth of blood and water from Christ's side which is itself a non-identical repetition of the water gushing forth from the rock of Horeb.[15] Ambrose noted that as eating the Passover lamb delivered the Israelites from the persecution of Pharaoh in Egypt so the consumption of the eucharistic bread and wine brings deliverance from sin. In this sense, the sacrament of the Eucharist is a non-identical repetition of the Fall, but with a critical difference. For as Satan tempted with food that brought death, so in the Eucharist does the Lord repair the damage wrought through food. What once brought death, now, in this repetition, brings eternal life.

As I noted at the beginning of this section, the significance of Ambrose is not to be underestimated. His eucharistic theology set the scene for over a thousand years of thinking on the

---

13 Ambrose, 'The Mysteries', Chapter 9, 57.

14 Finbarr G. Clancy, 'The Eucharist in St Ambrose's Commentaries on the *Psalms*', in *Studia Patristica*, ed. Markus Vinzent (Leuven, Paris, Walpole, MA: Peeters, 2011), 35–44, at 37.

15 Ambrose, 'The Mysteries', Chapter 8, 49.

matter. Ambrose laid the foundations for what would come to be considered the central elements of eucharistic theology – a proto-doctrine of Real Presence, and the significance of the words of consecration in effecting this Real Presence. Ambrose has a clear understanding of an actual transformation of the bread and wine into the body and blood of Christ and is able to identify the moment at which such a transformation takes place – the Words of Institution. Ambrose's theology of non-identical repetition within the Eucharist is similarly significant in the history of the Western Eucharist.

Having considered Ambrose's understanding of the sacrament of the Eucharist, it is clear that he considered the Eucharist (and in particular the twin orally fixated moments of consecration and consumption) to be the high point of theology. The sacrament itself is a typological fulfilment, a non-identical repetition, and a supra-expression of history, theology and language. It is in the human-Divine words of consecration and the human consumption of the Divine that, for Ambrose, we are united with the Lord. If we consider the Eucharist to be a repetition of a traumatic somatic memory, then we can see in microcosm that the memory is varied and by no means necessarily Pasch-focused.

The Annunciation-Incarnation as Eucharistic Reference Point

In the search for the somatic memory that is at the core of the traumatized Body of Christ and, therefore, non-identically repeated in the Eucharist, one event is prominent among many others in the early Church. From the time of the early Church onwards, Christian writers have engaged with the doctrine and event of the Annunciation-Incarnation in order to aid their understanding of the Eucharist. For example, in the early second century, Justin Martyr used the mystery of the Annunciation-Incarnation to explain what was happening in the Eucharist. He wrote:

[F]or not as common bread and common drink do we receive these; but in like manner as Jesus Christ our Saviour, having

been made flesh by the Word of God, had both flesh and
blood for our salvation, so likewise have we been taught
that the food which is blessed by the prayer of His word,
and from which our blood and flesh by transmutation are
nourished, is the flesh and blood of that Jesus who was made
flesh.[16]

This extract indicates that Justin viewed both the mystery of
the Annunciation-Incarnation and the mystery of the Eucharist
to be events in which the same process is being undertaken. As
Christ was made flesh and blood for our salvation, so are the
bread and wine made flesh and blood for our nourishment. In
the Latin Church, as we saw previously, Ambrose of Milan
was similarly keen to use the Annunciation-Incarnation to
elucidate the Eucharist:

Let us use the examples He gives, and by the example of the
Incarnation prove the truth of the Mystery (the Eucharist) . . .
this body which we make is that which was born of the
Virgin . . . It is the true Flesh of Christ which crucified and
buried, this is then truly the Sacrament of His Body.[17]

At the end of the fifth century, Pope Gelasius I further highlighted the connection between these two mysterious events:

Certainly the image and likeness of the body and blood
of Christ are celebrated in the action of the Mysteries [the

16 Justin Martyr, 'Apology 1', trans. Marcus Dods and George
Reith in *Ante-Nicene Fathers*, Vol. 1, ed. Alexander Roberts, James
Donaldson and A. Cleveland Coxe (Buffalo, NY: Christian Literature
Publishing Co., 1885), para. 66. Accessed online at http://newadvent.
org/fathers/0126.htm on 13/05/14.

17 Ambrose of Milan, 'On the Mysteries', trans. H. de Romestin,
E. de Romestin and H. T. F. Duckworth, in *Nicene and Post-Nicene
Fathers, Second Series*, Vol. 10, ed. Philip Schaff and Henry Wace
(Buffalo, NY: Christian Literature Publishing Co., 1896), Chapter
9, 53. Accessed online at http://newadvent.org/fathers/3405.htm on
13/05/14.

Eucharist] . . . Therefore it is shown clearly enough to us that we ought to think about Christ the Lord himself what we confess, celebrate and receive in His image [the eucharistic elements]; that just as they pass over into this, namely, divine substance, by the working of the Holy Spirit, yet remaining in the peculiarity of their nature; so they [the visible elements/eucharistic signs] demonstrate by remaining in the proper sense those things which they are, that the principal mystery itself, whose efficacy and power they truly represent to us, remains the one Christ, integral and true.[18]

The eucharistic theology of Gelasius is particularly helpful in the light of the current investigation in this chapter. In his brief elucidation of the eucharistic theology of Gelasius, Kilmartin specifically located Gelasius' 'eucharistic theology within the history of the theology of eucharistic incarnation'.[19] Gelasius understood the eucharistic consecration as analogous to the Incarnation of Christ. Furthermore, Gelasius specifically rejected any understanding of the bread and wine changing in their substances but rather suggested a hypostatic union of Christ's humanity and the substance of bread and wine. Ultimately, this view was rejected by the Council of Trent, but if we are to see the Eucharist as a non-identical repetition of the Annunciation-Incarnation event, then Gelasius' understanding of the change within the elements is a more accurate one than that described in discourses on transubstantiation. After all, in the hypostatic union of the Incarnation, the humanity of Jesus is not subsumed by the *Logos*, but rather exists alongside the Word. So too, then, in the Eucharist, does the fully hypostatically united being of the Word exist alongside the material nature of the bread and wine. In this sense the Eucharist, as a non-identical repetition

---

18 Gelasius, 'Tract 3, No. 14', trans. and cited in Edward J. Kilmartin and Robert J. Daly, 'The Eucharistic Theology of Pope Gelasius I: A Nontridentic View', in *Studia Patristica*, ed. Elizabeth A. Livingstone, Leuven: Peeters, 1997, 283–89, at 284–8.

19 Kilmartin and Daly, 'The Eucharistic Theology of Pope Gelasius I', 284.

of the Annunciation-Incarnation event, is a model for how unity and difference can co-exist together.

Each of these Christian writers has, when faced with incomprehension with regard to the Eucharist, turned to the mystery of the Annunciation-Incarnation event in order to grasp what is taking place on the altar. It seems that, for these theologians, the natural point of reference in aiding understanding of what was actually happening in the Eucharist and why it was happening was not to look to the Paschal suffering of Christ, as became common in later centuries, but rather to focus on the beginning of his life. The somatic memory at the core of the Christian faith is, therefore, the trauma of the Annunciation-Incarnation event.

The transformation of the earthly elements of bread and wine into eucharistic flesh and blood would seem, to these early writers, to bear something intrinsically in common with the Incarnation. To understand the Eucharist as a continuation, a re-actualization, or a 'non-identical repetition' of the Annunciation-Incarnation event would seem to have once been a legitimate understanding of the mysteries of this sacrament. As such, one can answer the question, 'What is the somatic memory of the Body of Christ?' The Annunciation-Incarnation event is the somatic memory that repeatedly makes itself known in this body. It is repeated in the celebration of the Eucharist as a repetition of this original traumatic event.

The Eucharistic Dough and the Nativity

While the connection between the Annunciation-Incarnation event and the Eucharist had a great deal of currency in the early Church's understanding of the Eucharist, the early Church theologians drew on other imagery, both natal and maternal, to convey this understanding. In considering a variety of early Church homilies, a number of connections between not just the Annunciation-Incarnation and the Eucharist but also the Nativity and the Eucharist are made apparent. For example, in the fourth-century work of John Chrysostom, we find that

'[F]or this reason He was placed in a manger, so that He who nourishes all might receive a child's nourishment from a virgin mother'.[20] The use of 'nourishing' imagery here draws an implicit connection between the Nativity of Christ and his subsequent designation as 'the Bread of Life', and, as such, directs the hearer to the Eucharist as a point of reference.

Furthermore, in the writings of Andrew of Crete regarding the Nativity, Andrew referred to the term 'dough' on a number of occasions. He wrote:

> [T]oday Adam, presenting [her] out of us and on our behalf as first-fruit to God, dedicates Mary, she indeed who was not mixed with the whole dough; through her is bread made for the remodelling of the race.[21]

At the time of Andrew's writing on the island of Crete, the bread predominantly eaten there was most likely bread made from barley. This barley bread would have been unlikely to be leavened. The more refined wheat bread was very costly as much of it had to be imported. This refined, white, purer, wheat bread would have been leavened and would have been consumed by even the poorest at festivals and holy days. It is this refined, purer wheat bread that Andrew is referring to when he uses dough imagery in his homilies. With this context in mind, then, Andrew seems to be implying that because Mary was not 'mixed with the whole dough', i.e. that she was conceived immaculately and not tainted with the stain of original sin, from her a new batch of bread is made – the 'race' of believers. Mary is a new starter dough which, when mixed with the dough of Christ, creates a new batch of bread. In this sense, then, as the starter dough from which the new race is formed, Mary is uniquely connected to the Eucharist. She

---

20 John Chrysostom, 'On the Birthday of Our Savior Jesus Christ a Sermon', www.tertullian.org/fathers/chrysostom_homily_2_on_christmas. htm, trans. Bryson Sewell. Accessed online on 24/11/15.

21 Mary Cunningham, *Wider Than Heaven: Eighth Century Homilies on the Mother of God* (New York: St Vladimir's Seminary Press, 2008), 75.

is, in this understanding, the key ingredient in the eucharistic bread, prior even to Christ. The consequence of (re)considering what might be being non-identically repeated in the celebration of the Eucharist, what the somatic memory at the core of the Christian faith might be, is to open up theology to new perspectives on traditional ideas.

In a later homily regarding the feast of the Annunciation, Andrew went on to note that 'it is therefore fitting that the current splendid and radiant festival is applauded today as it celebrates the acceptance in all its diversity of our dough'.[22] The translator, Mary Cunningham, noted that 'the vocabulary and metaphor used here are obscure: Andrew means that the feast is celebrating the Incarnation of Christ and his complete assimilation of human nature in becoming man'.[23] It is significant to note that in both of these instances, the metaphor of the dough, an image that early Christians would have associated with their regular eucharistic celebrations, is used in reference to the Incarnation. Andrew of Crete is, implicitly, drawing the connection between these two occurrences for his hearers. Following in the footsteps of Paul in his first letter to the Corinthian Church (1 Cor. 5.6–8), Andrew implied that there is something in the dough (perhaps the yeast) that is sinful – hence the immaculately conceived Mary is 'not mixed with the whole dough'. But the bread that is made from her – the Bread of Life received by the Church in the Eucharist – is bread that will reshape humankind.

Germanos of Constantinople, also writing in the eighth century, drew a connection between the foreshadowed eucharistic experience of the Hebrews in the desert, the body of Mary and the *Logos* when he noted: '[H]ail, favored one, the all-gold jar of manna . . . Hail, favored one, who brings Life and nourishes the Nourisher.'[24] For Germanos, drawing on the 'bread of life' imagery in chapter 6 of John's Gospel, the Eucharist is a non-identical repetition of the Nativity. Just as

---

22 Ibid., 198–9.
23 Ibid., footnote 11 on 199.
24 Ibid., 226.

Mary nourished Christ with the flesh and blood of her womb and the milk of her breasts, so now does Christ nourish all of humankind with his own flesh and blood. The implicit linking of these exaltations of Mary and food imagery once again draws together our understanding of both the Nativity and the Eucharist.

The use of terms related to bread, dough, nourishment, etc. in the early and the medieval Church draw, for the hearers of these homilies, implicit connections between the festivals at which these words were spoken – for example, the Feast of the Annunciation or the celebration of the Nativity – and their experience of the presence of Christ in the celebration of the sacrament of the Eucharist (regardless of whether, as laity, they were actually permitted or expected to receive this Eucharist). This connection certainly had currency in the eucharistic theology of the time alongside other, more widely known connections between the Eucharist and the Last Supper or the Eucharist and the Paschal experience of Christ.

The connection made by these Patristic writers in the early Church between the Nativity and the Eucharist is an important one, particularly when one begins to explore the implications. While certainly connected to the incarnational ideas of the Eucharist explored previously, understanding the Eucharist as a non-identical repetition of the Nativity draws some different conclusions. For example, if one considers the Eucharist to be a non-identical repetition of the Nativity, then by analogy Christ must already be present in the elements of bread and wine at the eucharistic table (as Christ was already present in Mary's womb). The mystery of the Eucharist in this interpretation, therefore, is not the transformation of the eucharistic elements into something else, but rather the *revelation* of the already-manifest presence of Christ in those elements. It is clear that some of the Church fathers viewed the Annunciation-Incarnation, itself, in precisely these terms. Athanasius, for example, noted that:

He was not far from us before. For no part of Creation is left void of Him. He has filled all things everywhere, remaining

31

present with His own Father. But He comes in condescension to show loving-kindness upon us, and to visit us.[25]

The implication in Athanasius' words is that although in the Annunciation-Incarnation event Christ became particularly present, he is universally present as the Word of God from the beginning of creation and eternally beyond. In the extended understanding of the Incarnation of Christ, of course, the Nativity is as much a part of the Incarnation of Christ as the moment of Annunciation is.

Furthermore, the shepherds' and Magi's experience of the Nativity offers, for them, a conversion experience. The shepherds leave the presence of the Holy Family, 'glorifying and praising God for all they had seen and heard' (Luke 2.20) and the Magi pay homage to the Christ-child (Matt. 2.11). If one understands the Eucharist as a non-identical repetition of the Nativity, then we might also understand that partaking of the Eucharist (as the Shepherds and the Magi did at the proto-table fellowship of the Nativity) is an experience that has the potential to convert non-believers into believers. The insistence, then, for example, that only those who have been baptized and made a sacramental confession of faith may receive the Eucharist, would seem to deny the power this sacrament has to convert non-believers. In the Gospel of Luke, the author specifically introduces the shepherds as trope of universal salvation – the inclusion of the shepherds suggests to the reader that the Christ-child is born for all. As the (most likely) Jewish shepherds and Gentile Magi were welcomed to the Nativity, so, perhaps, should our altar tables be open tables at which those of all faiths, and none, are welcome, with the expectation that an encounter with the transforming presence of Christ is available for everyone.

---

25 Athanasius, 'On the Incarnation of the Word', trans. Archibald Robertson, *Nicene and Post-Nicene Fathers*, Vol. 4, ed. Philip Schaff and Henry Wace (Buffalo, NY: Christian Literature Publishing Co., 1892), Chapter 8. Accessed online at www.newadvent.org/fathers/2802.htm on 01/03/16.

In locating the somatic memory at the core of Christianity in the extended incarnational event of the Nativity, once again it is possible to demonstrate that the theological consequences of such an interpretation of the Eucharist open up the boundaries of understanding and offer new perspectives on traditional doctrines.

The Eucharist and Mothers' Milk

When one considers the multi-faceted nature of somatic memory in the Eucharist, one is confronted with a wide array of bodies and memories. A distinct, but perhaps surprising, connection in early Christian writings is drawn between the milk of a nursing mother and the Eucharist. Milk manifests as a eucharistic element in two ways. First, milk features in some eucharistic liturgies up to the beginning of the fourth century. Second, the Eucharist as mothers' milk is also present as an image or symbol in early Christian writings. The prevalence of this milk image can prompt us to ask what its symbolism in literature, and presence in liturgy, mean. To put it another way, when milk is used as part of the instruction to 'do this in remembrance of me', what exactly is being remembered?

There is clear evidence that milk was used in a liturgical and sacramental manner by the early Christians. Andrew McGowan pointed out that there was a tradition of using cheese within Eucharist.[26] Epiphanius, writing in the fourth century, made reference to a group of Christians known as the 'Artotyritai' who were so called because 'in their rites they set out bread and cheese and thus celebrate their rites'.[27] This cheese was most likely a semi-solid cheese that may have been spread on the bread. This cheese is symbolically identified with milk and

---

26 Andrew McGowan, *Ascetic Eucharists: Food and Drink in Early Christian Ritual Meals* (Oxford: Clarendon Press, 1999), 95–8.

27 Epiphanius of Salamis, 'The Panarion of Epiphanius of Salamis Books 2 and 3', in *The Panarion of Epiphanius of Salamis Books 2 and 3: De Fide*, ed. Johannes van Oort and Einar Thomassen (Leiden and Boston, MA: Brill, 2013), 49.1.1.

indeed, for ancient cultures, the distinction commonly drawn between milk and cheese today would have been alien. Cheese was the best way of keeping milk without the aid of refrigeration. In the minds of these early Christians, it is also quite possible that cheese would have had explicit connection with the Incarnation itself. Aristotle noted:

> [W]hat the male contributes to generation is the form and the efficient cause, while the female contributes the material. In fact, as in the coagulation of milk, the milk being the material, the fig-juice or rennet is that which contains the curdling principle, so acts the secretion of the male, as it gets divided into parts in the female.[28]

Rennet is a key ingredient in the production of cheese. This image of curdling in the womb forming the foetus is later used by Tertullian[29] and indicates that the early Church understood the process of conception as similar to the process by which milk became cheese.

McGowan also noted that in some parts of the early Christian world there was a tradition of giving a cup of milk and honey to newly baptized Christians in their first celebration of the Eucharist, alongside a cup of wine.[30] The second-century writer Marcion clearly knew of this tradition, as did Tertullian in the third century. In this case, the use of a milk and honey cup would have been a once-only eucharistic event. This baptismal milk and honey cup is attested to in the most likely third-century text *The Apostolic Traditions*, wherein the clergy are instructed to prepare a cup of:

---

28 Aristotle, *Generation of Animals*, trans. A. L. Peck (Cambridge, MA: Harvard University Press, 1943), 106.

29 Tertullian, 'On The Flesh of Christ', trans. Peter Holmes in *Ante-Nicene Fathers*, Vol. 3, ed. Alexander Roberts, James Donaldson and A. Cleveland Coxe (Buffalo, NY: Christian Literature Publishing Co., 1885), Chapter 4. Accessed online at www.newadvent.org/fathers/0315.htm on 01/03/16.

30 McGowan, *Ascetic Eucharists*, 109.

milk and honey mingled together in fulfilment of the promise which was <made> to the Fathers, wherein He said I will
give you a land flowing with milk and honey; which Christ
indeed gave, <even> His Flesh, whereby they who believe
are nourished like little children, making the bitterness of the
<human> heart sweet by the sweetness of His word (λόγος).[31]

Teresa Berger, in her analysis of the significance of milk in such
eucharistic celebrations, suggested that the theological explanation of this milk and honey cup here comprises three themes.
First, it is connected to the eschatological promise of a land flowing with milk and honey. Second, this eschatological promise
points directly to the body of Christ who feeds the believers with
his sweet milk. The third theme is the evocation of a maternal
body that breastfeeds – indeed, the maternal imagery employed
by early Christian writers is explicit. Such imagery was a key
feature of the milk and honey cups shared in the celebration of
the Eucharist – a practice that receded in the late third century.[32]

Ultimately, milk used in liturgy is rich, not only in nourishment but also in theological meaning. Cheese, used as a milk
substitute in a pattern of repeated ascetic Eucharist, marked
a specific opposition to the eating of flesh and thus removed
the participant from society in general. This could be characterized as a deliberate distancing of the ritual from the sacrificial rituals of the pagans. It is possible to interpret such
distancing from sacrificial ritual as an indication that these
Christians did not view their ceremony as a repetition of the
sacrificial death of Christ, but rather as a repetition of something else. The somatic memory at the core of their faith is not
the trauma of Jesus' death. Given the use of milk, it seems that
they viewed their rituals as a repetition of something life-giving
and nourishing, and the actual somatic memory at the core of

---

31 Gregory Dix, ed. *The Treatise on the Apostolic Tradition of St.
Hippolytus of Rome, Bishop and Martyr* (London: SPCK, 1937), 40
(Apostolic Traditions XXIII: 2).

32 Teresa Berger, *Gender Differences and the Making of Liturgical
History: Lifting a Veil on Liturgy's Past* (Farnham, Surrey: Ashgate
Publishing, 2011), 82.

their Christian faith appears to be more strongly connected to the Annunciation-Incarnation event. However, milk used in a once-only baptismal Eucharist was full of eschatological, incarnational and eucharistic overtones. In the light of this evidence of practice, it is worth considering whether, when New Testament writers and early Church theologians use milk imagery in their writings, they are making eucharistic references.

The first extant theological reference to breast milk in Christian writings comes towards the end of the first century in the first Epistle of Peter. The author of the Epistle encourages believers to '[L]ike newborn infants, long for the pure, spiritual milk, so that by it you may grow into salvation' (1 Pet. 2.2). Rather than offering these new Christians a simple form of Christianity as opposed to a more advanced form (or solid food) of Christianity they might be ready for later (as Paul's use of the term 'milk' indicates in 1 Cor. 3.2), the milk, in this verse, appears to be the simplicity of the Christian way of life as opposed to the guiles of the world around them. There is no explicit connection made with the Eucharist here but the connection between this milk and salvation is an important one and one that is frequently repeated. Karen Jobes, in her analysis of this verse and its relationship to Septuagint Psalm 33, suggested that:

> Peter is not describing the recent conversion of his readers for he has already described all believers as new-born children of God, and uses the metaphor to instruct them to crave pure spiritual milk, even as a newborn baby craves its mother's milk, that is, instinctively, eagerly, and incessantly. Although milk is elsewhere in the New Testament used as a metaphor for teachings suitable for immature Christians (Heb. 5.12) and worldly Christians (1 Cor. 3.1) such a negative connotation is not found here. Rather Peter presents pure spiritual milk as that which all Christians need in order to grow up in their salvation.[33]

---

33 Karen H. Jobes, 'Got Milk? Septuagint Psalm 33 and the Interpretation of 1 Peter 2.1–3', *Westminster Theological Journal* 64, no. 1 (2002), 1–14, at 1–2.

The referent of the pure spiritual milk metaphor is not imme-diately clear but Jobes concluded that most interpreters under-stand the referent to be the word of God. The interpreters predominantly conceive of this with regard to apostolic preach-ing or the Bible. Although there is not an explicit connection to the Eucharist made here, the connection between milk and the Word, or rather the *Logos*, is clear. To feed on the Word is to consume Christ in the eucharistic ritual. Thus, the pure spiritual milk is the body and blood of Christ.

Clement of Alexandria also used the imagery of breast milk. In this case, Clement drew a connection between the spiritual teaching believers receive and the nourishment provided to infants through breast milk. Clement did not leave the image there but extended the symbolism of the image to drawing a distinct link between this breast milk and 'the Word, the milk of Christ'.[34] Drawing on the ancient belief that breast milk was heated or frothed blood, for Clement this milk was clearly sac-ramental. He noted:

> '[F]or my blood', says the Lord, 'is true drink.' In saying, therefore, 'I have given you milk to drink', has he not indi-cated the knowledge of the truth, the perfect gladness in the Word, who is the milk?[35]

It seems that Clement is quoting the words of the apostle Paul here from 1 Corinthians 3.2: 'I fed you with milk, not solid food.' This is a curious choice on the part of Clement as Paul is referring here to giving new Christians simple teaching because they were not yet ready for the more challenging doctrines. However, if this is the verse that Clement is referring to, then he seems to be doing so in a positive and eucharistic manner.

---

34 Clement of Alexandria, 'The Instructor Book I', trans. Revd William Wilson, in *Clement of Alexandria, Vol. IV, Ante-Nicene Christian Library: Translations of the Writings of the Fathers Down to AD 325*, ed. Alexander Roberts and James Donaldson (Buffalo, NY: Christian Literature Publishing Co., 1885), Chapter 6. Accessed online at www.newadvent.org/fathers/02091.htm on 01/03/16.

35 Ibid.

Drinking the Word, the Christ, is the action Christians share in at the Eucharist. This explicit connection of milk with the drinking of Christ's blood in the sacrament of the Eucharist transforms Clement's use of the image of breast milk from the realm of metaphor into the realm of sacrament.

The writer of the first Petrine Epistle and Clement are not alone in this use of the breast milk imagery. Similar imagery can be found in the writings of Irenaeus:

> He, who was the perfect bread of the Father, offered Himself to us as milk, [because we were] as infants. He did this when He appeared as a man, that we, being nourished, as it were, from the breast of His flesh, and having, by such a course of milk-nourishment, become accustomed to eat and drink the Word of God, may be able also to contain in ourselves the Bread of immortality, which is the Spirit of the Father.[36]

This curious image combines references to the Incarnation, the Eucharist, spiritual growth, and Spirit-indwelling. Christ is milk. He feeds us from his breast with milk – the breast of His flesh being a reference to the Eucharist. The reference to 'flesh' here recalls the repeated use of the term in chapter 6 of John's Gospel, where Jesus exhorts his followers to feed on his flesh, and, by extension, makes the connection with the early Christian understanding of the Eucharist. This understanding of the Eucharist is not couched in sacrificial or Last Supper overtones, but rather in an eschatological hope of eternal life. By this nourishment at his breast, Christians are able to digest the Bread of immortality, presumably indigestible to them in any other format.

Each of these writers draws a parallel between the milk they are referring to and the Word or the *Logos*. In the Western, Latin tradition, particularly in the light of the Reformation, sharp distinctions are drawn between the Word and the Eucharist. In response to the perceived over-sacramentalism of the medieval Church, the Protestant Reformers elevated the

---

36 Irenaeus, 'Against Heresies', Book IV, Chapter 38.

reading of the Word as the pure, unadulterated mode of worship and advocated a theology of the Eucharist that moved away from the doctrine of transubstantiation. Many contemporary evangelical Protestant churches prioritize the reading and preaching of Scripture at the expense of the celebration of the Eucharist to the extent that the Eucharist, in some cases, is celebrated perhaps once a year. Even now, within the Catholic Church (and indeed, in most Anglican services) the Mass is divided into the Liturgy of the Word followed by the Liturgy of the Eucharist. But in the early Church not so sharp a distinction was drawn. The consumption of the Word was seen as a necessary pre-requisite for the consumption of the Eucharist and the two 'eatings' were two courses of the one meal. For example, Ambrose encouraged believers to 'eat this food first [the scriptures], in order to be able to come afterward to the food of the body of Christ'.[37] Similarly, Augustine noted:

> let all this, then, avail us to this end, most beloved, that we eat not the flesh and blood of Christ merely in the sacrament, as many evil men do, but that we eat and drink to the participation of the Spirit, that we abide as members in the Lord's body, to be quickened by His Spirit.[38]

Chauvet considered this connection between the Word and sacrament, specifically the Eucharist, in the context of the Bread of Life discourse in the sixth chapter of John's Gospel. Chauvet contended that this discourse is not solely about the Eucharist but rather it is a discourse about faith in Jesus as the Word of God expressed in eucharistic language. From start to end it is a discourse about eating set against the backdrop of

---

37 Ambrose, 'Homily on Psalm 118', in *Patrologiae Cursis Completus: Series Latina*, ed. Jacques-Paul Mignes (Paris: Migne, 1844–91), 15:1197–1526. Cited in and trans. Chauvet, *Symbol and Sacrament*, 214.

38 Augustine, 'Tractate 27 (John 6.60–72)', trans. John Gibb, in *A Select Library of the Nicene and Post-Nicene Fathers*, Vol. 7, ed. Philip Schaff (Buffalo, NY: Christian Literature Publishing Co., 1888). Accessed online at www.newadvent.org/fathers/1701027.htm on 01/03/16.

the Jewish narrative of God's provision of manna from heaven in the Exodus story. Both eating the word (or 'chewing the book' as Chauvet entitled it) and eating the Eucharist are sacramental actions and intimately associated with one another. Thus, he concluded:

> In the sacraments, as in all other ecclesial meditations, it is always as *Word*, bitter and sweet at the same time, that Christ gives himself to be assimilated . . . the efficacy of the sacraments cannot be understood in any other way *than that of the communication of the Word.*[39]

To understand the milk as the *Logos* is to understand that the Eucharist enables the text of the Scriptures to become reality in the body of each believer who receives the sacrament. For Chauvet, the reception of the sacrament is the bridge between the Scriptures in writing and the Scriptures in action – or ethics – because of the connection he draws between bodies and words; corporality is the speech of the body.

Perhaps one of the most significant and challenging uses of breast milk imagery, to the contemporary interpreter at least, is that presented in the Odes of Solomon, specifically in the nineteenth Ode. The Odes of Solomon are the oldest extant collection of Syriac poems.[40] Numbering 42 in total, they are powerful and haunting in both their imagery and their theology. There is much scholarly debate on the date of composition but, as a starting point, Michael Lattke, in his commentary on the Odes, noted that 'a *Greek* version of the *Odes of Solomon* was in circulation no later than the end of the second/beginning of the third century CE.'[41] By process of elimination, Lattke further refined the date of composition to the first quarter of the second century. Most scholars tentatively agree that by the

---

39 Chauvet, *Symbol and Sacrament*, 226.

40 G. K. Taylor, 'The Syriac Tradition', in *The First Christian Theologians*, ed. G. R. Evans (Oxford: Blackwell Publishing, 2004), 201–24, at 207.

41 Michael Lattke, *Odes of Solomon: A Commentary* (Minneapolis, MN: Fortress Press, 2009), 6. Emphasis Lattke's own.

mid to late third century copies of the *Odes of Solomon* were circulating in various languages in North Africa. The *Odes of Solomon* can, therefore, be considered to be contemporary to evidence of liturgical practice that included milk and/or cheese in the Eucharist which we have already considered in this chapter. It is worth reading Ode 19 in its entirety to fully appreciate the 'dissonant gender imagery'[42] at play there and the extent of the metaphor in use.

A cup of milk was offered to me
And I drank it in the sweetness of the Lord's kindness.
The Son is the cup
And he who was milked, the Father,
And [the one] who milked him, the Spirit of holiness.
Because his breasts were full
And it was not desirable that his milk should be poured out/discharged for no reason/uselessly,
The Spirit of holiness opened his [viz., the Father's] bosom
And mixed the milk of the two breasts of the Father.
And she/it gave the mixture to the world, while they did not know,
And those who receive [it] are in the pleroma of the right [hand].
The womb of the Virgin caught [it],
And she conceived and gave birth.
And the Virgin became a mother in great compassion
And she was in labor and bore a son.
And she felt no pains/grief,
Because it was not useless/for no reason.
And she did not require a midwife
Because he [viz., God] kept her alive.
Like a man
She brought forth by/in the will [of God]
And brought forth by/in [his] manifestation
And acquired by/in [his] great power

42 Jennifer A. Glancy, *Corporal Knowledge: Early Christian Bodies* (Oxford: Oxford University Press, 2010), 96.

And loved by/in [his] salvation
And guarded by/in [his] kindness
And made known by/in [his] greatness.
Hallelujah.[43]

While the milk imagery is used in other Odes, it is here in Ode 19 that the most pronounced development of the imagery takes place. A beautiful, if unusual, image of Trinitarian incarnation, this image has been dismissed by some as being too explicit for modern tastes. James Harris and Alphonse Mingana noted that '[T]his Ode is, in modern eyes, altogether grotesque, and out of harmony with the generally lofty strain of the rest of the collection.'[44] While the Father and the Son both have bosoms that are brimming over with milk, Mary brings forth her child 'like a man' with God the Father as her midwife. The gender imagery here is 'played with for all participants in the salvation drama, both human and divine'.[45]

Here we see the Spirit milking the two breasts of the Father. The milk, when mixed together in a foreshadowing of the two natures of Christ – one Divine and the other human – is Christ the cup. This milk, that the Spirit expresses from the Father's bosom, has generative capabilities. In the ancient world, there was a close relationship between breast milk and semen. Aristotle, for example, understood semen to be heated blood and that menstrual blood, when heated by contact with semen, turned into milk.[46] Thus the liquid offered from the breasts of a nursing mother was the result of contact between menstrual blood and semen.[47] It is entirely reasonable then, given this

---

43 Lattke, *Odes of Solomon: A Commentary*, 268.

44 James Rendel Harris and Alphonse Mingana, *The Odes and Psalms of Solomon*, Vol. 2 (California: The University Press, 1916), 304.

45 Susan Ashbrook Harvey, 'Feminine Imagery for the Divine: The Holy Spirit, the Odes of Solomon, and Early Syriac Tradition', *St Vladimir's Theological Quarterly* 37 (1993), 111–39, at 126–7.

46 Aristotle, *Generation of Animals*, 172.

47 Alicia D. Myers, '"In the Father's Bosom": Breastfeeding and Identity Formation in John's Gospel', *The Catholic Biblical Quarterly* 76 (2013), 481–97, at 484–5.

connection, that the Odist should note that this milk should not be 'poured out for no reason' in the same way that semen must not be discharged fruitlessly.

In the case of the nineteenth Ode, the milk here is specifically connected to the Incarnation and only secondarily to the Eucharist (as it [the body and blood of Christ] is given to those who will receive it). This corresponds to early Christian celebrations of the Eucharist in which the bread and cup ritual is not primarily viewed as being connected to the Last Supper. Instead these early Christians 'view[ed] the eucharistic elements as life-giving and spiritually nourishing rather than in sacrificial terms'.[48] It would seem that even the early Christians sought to view the primary ritual of intimacy with the Divine not in terms of the horror and violence of the Cross, nor making any connection with the pagan sacrificial activity of their contemporaries, but rather with the miracle of the Annunciation-Incarnation event with all its generative and life-giving promise. The spiritually nourishing image of milk would sit well in this understanding of the significance of the Eucharist. If one considers this imagery of the milk in connection with a search for the somatic memory at the core of Christian faith and in dialogue with the multivalent options for understanding the Eucharist, one arrives, once again, not at the Cross but at the Annunciation-Incarnation event. The nineteenth Ode provides strong indications that the Eucharist and the Incarnation cannot be separated. Indeed, we see in this Ode that the Eucharist and the Annunciation-Incarnation event are two parts of the same happening – the Odist is offered a cup of milk even as the milk (or the *Logos*) is given to the world. Edward Engelbrecht concluded his analysis of the milk imagery in the *Odes of Solomon* by noting that:

> [I]f the Odist's uses of milk analogy are read in isolation from one another, there is no obvious reference to the eucharist. But when read together, a pattern emerges. Baptismal

---

48 Paul Bradshaw and Maxwell E. Johnson, *The Eucharistic Liturgies: Their Evolution and Interpretation* (London: SPCK, 2012), 21.

language is followed by the milk analogy. This suggests the author's familiarity with the cup of milk and honey in the baptismal eucharist. The passages may be eucharistic after all.[49]

If this is the case, then such an interpretation raises the question – what is being remembered in the celebration of the Eucharist?

There is a further element to this connection between the Eucharist and breast milk. Breastfeeding in the biblical narrative is an important element in the formation of identity. In the Hebrew Bible, there are a number of accounts of unusual breastfeeding narratives. For example, Sarah nurses Isaac when her age, status and the presence of her slave Hagar would have indicated the role could be delegated to a wet nurse. Similarly, Moses is nursed by his actual mother – a Hebrew – rather than one of the Egyptian wet nurses. Furthermore, Obed is not nursed by his mother Ruth – the Moabite – but rather by his grandmother Naomi – an 'Ephrathite[s] from Bethlehem of Judah' (Ruth 1.1). In all these cases, to be nursed by any of the alternatives would be to have been nursed by a tribal outsider. Thus, Cynthia Chapman concluded that the 'Hebrew narrative provides evidence for the understanding of breastfeeding as a practice that conferred upon sons tribal identity, royal or priestly status, and ritual purity.'[50] It clearly matters who breastfeeds a child, which makes it significant that none of the canonical Gospels record Mary breastfeeding Jesus. In contrast, the beginning of John's Gospel, full of generative imagery, presents Jesus as one breastfed by God – one who is in the bosom of the Father (John 1.18).

In contrast to this omission in the New Testament writings, the Church Fathers were keen to emphasize that Mary had,

49 Edward Engelbrecht, 'God's Milk: An Orthodox Confession of the Eucharist', *Journal of Early Christian Studies* 7, no. 4 (1999), 509–26, at 517.

50 Cynthia Chapman, '"Oh That You Were Like a Brother to Me, One who Had Nursed at My Mother's Breasts": Breast Milk as a Kinship-Forging Substance', *Journal of Hebrew Scriptures* 12 (2012), 1–41, at 39.

indeed, breastfed Christ as part of their insistence that Christ was truly formed from her flesh and therefore truly human. For example, Tertullian interpreted Psalm 22.9, 'And my hope is from my mother's breasts', as being words from Christ directed to the Father and thus indicating that Jesus had suckled at the breasts of Mary. Mary could not, Tertullian argued, have produced any milk for Christ to drink, if she had not truly been pregnant and given birth to Him.[51]

In this context, then, if the eucharistic cup is identified with breast milk rather than sacrificial blood, there is a profound implication for all those who receive it. Those who suckled at the same breast were, in ancient cultures, considered to be milk siblings. Indeed:

> nursing from the same mother or within the same maternal clan establishes a kinship bond; milk siblings form an alliance with one another against outsiders, and opposite-sex milk siblings enjoy social access to one another that extends into the private and intimate space of their mother's house.[52]

For the early Christians, who associated the eucharistic chalice with a mother's milk, to share this nourishment from the same breast (or cup) was to forge strong familial bonds and enabled them to look upon one another as true siblings. As early Church communities were organized along the lines of households, this 'brother and sister' sibling language would have been entirely appropriate in the familial community setting in which the early Church functioned. Breast milk conferred not only kinship but also characteristics of the mother – the one providing the milk. Therefore in 'the ancient Near East and Jewish world, as well as the world of the Greeks and Romans, it [breast milk] is also a substance that communicates essential characteristics'.[53] To drink of the eucharistic cup full of the milk provided through the flesh of Jesus is to consume

---

51 Tertullian, 'On the Flesh of Christ', Chapter 20.
52 Chapman, '"Oh That You Were Like a Brother to Me"', 21.
53 Myers, '"In the Father's Bosom"', 486.

milk that is full of the essential characteristics of Christ. Just as babies bonded with their nurse or mother through breast-feeding and so were made in her likeness, so too do Christians forge familial bonds with Christ and the Christians around them, through sharing the eucharistic cup, and become more conformed to the likeness of Christ.

The metaphor of (breast) milk is an undeniably powerful one. The provision of spiritual nourishment through the flesh (or breast) of Christ draws striking connections to the Eucharist in an image that is replete with incarnational and eschatological references. With regard to the Eucharist as non-identical rep-etition of the Annunciation-Incarnation event, the use of milk in both eucharistic liturgical practice and in the writings of the early Church indicates that for some early Christians the Eucharist was not connected to the sacrificial imagery of blood but rather with the generative and incarnational imagery of milk, with all its heated blood and semen connotations. In fact, the use of milk in the place of wine might be thought to be a deliberate attempt to draw away from sacrificial imagery that is now so prevalent in eucharistic theology. This metaphor relies on the connection between the nursing mother and her child and yet it is entirely removed from the feminine world of breastfeeding. The image, as we have seen it presented here, is detached from the lived experience of women and dislocated from their reality. Gail Paterson Corrington pointed out that 'the detachment of the mother from the actual role of nurse seems to enable the metaphor of nursing to be applied to males as imparters of life and saving knowledge'.[54]

Milk, and especially breastfeeding, has particular somatic overtones given its natural production by the female body and its universal trait as nourisher of infants. Milk and bodily memory seem to be closely entwined. If (breast) milk is a part of eucharistic theology, what is being remembered on the altar? Are we remembering Christ's feeding on his Father, as

---

54 Gail Paterson Corrington, 'The Milk of Salvation: Redemption by the Mother in Late Antiquity and Early Christianity', *The Harvard Theological Review* 82, no. 4 (1989), 393–420, at 406.

seems to be indicated in the opening of John's Gospel? Or are we remembering the nourishing of Christ by Mary which is never mentioned in the Gospels? The connection of milk with the Eucharist encourages *both* of these meanings, and additionally draws attention to the effects of milk on Jesus' (and our) body. Milk nourishes and strengthens and is necessary throughout life. Rather than remembering, simply, the birth of Christ, or his infancy, the use of milk in the Eucharist encourages us to remember the whole Annunciation-Incarnation event – gestation, birth, growth, life, death and resurrection. It incorporates the trauma of these events alongside the familiar and the natural.

The Consecratory Epiclesis

As has already become clear, the variety of meaning and repeated memory remembered in the Eucharist is wide. Many of these patterns of non-identical repetition point towards the remembering of an event more aligned with the Annunciation-Incarnation event than with the Pasch of Christ. These patterns can also be identified in the liturgy of the Eucharist. Some of the implications of such patterns of repetition for contemporary eucharistic theology have already been considered but it is also possible to see the epiclesis in the anaphora as a non-identical repetition of the Annunciation-Incarnation event. The epiclesis is usually understood in the contemporary Church to be the invocation of the Holy Spirit by the priest upon the eucharistic bread and wine.

I have already explored the consecratory epiclesis in the writings of Ambrose. While helpful in outlining the varying ways in which non-identical repetition was employed by early Christian writers, consideration of Ambrose's approach to the epiclesis is not as fruitful as that of some of his contemporaries. Ambrose makes no mention of the Spirit in his consideration of the moment of consecration. Indeed, Ambrose's epiclesis seems to be entirely Christ-focused. And for Ambrose, the transformation of the eucharistic elements takes places in the speaking of the Words of Institution by the priest *in persona Christi*. This is characteristic of an earlier eucharistic theology.

Some of the early Church theologians commented on the epiclesis and drew parallels between this moment as, on the one hand, a descent of the Word of God through the power of the Holy Spirit on the eucharistic elements and, on the other, the incarnational activity of the Word of God, forming Himself a body in the womb of Mary as the Holy Spirit overshadowed her. All of these moments are somatic. Described in philosophical or theological terms, they are, at their core, embodied experiences of flesh and blood. It is, therefore, essential to consider the theological significance of such a connection with regard to our investigation of the somatic memory at the core of the Christian faith – that which is repeated in the celebration of the Eucharist.

In the writings of John Damascene the explicit connection made between the Annunciation-Incarnation event and the consecration is clear. John noted:

> [A]nd now you ask, how the bread became Christ's body and the wine and water Christ's blood . . . it is enough for you to learn that it was through the Holy Spirit, just as the Lord took on Himself flesh that subsisted in Him.[55]

The language that John Damascene uses, in this extract, is significant in itself. John indicates that it is the Word who forms 'for Himself' flesh. This seems to be indicative of a *Logos* epiclesis which will be explored further below. However, John also makes it clear that with regard to the Eucharist, it is the Spirit who effects the transformation of the elements. The relationship between the *Logos* and the Spirit in these two events seems unclear. In both cases, the relationship between earthly

---

55 John Damascene, 'An Exposition of the Orthodox Faith, Book 4', trans. E. W. Watson and L. Pullan, in *Nicene and Post-Nicene Fathers, Second Series*, Vol. 9, ed. Philip Schaff and Henry Wace (Buffalo, NY: Christian Literature Publishing Co., 1899), Chapter 13. Accessed online at http://newadvent.org/fathers/33044.htm on 13/05/14.

materials (the bread and wine or the womb of the Virgin) and the Divine is altered by the activity of the Holy Spirit.

While it would seem logical in the modern context to identify the link between the epiclesis and the event of the Annunciation-Incarnation given our developed understanding of Pneumatology and Trinitarian theology, this was not always the case. In the early Church the epiclesis was, at first, not consistently given as an epiclesis of the Spirit. That is to say, rather than calling down the Holy Spirit upon the offerings of bread and wine on the altar, some of these early liturgies included a petition for the *Logos* to come and effect some change on these earthly elements. Earlier in this chapter it was noted that Justin Martyr drew a connection between the Annunciation-Incarnation and the Eucharist. Returning to this quotation we see that he wrote:

> but in like manner as Jesus Christ our Saviour, having been *made flesh by the Word of God*, had both flesh and blood for our salvation, so likewise have we been taught that the food which is blessed by the prayer of His word, and from which our blood and flesh by transmutation are nourished, is the flesh and blood of that Jesus who was made flesh.[56]

Justin Martyr's words reveal the emphasis on the action of the *Logos* – the action is his, not that of the Holy Spirit. Just at the time when discussions about the nature and divinity of the Holy Spirit reach their peak (mid fourth century), so we begin to see the decline in *Logos* epiclesis and the rise of appeals to the Holy Spirit. It would seem that as early Christians gained confidence in their understanding of the Trinity and the consubstantial nature of the Holy Spirit, so they seemed more inclined to pray to the Spirit. Kilmartin noted that, subsequent to the middle of the fourth century, 'the Holy Spirit is assigned both the role of effecting the incarnation and the

---

56 Justin Martyr, 'Apology 1', Chapter 66. Emphasis my own.

transformation of the Eucharistic gifts in Greek theology'.[57] It must be noted that Greek and Latin theologians (and thus the Orthodox and Roman Churches) differ in their understanding of the precise moment of consecration. For the Latin theologians, this happens with the Words of Institution but for the Greek theologians there is no moment of consecration, rather the whole eucharistic prayer is considered to be consecratory. The mystery is completed in the 'Amen' of the gathered people. In many eastern rites there are, in fact, two epicleses – one before the Words of Institution and a second after.

This characterization of the shift in emphasis from *Logos* to Spirit seems to imply some clear point of transition in thought, but the reality of this change is a more gradual movement in thinking. John McKenna offered a more nuanced view of this transition. In his examination of these early epicleses, he concluded that the evidence seems to suggest the consecratory epiclesis of the Holy Spirit that came to popularity in the middle of the fourth century developed out of an earlier epiclesis of sanctification which already contained implicitly an idea of the Spirit's transforming, consecratory action.[58] Here one can see a transition in doctrine regarding the Spirit – as the understanding of the role of the Spirit in the Incarnation changes so also does the understanding of the role of the Spirit in the Eucharist. As the role of the Spirit is increased and given primacy in the event of the Annunciation-Incarnation, so these early theologians feel the need to revise their understanding of the event of the Eucharist and to clarify the role the Spirit has here too. It would seem clear that these two events were intimately connected together in the minds and the theology of the church fathers.

With regard to our question of what is being remembered at the altar and the search for the traumatic somatic memory that is repeatedly played out in the Body of Christ, this analysis

---

57 Edward Kilmartin, *Christian Liturgy 1* (Kansas City: Sheed & Ward, 1988), 166.

58 John McKenna, *The Eucharistic Epiclesis: A Detailed History from the Patristic to the Modern Era* (Chicago: Hillenbrand Books, 2009), 121.

of the significance and meaning of the epiclesis offers salient insight. The development of the epiclesis is clearly linked to the development of Pneumatological and Trinitarian doctrine. As understanding of the Spirit's role in the Incarnation took clearer shape, theologians felt the need to give greater clarity to the Spirit's role in the Eucharist. Why would they seek to do this if they did not already understand the Eucharist to be intimately intertwined with the Annunciation-Incarnation event?

The Eucharist and the Kollyridians

Much of our consideration of eucharistic theology in this chapter has, thus far, been focused on what can be regarded as reasonably mainstream practice. It is helpful, therefore, to consider eucharistic practice at the fringes of the theological milieu of the writings we have considered. Our search for somatic memory and our exploration of what is being repeated in the celebration of the Eucharist must not be removed from the wide variety of practice found in the early Church. We have already explored the practice of a milk cup in eucharistic celebrations, but most challenging, in the fourth century, is the practice of the Kollyridians.

There is a surprising paucity of written analysis of Epiphanius of Salamis' reference in his *Panarion* – his medicine chest of heresies (and, one can speculate, of Epiphanius' preferred remedies for such illnesses) – to the Kollyridian women devoted to Mary. Epiphanius wrote of a group of women, first in Thrace, then in Scythia and on to Arabia, who 'decorate a barber's chair or a square seat, spread a cloth on it, set out bread and offer it in Mary's name on a certain day of the year, and all partake of the bread'.[59] Epiphanius has two issues with the actions of these women: first, they appear to be allowing women to function in liturgical office, and second, they are, in the view of Epiphanius at least, substituting Mary for God; he

---

59 Epiphanius, 'The Panarion of Epiphanius of Salamis Books 2 and 3', 637.

wrote: 'Even though the tree is lovely, it is not for good; and even though Mary is all fair, and is holy and held in honour, she is not to be worshipped.'[60]

One can, perhaps, account for the lack of scholarly work focused on the Kollyridians by noting some of the attitudes that accompany any such discussion of this part of Epiphanius' text. For example, Averil Cameron, in an essay published in 2004, dismissively noted that 'we should probably leave aside the claim made in Epiphanius of Salamis's list of heresies that there was an obscure group of women, the Collyridians [sic], who particularly venerated her [the Virgin Mary]'.[61] And with this, Cameron passes over this text as an invention of Epiphanius – a piece of fiction.

Other scholars appear to discount the account of the Kollyridians as being evidence of 'popular' belief and thus not worthy of serious consideration. In contrast to Cameron, the historian Stephen Benko did suggest that the Kollyridians were a real group of women. In fact, he seems to give great credence to Epiphanius' account and takes little heed of any potential rhetoric at work in Epiphanius' writing. Benko presented the Kollyridians as a group of probably poorly educated women who were influenced by their local experience of pagan goddess worship and developed a ritual dedicated to Mary as a continuation of this pagan goddess worship they were familiar with in their milieu – a form of syncretism he believes was exceedingly common in the ancient world. He concluded that '[The] Kollyridians were Christians, but they were an extremist fringe and their story soon leads the historian into a blind alley.'[62] Benko dismissed the Kollyridians, not in the same way as Cameron did by implying they are fictional, but rather by

---

60 Ibid., 644.

61 Averil Cameron, 'The Cult of the Virgin in Late Antiquity: Religious Development and Myth-Making', in *The Church and Mary: Papers Read at the 2001 Summer Meeting and the 2002 Winter Meeting of the Ecclesiastical History Society*, ed. R. N. Swanson (Suffolk: The Boydell Press, 2004), 1–21, at 6.

62 Stephen Benko, *The Virgin Goddess: Studies in the Pagan and Christian Roots of Mariology* (Leiden and Boston, MA: Brill, 1994), 194.

suggesting that they are on the edges of 'orthodox' Christian worship and thus should be ignored.

There are a number of problems with Benko's argument: it is patronizingly condescending in its regard to early religious practices, deliberately one-sided in its choice of texts, and seemingly uncritical in its analysis of primary sources. It is surprising that Benko could see fit to write such an analysis in the light of Peter Brown's ground-breaking work on the cult of the saints published some thirteen years earlier. In his analysis of the rise of veneration of the saints within Latin Christianity, Brown began by pointing out in his first chapter that it had been a tendency of scholars to assume that 'popular' beliefs and religion are uniformly unsophisticated and old-fashioned and that such beliefs can only really show themselves in a monotonous continuity with older, pagan beliefs. This tendency must, Brown argued, be challenged. With regard to the cult of the saints, and for our concerns, the veneration of the Virgin Mary, he concluded:

> [Y]et we have seen . . . that the rise of the cult of saints was sensed by contemporaries, in no uncertain manner, to have broken most of the imaginative boundaries which ancient men had placed between heaven and earth, the divine and the human, the living and the dead, the town and its antithesis.[63]

We cannot, therefore, suggest that the ritual performed by the Kollyridians was merely a continuation of pagan goddess worship. Brown has made it clear that the development of veneration of the saints was a moment of radical discontinuity with the kind of 'popular' belief that had gone before in the ancient world. To argue, as Benko did, that the kind of ritual action performed by the Kollyridians is nothing more than the continuation of pagan goddess worship, is to do a great disservice to the undoubtedly Christian milieu in which the Kollyridians,

---

63 Peter Brown, *The Cult of the Saints: Its Rise and Function in Latin Christianity* (Chicago: University of Chicago Press, 1981), 21.

whomever they were and whatever name they went by, lived and worshipped.

A more nuanced reading of Epiphanius comes from the work of Stephen Shoemaker, who has focused on the texts of the earliest Dormition narratives in examining the rise of the Marian cult in the patristic period. Shoemaker agreed with Benko in suggesting that the Kollyridians were a real group (albeit one named by Epiphanius himself!) but he suggested that rather than worshipping Mary as a goddess, 'the Kollyridians merely were offering Mary a kind of veneration that during the late fourth century was increasingly directed towards Christian saints'.[64] In his analysis of the text of the Kollyridian 'heresy' in Epiphanius' *Panarion*, Shoemaker indicated that while Epiphanius felt that the Kollyridians were 'worshipping Mary in the place of God, his charge offers no assurance that these opponents . . . understood their ritual practices this way'.[65] Shoemaker demonstrated that other sources, specifically early narratives of the Dormition of Mary, attest to the existence of a remarkably similar ritual enacted three times a year and observed in honour of Mary.[66] He concluded that this understanding of Epiphanius' comments indicates that there is evidence of cultic veneration of Mary half a century prior to the council of Ephesus – the point at which the cultic veneration of Mary was thought to get its real boost with the affirmation of the title *Theotokos* for Mary.

One is left, after following Shoemaker's line of thought, with an impression of Epiphanius as a lone voice in criticizing this early veneration of the saints. Such veneration

---

64 S. J. Shoemaker, 'Epiphanius of Salamis, the Kollyridians, and the Early Dormition Narratives: The Cult of the Virgin in the Fourth Century', *Journal of Early Christian Studies* 16, no. 3 (2008), 371–401, at 371.

65 Ibid., 374.

66 S. J. Shoemaker, 'The Cult of the Virgin in the Fourth Century: A Fresh Look at Some Old and New Sources', in *The Origins of the Cult of the Virgin Mary*, ed. Chris Maunder (London: Burns & Oates Ltd, 2008), 71–88, at 78.

was certainly, by the end of the fourth century, becoming more commonplace in the Christian world. The Kollyridians were, perhaps, simply ahead of the game in terms of their veneration and, tellingly, Epiphanius' attack on their practices is located in a broader critique of the veneration of the saints. After outlining the features of the Kollyridian ritual, Epiphanius goes on to recount all the reasons why women can have no priestly function before drawing comparisons between Mary and Elijah, John and Thecla.[67] None of these others are to be worshipped and, thus, neither is Mary. Epiphanius is not merely rejecting the veneration (or, in his mind, the worshipping) of Mary, he is rejecting the emerging cult of the saints as offering worship to the created rather than the Creator.

What, then, are the implications of this consideration of the Kollyridians for our question? What is the somatic memory being repeated in their celebration of this Marian-focused Eucharist? It is significant that in this earliest of testaments to Marian veneration the Eucharist is intimately involved. Bodily memory recalled in the Eucharist cannot be separated from the Marian body. The Annunciation-Incarnation event depends upon it. The fact that the Dormition narratives recommend the celebration of this 'bread ritual' in the name of Mary in connection with agricultural markers in the course of the year indicates that there is some connection, at least in the minds of believers, between Mary, the Eucharist, and successful generation of crops. Is it, perhaps, likely that they were remembering the fecundity of Mary, imaged in the Eucharist and prayed for, analogously, in the harvest? In which case, the Eucharist is, for these so-called Kollyridians, a re-actualization, a non-identical repetition, of the Annunciation-Incarnation event. The somatic memory in this eucharistic practice is not Cross-focused, but rather focused on the holistic concept of the Incarnation.

---

67 Epiphanius, 'The Panarion of Epiphanius of Salamis Books 2 and 3', 641.

The Implications of Non-Identical Repetition and the Search for Somatic Memory

In the early Church the reference point for the meaning of the Eucharist was not fixed and was certainly not as fixed on the death of Christ as Eucharist celebrations in the contemporary Church are. Something is clearly being repeated in the celebration of the Eucharist in line with Jesus' command to 'Do this in remembrance of me.' Of course, the context in which that command was given was, itself, a non-identically repeated event – the Last Supper – that drew on the Passover as its reference point. Heaney referred to this as a 'retrospectively restructured annual Passover meal'.[68]

If, however, we see the Eucharist as a non-identical repetition of the Annunciation-Incarnation event (in the full sense I have proposed here) then we can suggest that in the repeated celebration of this event (both Eucharist and Annunciation-Incarnation), the eucharistic self is formed. The sacrament of the Eucharist is, at its core, a generative experience in which one is born and reborn. The critical difference in this repetition is the life of the *Logos*, first only experienced in one woman, Mary, but now available to all who will receive.

David Ford identified the eucharistic self as 'being face to face (in faith and hope) with the one who commands that this be done in memory of him . . . the baptized self in the routine of being fed and blessed.'[69] Ford viewed the Eucharist as creating an expectation of death in its focus on the Last Supper and thus this non-identical repetition celebrates the Lord's death until he comes. However, if one considers the Eucharist as the non-identical repetition of the Annunciation-Incarnation event we see the thoroughly New Testament declaration of life in abundance (John 10.10). In his exegesis of 2 Corinthians 4.16, Ford concludes that the Eucharist 'is the sacrament of human flourishing'.[70] Ford himself is focused on the Eucharist

---

68 Heaney, *Beyond the Body*, 98.

69 David F. Ford, 'What Happens in the Eucharist?', *Scottish Journal of Theology* 48, no. 3 (1995), 359–81, at 379.

70 Ibid., 380.

as death, but this declaration makes much more sense if the Eucharist is understood in the context of the Annunciation-Incarnation. The Annunciation-Incarnation event *is* the location of the traumatic somatic memory at the core of Christian belief. The somatic memory, even here, is that of the full life of Christ – this is the heart of the Christian faith.

Re-Membering the Body of Christ

Situating the Eucharist as the place where bodies and memories come together in a way that appears symptomatic of the repetition and rupture inherent in trauma has led us to the traumatic somatic memory of the Body of Christ. It is not, surprisingly, the horrific trauma of the Cross, but rather the understated trauma of the Annunciation-Incarnation event. By examining the use of generative Incarnational imagery, alongside bread/dough and milk in both eucharistic imagery and eucharistic practice, it becomes clear how wide an Incarnational perspective these early Eucharists had. The epiclesis in the anaphora can be understood as making a specific connection between the events on the altar and those at the Annunciation. It is clear then, that within Christian thought, there is a strong tradition of viewing the Annunciation-Incarnation event with the same theological imagination that one considers the Eucharist. As an act of non-identical repetition, the Eucharist repeats the events of the Annunciation-Incarnation event but with a critical difference – not becoming present in one, immaculately conceived woman but becoming present in all bodies who receive his flesh.

Bodies and memories come together in the celebration of the Eucharist. For this reason, as I demonstrated at the outset of this chapter, the Eucharist becomes the ideal place to search for the somatic memory at the heart of the Christian faith. Continually repeated and allowed to rupture our identities afresh in each celebration, the somatic memory isn't what we might assume. It is tempting to make an easy connection between the Eucharist and the Pasch of Christ. After all, here is a body suffering trauma and, just the night before, Jesus has asked his followers to engage in collective memorial practice as they think of him. But they cannot be remembering his death at the Last Supper because it hasn't happened yet! Instead, Jesus is instructing them to remember Him. All of Him. His full life from Annunciation to the sharing of this final Passover meal. We can certainly extend the memory to incorporate the trauma of the Pasch and the joy of the resurrection but we should be cautious in *only* remembering those events when we celebrate the Eucharist. The somatic memory that underpins the Christian faith is much bigger than the final weekend of Christ's life.

3

Christ is One:
The Unity of the Body in the
Theology of Cyril of Alexandria

Blessing through the mystery of the Eucharist those who believe in Him, He makes us of the same Body with Himself and with each other. For who could sunder or divide from their natural union with one another those who are knit together through His holy Body, which is one in union with Christ? For if we all partake of the one Bread, we are all made one Body; for Christ cannot suffer severance. Therefore also the Church is become Christ's Body, and we are also individually His members, according to the wisdom of Paul. For we, being all of us united to Christ through His holy Body, inasmuch as we have received Him Who is one and indivisible in our own bodies, owe the service of our members to Him rather than to ourselves.[1]

The Body of Christ is a traumatized Body. We have located the trauma of this Body by examining the Eucharist as the somatic memory of a traumatic event; not the Crucifixion, but rather the Annunciation-Incarnation event. What happens to theological endeavour, then, when not only the Eucharist but the Eucharist as repetition of the Incarnation is taken as the central point of theology? Before I set out on constructing a theological response to this location of trauma in the Body of Christ,

---

1 Cyril of Alexandria, *Commentary on the Gospel According to S. John*, 2 vols, Vol. 2, trans. T. Randell (London: W. Smith, 1885), 550.

59

let us consider the theology of Cyril of Alexandria. Although he has no language for, nor interest in, trauma, Cyril performs similar theological moves to those undertaken in the following chapters. Such a consideration helps to shape our expectations of what the consequences of such a theological move might be. For Cyril, an emphasis on the Eucharist as repetition of the Annunciation-Incarnation event, and a foregrounding of this event as the central moment of theology, leads to a strong concern for the unity of the body.

Cyril of Alexandria was one of the key protagonists in the Nestorian Controversy – a dispute over the somatic memory of the Church which can be viewed as an episode where bodies, and disagreements over how we remember them, threatened to cause traumatic rupture in the body of the Church itself. Beneath the well-trodden history of the Nestorian Controversy, there is a unified theological driving force apparent in the thinking of Cyril of Alexandria.

This chapter will outline Cyril's understanding of the eucharistic Body of Christ, the historical, physical body of Jesus, the corporate body both in terms of the Church and the Empire, and finally, the female bodies of both the women of Byzantium and the *Theotokos*. In each case, these bodies will be considered in relation to Cyril's position in the Nestorian Controversy. Beginning theological endeavour at the Eucharist, as a non-identical repetition of the Annunciation-Incarnation event, Cyril is the model and example of what such a shift in theological method might accomplish.

The Nestorian Controversy: The Issues at Stake

The Nestorian Controversy, regardless of the variety of opinion of its actual causes, was focused on the understanding of the incarnational union of the Divine and human in the person of Jesus Christ and consequently on the issue of appropriate terminology for his mother, Mary. Nestorius, in 428 CE, waded into an already active debate on whether it was appropriate to refer to Mary as the *Theotokos* – the God-bearer.

Arguing that this title was not appropriate, Nestorius believed that the title *Theotokos* implied a gestation of God in the womb of Mary. He believed this seemed to indicate that God was changing in some way. Nestorius was not simply attacking one name given to Mary among many others. Rather, his argument had implications for both the nature of Christ and the person of Mary. The development of the use of the term *Theotokos* was a natural part of kerygmatic evolution and already an established part of theological language by the time of the controversy.[2]

Nestorius' attempted prohibition of the title *Theotokos* in Constantinople reached the attention of the Bishop of Alexandria, Cyril, who immediately took the opportunity to write to Nestorius and correct his theology. Cyril claimed that Nestorius' proclamations against the *Theotokos* were a revival of the heretical concept of a union that was entirely, and merely, moral. In the fourth book of his *Five Tomes Against Nestorius*, written around 430 CE and roughly contemporaneous with the controversy, Cyril used the analogy of fire to make his position regarding the unity of Christ clear for Nestorius.

> It is the flesh united to him and not someone else's flesh that has the power to endow with life, in the sense that it became the peculiar property of him who has the power to endow all things with life. For if ordinary fire transmits the power of the natural energy inherent within it to the material with which it appears to come into contact, and changes water itself, in spite of its being cold by nature, into something contrary to its nature, and makes it hot, what is strange or somehow impossible to believe about the Word of God the Father who is Life by nature, rendering the flesh united to him capable of endowing with life? For it is his own flesh and not that of another conceived of as separate from him

---

2 Aloys Grillmeier, *Christ in Christian Tradition: From the Apostolic Age to Chalcedon (451)*, trans. J. S. Bowden (London: A. R. Mowbray & Co. Ltd, 1965), 370.

and as the flesh of someone like ourselves. If you detach the life-giving Word of God from the mystical and true union with body and separate them entirely, how can you prove that it is still life-giving?[3]

For Cyril, then, Nestorius' attack on the use of the title *Theotokos* seemed to reduce the connection of the Divine and the human in the person of Jesus Christ to simply an external, illusory association. To reduce the Incarnation to such a level undermines the possibility of redemption and deprives the Eucharist of its energizing force. The act of eating the Eucharist, if Jesus is just a man, becomes cannibalistic. Eventually, the discord resulted in the calling of the Council of Ephesus in 431 CE and the subsequent victory of Cyril's theology over Nestorius and the Antiochene School.

The war of words resulted from a lack of understanding on both sides and it would seem, in retrospect, that the two bishops were likely much closer in their theology than either would have conceded at the time. Indeed, within two years following the Council, Cyril and leading members of the Antiochene Church had agreed on the Symbol of Union – a statement encapsulating orthodox belief regarding the union of the Divine and the human in the person of Christ. At first glance this statement appears to make major concessions on the part of Cyril towards the Antiochene position. Cyril's favoured terms of 'one nature' and 'hypostatic union' were displaced by Antiochene terms such as 'union of two natures' and 'one *prosopon*'. The title *Theotokos* was admitted but only with safeguards that pleased the Antiochenes. It would seem that some of the tenets Cyril had considered to be non-negotiable became, away from the heat of controversy, more open to discussion.

---

3 Cyril of Alexandria, *Five Tomes against Nestorius*, trans. P. E. Pusey, *A Library of the Fathers of the Holy Catholic Church* (Oxford: James Parker & Co., 1881), Book IV, 125–52, at 142.

Eucharistic and Incarnate Body

Cyril's reaction to Nestorius' attack on the use of the title *Theotokos* is firmly grounded in his theology. In his *Commentary on the Gospel of John*, Cyril demonstrated very clearly what he considered to be important in his Christology. The whole work (and indeed much of his other work) is characterized by a strong eucharistic theology. He noted, for example, when commenting on chapter 6 of the Gospel (the Bread of Life discourse), that when Jesus said, 'I am the Bread of Life', he meant:

> not bodily bread, which cutteth off the suffering from hunger only, and freeth the flesh from the destruction therefrom, but remoulding wholly the whole living being to eternal life, and rendering man who was formed to be forever, superior to death. By these words He points to the life and grace through His Holy Flesh, through which this property of the Only Begotten, i.e., life, is introduced to us.[4]

Henry Chadwick noted that the Eucharist:

> is the heart of Cyril's faith, the dynamic which imparted such intense religious fervour to his monophysite monks. Every eucharist is a reincarnation of the Logos who is there πάλιν ἐν σώματι, and whose ἰδία σάρξ is given to the communicant.[5]

The mystery by which the bread becomes the body and the wine becomes the blood is the same mystery as when the *Logos* became the person of Jesus. Every celebration of the Eucharist is, for Cyril, a non-identical repetition of the Annunciation-Incarnation event.

---

4 Cyril of Alexandria, *Commentary on the Gospel According to S. John*, 373–4.

5 Henry Chadwick, 'Eucharist and Christology in the Nestorian Controversy', *Journal of Theological Studies* 2, no. 2 (1951), 145–64, at 155, 'Every eucharist is a reincarnation of the *Logos* who is there again in body, and whose same flesh is given to the communicant'. Translation of Greek my own.

In Cyril's theology, one finds the somatic memory of the Annunciation-Incarnation event intimately entwined with his theology of the Eucharist. The bodily memory of the Incarnation is celebrated and remembered repeatedly in each Eucharist. Not only are the two mysteries (the Incarnation and the Eucharist) linked in their theology, they are also linked in the believers' embodied experience of each of them. Cyril's eucharistic theology is a mirror image of, and identical with, his theology of the Incarnation.

The theme of unity in Cyril's writings rings clear; Christ is One. This is evident in the sense of both the unity of humanity and divinity in the person of Christ, and in the 'unabridged unity of God and Man, Spirit and body'[6] of the Eucharist. This unity in the person of Christ creates, in the context of the Eucharist, a vertical dynamic of unity between the participating believer and God, as well as a horizontal dynamic of unity between the body of participating believers as they share in the eucharistic flesh and blood of the one Christ. The believers are one body *because* they all share in one bread. The bodily integrity of the communal Body of Christ is established in the sharing of the Eucharist, even as the reception of the Eucharist, as we shall see later on, causes a rupture in the bodily integrity of the individual believer.

There is a distinct soteriological train of thought to Cyril's theology of the Eucharist:

> Christ therefore gave His Own Body for the life of all and again through It he maketh Life to dwell in us . . . For since the life-giving Word of God indwelt in the Flesh, He transformed it into His own proper good, that is life, and by the unspeakable character of this union, coming wholly together with it, rendered It life-giving, as Himself is by Nature. Wherefore the Body of Christ giveth life to all who partake of It. For it expels death, when it cometh to be in dying men,

---

6 Ezra Gebremedhin, *Life-Giving Blessing: An Inquiry into the Eucharistic Doctrine of Cyril of Alexandria* (Uppsala: Uppsala University Press, 1977), 110.

and removeth corruption full in Itself perfectly of Word which abolisheth corruption.[7]

Participation in the incarnate Christ through the bread of the Eucharist is the essential means of salvation. The reality of the Incarnation, the union of the Word with flesh, serves to make the reception of the Body of Christ in eucharistic form life-giving and therefore salvific. Patrick Gray concludes that, for Cyril, '*because* one experiences participation in the life-giving Body of Christ [in the Eucharist], *therefore* the life-giving divine Word Himself really must have become incarnate'.[8] It is the reality of the power of the Eucharist that proves the union of the two natures in the Incarnation. The Eucharist is the driving force behind Cyril's theology.

Cyril's discussion of the Eucharist is not always explicit, but it can be detected as an underlying theme in Cyril's Christological thinking. Indeed, the location of Cyril's rare references to the Eucharist makes it clear that it is of foundational and pivotal importance. Therefore, 'any division of Christ, of the Word from his flesh, leads to the reception of mere lifeless flesh in the Eucharist. This renders the Incarnation and the Pasch without fruit and destroys the whole economy of our salvation.'[9]

Cyril felt that Nestorius and the Antiochene School were straining the unity of the person of Christ to its very limits, if not beyond. The Antiochenes could be seen to have made Christ into a dual personality that in one moment acted as the *Logos*-Incarnate, and in the next moment was merely human.

---

7 Cyril, *Commentary*, 410.

8 Patrick R. T. Gray, 'From Eucharist to Christology: The Life-Giving Body of Christ in Cyril of Alexandria, Eutyches and Julian of Halicarnassus', in *The Eucharist in Theology and Philosophy: Issues of Doctrinal History in East and West from the Patristic Age to the Reformation*, ed. Istvan Percvel, Reka Forrai and Gyorgy Gereby (Leuven: Leuven University Press, 2005), 25–36 at 28. Italics Gray's own.

9 Ellen Concannon, 'The Eucharist as Source of St Cyril of Alexandria's Christology', *Pro Ecclesia* 18, no. 3 (2009), 318–36 at 335.

This, for Cyril, was unacceptable. Concern for the eucharistic Body of Christ is certainly central to Cyril's rejection of Nestorius' argument. For Cyril, it is the union of two natures in the flesh of Christ that provides the life-giving bread and wine of the Eucharist. Without the physical body of Jesus, one cannot be saved.

With regard to the body, the dispute can be characterized as, on the part of Nestorius, a denial of the *Logos* as the ultimate subject of the human attributes of Jesus and, simultaneously, a concern to 'provide for a clear distinction of the natures in the face of the heretical tendencies of his time'[10] that might suggest some sort of altering of the deity of Christ. The argument between the two can be couched in the terms of the Arian debate; Cyril believed that Nestorius' position made Jesus not Divine, whereas Nestorius was concerned that Cyril was making Jesus into some sort of demi-God. On Cyril's part, at least until the formula of union, there was a fierce refutation of anything less than one incarnate nature of the Divine *Logos*. He believed that, while remaining God, the *Logos* took on and became the subject of human life. For Cyril, humanity belonged so completely to the *Logos* that there was only one subsistent reality in Jesus. To refuse the title *Theotokos* to the mother of Christ implied, to Cyril at least, that the divinity of the *Logos* and the humanity of Jesus were separated. The soteriological, and thus eucharistic, implications of such a statement were catastrophic. If the body of Jesus is not fully Christ but merely inhabited by the *Logos*, then the Annunciation-Incarnation event non-identically repeated in the celebration of the Eucharist and received into the physical body of the believer is a sham. Cyril himself noted:

It was not otherwise possible for man, being of a nature which perishes, to escape death, unless he recovered that ancient grace, and partook once more of God who holds all things together in being and preserves them in life through the Son in the Spirit. Therefore his Only-begotten Word has

10 Grillmeier, *Christ in Christian Tradition*, 379.

become a partaker of flesh and blood (Heb. 2.14), that is, he was become man, though being Life by nature, and begotten of the life that is by nature, that is, of God the Father, so that, having united himself with the flesh which perishes according to the law of its own nature . . . he might restore it to his own Life and render it through himself a partaker of God the Father . . . And he wears our nature, refashioning it to his own Life. And he himself is also in us, for we have all become partakers of him, and have him in ourselves through the Spirit. For this reason we have become 'partakers of the divine nature' (2 Peter 1.4), and are reckoned as sons, and so too we have in ourselves the Father himself through the Son.[11]

The physical, historical body (or flesh) of the Divine Son is clearly essential for Cyril. It is through this union of God with humanity's flesh and blood that redemption becomes possible.

This eucharistic thought draws an inextricable link with the Annunciation-Incarnation event. This theology is entirely body-focused – not just on the Incarnate Body of Christ but also on the eucharistic body and the physical body of the believer. At every stage, Cyril is keen to emphasize the significance of bodily integrity – a key theme in the recovery from trauma. Bodily division and disunity are unacceptable in this theology of wholeness. Indeed, it seems almost impossible to apply modern distinctions of sub-genres of theology to Cyril's thought – each aspect is tightly interwoven with the next. There is, for Cyril, an interpenetrative relationship between all aspects of his theology. Although his doctrine of the Eucharist is a strong driving force in his thinking, one cannot, in the case of Cyril, separate this from any other aspect of his theology.

For Cyril, the Body of Christ, in its incarnate sense, is not incidental but essential. This body must have its own

---

11 'In Jo. 14.20', trans. Thomas G. Weinandy, 'Cyril and the Mystery of the Incarnation', in *The Theology of St Cyril of Alexandria: A Critical Appreciation*, ed. Thomas G. Weinandy and Daniel A. Keating (London & New York: T & T Clark, 2003), 23–54, at 24–5.

integrity; it cannot be divided in its essence from the divinity of the *Logos*. The somatic memory of the Annunciation-Incarnation event, and the later non-identical repetition of this event in the Eucharist, thus stems from the bodily integrity of Jesus Christ.

The Corporate Body

If beginning our theological endeavour from the starting point of the Eucharist allowed us to view the Incarnation of Christ in its fullest sense – from the moment of the Annunciation to the Ascension of Christ – so, too, does it require us to consider bodies in their broadest sense. In exploring Cyril's theology and faith we have already considered the eucharistic, Incarnate Body of Christ; but other bodies were similarly significant in Cyril's theological universe, and the eucharistic drive, which is the core of Cyril's theology, can be seen in these bodies too.

The holistic image of the united body of Jesus, in terms of both the Eucharist and the body of the Incarnate Word, is an image that extends beyond these realities and into the realm of symbol for Cyril of Alexandria. The symbol of the body must not be underestimated in its role in the Nestorian Controversy. Nor should one underestimate the extent to which the affairs of the Church were connected with the business of the Imperial family. Susan Wessel noted that:

[T]o warn the Emperor of a divisive heresy that separated the humanity and divinity of Christ, Cyril reminded him [the Emperor] that Jude had predicted that false teachers would appear at the end of time, and that they would create divisions within the church. The ecclesiastical political implications seemed clear. Just as the unnamed Nestorius claimed that there was division within the person of Christ, so could that division insinuate itself into the social fabric of the church. And a church so divided would threaten the stability of the emperor's reign. Athanasius had similarly invoked the metaphor of a unified Christ when he compared Christ's body, undivided at death, to a unified, orthodox church free from schism.[12]

The significance of the unity and the holistic understanding of the corporate body, in both its imperial and its ecclesial contexts, is another factor in understanding the driving forces of the Nestorian Controversy. Agreement, peace and unity in the ecclesial and imperial bodies seem, in this sense, to be grounded on 'correct' theology. This certainly appears to be the attitude of both Cyril and the Emperor – Theodosius. Perceiving a rift in the imperial family, Cyril wrote separate letters, stating his case and carefully opposing Nestorius, to Emperor Theodosius, his wife Eudocia and his sister Pulcheria, and a further letter for the younger princesses.[13] Cyril told the women that:

> [I]t is very impious to divide into two sons and two Christs after the inseparable union . . . for if Christ thus finds your faith is steadfast and pure, he will honour you abundantly with good things from above and you will be fully blessed.[14]

Cyril drew the connection for the female members of the imperial family clearly. If they support Cyril's Christology then their family, and thus by extension the Empire, will flourish. If they support Nestorius they will not be blessed. A divided Christ will bring division to the Empire. In these letters, Cyril drew a direct line between the belief in the united nature of Christ and the fortune of the imperial women.

In this respect, Cyril drew on Paul's body theology, particularly as expressed in 1 Corinthians 12. Dale Martin, in his analysis of Paul's Corinthian body, noted a relationship

---

12 Susan Wessel, *Cyril of Alexandria and the Nestorian Controversy: The Making of a Saint and of a Heretic* (Oxford: Oxford University Press, 2004), 98.

13 Ibid., 98.

14 Cyril of Alexandria, 'Cyrilli oratio ad augustas de fide', *Acta Conciliorum Oecumenicorum* I.I.5, ed. Edward Schwartz (Berolini: W. de Gruyter, 1927), 26–61, cited and trans. Wessel, *Cyril of Alexandria and the Nestorian Controversy*, 112, n. 84.

between the divided church body in the city of Corinth and the celebration of the Eucharist. He argued that:

> Paul focuses his argument on the fracturing of the church, the body of Christ. His solution to the problems surrounding the Lord's Supper is a social one: heal the fragmented body and restore unity . . . The Strong at Corinth, by reinforcing social distinctions in the church, divide the church. They are quite literally, in Paul's view, 'killing' Christ by tearing apart his body. They pervert the meal of unity, the 'common meal', by making it an occasion for schism and difference.[15]

The corporate body, for Paul, was clearly not distinct from the eucharistic body. And one's actions towards one body had the potential to affect the other bodies too.

Theodosius was influenced by the powerful imperial theology espoused by Cyril. In a letter written to Cyril and the Metropolitan Bishops in November 430 CE, Theodosius linked the condition of the state to godly piety and the acceptability of the state to God. It was this desire for a peaceful state in the eyes of God that prompted Theodosius to convene a synod in the following year to draw this dispute to a close. Wessel drew the connection between these two bodies to a dramatic conclusion: '[M]ore than a matter of ecclesiastical division, the potential conflict was thought to disrupt the very foundations of Theodosius' imperial reign, which rested on divine sanction.'[16]

The issue of bodily unity clearly stretched beyond the unity of divinity and humanity in the eucharistic and Incarnate Body of Christ and into the symbolic bodies of the Church and the Empire. Here, too, unity cannot be divided from correct doctrine and the two seem to have an interpenetrative relationship in the thought of Cyril. The eucharistic, Christological, ecclesiological and imperial elements of this bodily unity cannot

---

15 Dale B. Martin, *The Corinthian Body* (New Haven, CT and London: Yale University Press, 1995), 194.

16 Wessel, *Cyril of Alexandria and the Nestorian Controversy*, 99.

be easily separated and this desire for unity is driven by Cyril's understanding of the relationship between the Eucharist and the Incarnation. The unity of these corporate bodies is entirely connected to the Annunciation-Incarnation event. The drive for wholeness and fullness entwined with Cyril's understanding of the importance of unity for all bodies.

Women's Bodies

The Annunciation-Incarnation event goes beyond the moment of Jesus' becoming human and our understanding of Incarnation stretches far in two directions. In one direction, the Incarnation stretches to the Ascension of Christ into heaven and infinite existence in his human body. In the other direction, the Incarnation encompasses the Annunciation and the body of Christ's mother, Mary. This event, so central to both Cyril's theology and my own theological endeavour, is not, however, solely the preserve of the male body of Jesus. What is non-identically repeated in the celebration of the Eucharist is not only significant to the male body.

The female body is not absent from the Nestorian Controversy. The Nestorian Controversy arose over the use of a title for Mary – *Theotokos* – meaning 'god-bearer'. It would be a mistake to argue that the Nestorian Controversy was a Mariological issue – it was not. It was, primarily, a long-standing Christological one, that had found its most recent expression in an issue regarding appropriate titles of Mary. However, while the debate was not, in truth, about Mary, it is not possible to separate out the female body from the male one; the mother's body from the child's. The discussions about the way in which the Body of Christ was to be remembered and worshipped had direct implications for the body of Mary also. Similarly, debate about the nature and person of Mary impacted upon Christology.

In her exploration of the significance of the title *Theotokos* within the wider rhetoric of soteriology and eschatology in fifth-century Byzantium, Frances Young noted the essential

nature of Mary's physical, female flesh for Cyril: '[T]he crucial thing for Cyril is that the Word dwelt in flesh, "using
as his own particular body the temple that is from the holy
Virgin".'[17] Acknowledging that it is neither possible nor profit-
able to attempt to separate Cyril's Christological position from
his understanding of the Eucharist, Young outlined the significance of the flesh of Christ and concluded that there 'are many
indications that the flesh is vital as the medium of this eternal
life. So Mary *Theotokos* is essential as the vehicle of the Word's
enfleshment.'[18] The physical, female flesh of Mary cannot be
separated from Cyril's Christology, his understanding of the
Eucharist or his conception of salvation. Therefore, the female
flesh of Mary and her participation in the mysteries of the
Incarnation (and in the Eucharist if one follows Cyril's understanding of the connectedness of these two mysteries) must be
taken seriously in exploring the Nestorian Controversy. For
Cyril, the unity and integrity of the body is not a gendered
issue; it is significant for all bodies.

If the dispute was not exclusively a Mariological one, the
Marian influence, however, can be argued to be at the heart of the
actions of principal players in the crisis. The Emperor's sister –
Pulcheria – was key to the events surrounding the Nestorian
Controversy. Kenneth Holum painted a picture of Pulcheria as
a Marian impresario who wields her virginity and devotion to
Mary as political tools and weapons of power. Pulcheria swore
an oath of virginity in emulation of the Virgin that not only pro-
tected her independence as an imperial woman, but also pro-
tected her brother's imperial courts from the external influence of
her potential husband. Furthermore, in appealing to the Virgin,
Holum argues that Pulcheria and her sisters solidified their
sacred *basileía* (a form of royal charisma essential for activating

---

17 Frances Young, '*Theotokos*: Mary and the Pattern of Fall and
Redemption in the Theology of Cyril of Alexandria', in *The Theology
of St Cyril of Alexandria: A Critical Appreciation*, ed. Thomas G.
Weinandy and Daniel A. Keating (London and New York: T & T
Clark, 2003), 55–74, at 71.

18 Ibid., 73.

cooperation from imperial subjects) through their devotion to the Virgin Mary.[19]

Pulcheria appears to have had running clashes with Nestorius from the time of his appointment as Bishop of Constantinople. Nestorius accused her of immorality and adultery, refused to entertain her and her ladies, as had been the custom of the former bishop, and removed her portrait and donations from the altar of the Great Church. The most dramatic encounter occurred on an Easter Sunday, only a few days after Nestorius had been ordained as Bishop of Constantinople.

> Pulcheria appeared at the gate to the sanctuary of the Great Church, expecting to take communion within in the presence of the priests and her brother the emperor. The archdeacon Peter informed Nestorius of her custom, and the bishop hurried to bar the way, to prevent the sacrilege of a lay person and woman in the Holy of Holies. Pulcheria demanded entrance, but Nestorius insisted that 'only priests may walk here'. She asked: 'Why? Have I not given birth to God?' He replied: 'You? You have given birth to Satan!' And then Nestorius drove the empress from the sanctuary.[20]

There is some doubt as to whether or not this incident can be treated as historical fact or if it is an apocryphal contribution to the Pulcheria legend that grew in the centuries following her death. Regardless of the veracity of the statement, it is a revealing anecdote. Pulcheria's appeal to her imitation of Mary's virginity appears to furnish her with a power that would otherwise have been inaccessible to a woman, even an imperial one. However, Maxwell Johnson interpreted this statement as a purely spiritual one. He concluded:

---

19 Kenneth Holum, *Theodosian Empresses: Women and Imperial Dominion in Late Antiquity* (Berkeley, Los Angeles and London: University of California Press, 1982), 93.

20 *Lettre à Cosme* 8 (PO, XII, 279), cited in Holum, *Theodosian Empresses*, 153.

consistent with the Marian theology of Nestorius's predeces-
sor, Atticus of Constantinople (d. 425), who had instructed
Pulcheria and her sisters, Arcadia and Marina, that if they
imitated the virginity and chastity of Mary they would give
birth to God mystically in their souls, Pulcheria's Marian
self-identification ('have I not given birth to God?') indicates
that such personal or popular devotion to the *Theotokos*
could even become a kind of Marian mysticism.[21]

Once again, it would seem to be difficult to distinguish the
political realm from the theological one. The true explanation of Pulcheria's self-identification with the figure of Mary
is, most likely, both political and theological; her identification with Mary's virginity gives Pulcheria both political and
theological authority. It seems that the boundaries between
the political, familial and spiritual bodies are blurred, as has
been demonstrated throughout this exploration of Cyril's
theology.

What is, however, certain is that the two (Nestorius and
Pulcheria) did not get off to a good start. This fact was exploited
by Cyril who sought to curry favour with Pulcheria directly
through letters sent to her and her sisters, vilifying Nestorius
and his teachings. With regard to the issue of Mary *Theotokos*,
Pulcheria intervened even before the Council tasked to consider the issue took place and influenced the arrangements in
her favour (and thus, presumably, not in Nestorius' favour).
The Council itself took place in Ephesus, an ancient centre of
virgin goddess worship which had already devoted itself to the
cult of the *Theotokos*, and the meetings themselves took place
in a church dedicated to Mary.

The influence of Pulcheria on the arrangements for the
Council go some way to demonstrate just how united the
imperial body was. Pulcheria clearly had the ear of her brother

---

21 Maxwell E. Johnson, 'Sub Tuum Praesidium: The Theotokos in
Christian Life and Worship before Ephesus', in *The Place of Christ in
Liturgical Prayer: Trinity, Christology, and Liturgical Theology*, ed. Bryan
D. Spinks (Collegeville, MN: Liturgical Press, 2008), 243–67, at 261.

and was devoted to seeing unity – albeit the unity she had already staked her claim on. Pulcheria did not just play a political role in the resolution of this controversy; her Marian piety, her devotion to Jesus' mother, had a profound influence on the people of Constantinople and the eventual resolution of the dispute.

> Pulcheria had a more important function in the *Theotokos* controversy than backstage manoeuvring and attempts to exert influence. More than anyone else in Constantinople, she embodied the fullness of Mary piety – in her womanhood, in her spectacular asceticism, and in her claims to Marian dignity. The *voces populi* of July 5 prove that the people of Constantinople responded to her piety, and that this response contributed to their hatred of Nestorius. Thus Mary's victory became her victory as well. In contemporary thinking this victory conferred legitimacy as effectively as any battlefield success. To judge from the *Theotokos* controversy, Pulcheria's sacral *basileía* encompassed resources better emulated than resisted by an imperial person of either sex.[22]

It is important to note that this analysis of Pulcheria and her role in the Nestorian Controversy cannot be separated out from the significant Pulcherian legend that grew up around her in the years following her death. It is perhaps impossible to know historically whether she did behave in the way she has been portrayed or said the words that we have recorded. Even if one assumes that none of these events are true and they are all later inventions of rhetoricians and historians, the foundation for such stories must have been laid in truth. It is likely that, even if Pulcheria did not claim to have given birth to God, even if she did not self-identify with the *Theotokos*, even if the crowds did not cry out to her as their hero after the Council of Ephesus, these actions are not beyond the realm of historical imagination. To posit these stories into history,

---

22 Holum, *Theodosian Empresses*, 174.

there must have been a basis of reality on which they could lie. They cannot be so far removed from reality as to make them implausible. Our interest is not in Pulcheria herself, *per se*, but rather in the theology and mythology that surrounds her and these actions.

Pulcheria was not the only woman of significance in Constantinople in the time of the Nestorian Controversy. Pulcheria's power and influence owed much to her patronage relationships throughout the church. Pulcheria was the leader of an important network of aristocratic women. These women were equally distressed at the actions and proclamations of Nestorius in Constantinople. As well as denouncing the title *Theotokos* and publicly snubbing Pulcheria, Nestorius subjected all the women of the city to a curfew, suggesting that no respectable woman should be out in the city after dark. This curtailed these women's habit of attending vespers. John McGuckin concluded:

> [T]he assault on the validity of the *Theotokos* title could only have been interpreted by these powerful women (particularly the virgins and deaconesses among them) in the light of their own mimesis of the fertile and sacral virginity of the Mother of God. It seemed abundantly clear to them that Nestorius's assault on the honour of the Virgin went hand in hand with his attack on their own sources of honour and patronage, their own derived sacral basileia that reflected the glory of the Mother of God . . . It is probably no exaggeration to think that this party of aristocratic women gathered around Pulcheria was primarily responsible for the downfall of Nestorius.[23]

The actions of Nestorius on the women of Constantinople at this time can be understood as an 'assault' and can be read, in hindsight, as a traumatic experience. The women experience the

---

23 John McGuckin, 'The Paradox of the Virgin Theotokos: Evangelism and Imperial Politics in the Fifth Century Byzantine World', *Maria* 2 (2001), 8–25 at 20.

rupture of their identities as Nestorius attacked their (already limited) power through his assault on the *Theotokos*. The downfall of Nestorius and the preservation of the title *Theotokos* is, perhaps, the establishment of the integrity of the feminine body in Constantinople – the first stage of their recovery from the trauma from this assault. The significance of the female body in Constantinople during this period is not to be underestimated. Regardless of whether one attributes to the female a primary role in the Nestorian controversy, it is clear that this body of women within the city and the person of Mary from whom they took their inspiration must be considered in a holistic interpretation of the events of this period.

Furthermore, if, as Cyril believed, the Incarnation and the Eucharist are intimately connected, then it would seem that these female bodies, acting in imitation of Mary, who cannot be discounted from the Annunciation-Incarnation event herself, are intimately connected to Cyril's eucharistic theology too. A holistic view of the Incarnation inevitably leads to a holistic view of theology as well.

Bodily Unity

Cyril of Alexandria had neither interest in, nor language for, an exploration of the impact of trauma on theological discourse. But he did have absolute faith in the life-giving, salvific efficacy of the Eucharist. It is this theological concept that drives the rest of his theology. Beginning his theology at the Eucharist, Cyril allowed his belief in the life-giving effect of the bread and wine to shape his Christology and soteriology. The impact of this is to mould a theology that has a profound concern for the holistic unity and integrity of the body. This concern begins with the eucharistic Body of Christ shared in bread and wine in each celebration of the Eucharist but spreads its theological tendrils into understandings of the Incarnation, the Church, the State, the perceived differences between gendered bodies.

Significantly, then, understanding the Eucharist as a non-identical repetition of the Annunciation-Incarnation event

provides a great impetus for exploring the surrounding theological issues of unity and salvation. The Eucharist remem-
bers the life of Christ including, but not solely focused on, his
Passion, death and resurrection. The somatic memory repeatedly enacted is one of Jesus' life – his whole life. Understanding
the unity of the eucharistic body provides, both for Cyril and
for the contemporary reader, the key to understanding bodily
unity and integrity in all its forms. Cyril would have agreed
with the later assessment of David Ford when Ford concluded
that the Eucharist 'is the sacrament of human flourishing'.[24]
It is in the Eucharist that bodies flourish. Understanding the
(eucharistic, physical, historical) bodily integrity of Christ
becomes a model for all Christian understanding of bodily
integrity. For Cyril, therefore, there is an overriding theme of
bodily unity and a holistic approach to objective reality – it
is imperative, for Cyril, that the body, in all its manifesta-
tions, is one. It is this concern for the body, particularly a
holistic concern for bodily integrity, that we shall similarly
see as an outworking of the theological moves I will take in
the subsequent chapters exploring the impact of trauma on
our theology.

---

24 Ford, 'What Happens in the Eucharist?', 380.

Rupture

The experience of trauma is a rupturing event. Like an earth-quake rolls through a landscape and radically alters the topo-graphical features, so does trauma roll through lives, stories, memories and bodies, leaving them radically altered. Allowing the traumatic memory of the Body of Christ to be framed in terms of the Annunciation-Incarnation event and moving it away from the destructive power of the Cross causes a rup-ture in traditional Christian narratives. The way in which the Christ-event has been understood, along with the intertwined narratives of priesthood, sacrifice, and the Eucharist, are rad-ically altered in the light of this traumatic reframing. It is from this rupture that new, fresh, life-giving theological narratives come forth. They blossom in the space cleared by the rupture of trauma. Like a forest awakening in the aftermath of a fire, or a trauma survivor stirring up a survivor's gift in the after-math of trauma, some stories can only be told in the wake of the rupture. These are those narratives.

4

Priesthood

What is a Priest?

In the Hebrew Bible, the priests of the Temple had a two-fold function. Primarily, they acted as intermediaries. Broadly speaking, one can conceive of the priesthood at this time as:

> [a] bridge from God to the people through teaching, judging, mediating, and conferring the priestly blessing. It also serves as a bridge from the people to God through participation in the Temple service and wearing garments inscribed with the names of the twelve tribes.[1]

Much of this fluidity and twofold nature is transferred into the contemporary understanding of the priest, particularly with regard to their function in the eucharistic celebration. Indeed, one can still consider the role of the priest today to be one of mediation. For example, Rowan Williams noted that the fundamental task of priesthood is to mediate between the orders of reality (the Divine order and the human order). He wrote, poignantly, that the priesthood is:

> crucially to do with the service of the space cleared by God; with the holding open of a door into a place where a damaged and confused humanity is able to move slowly into the room made available, and understand that it is accompanied

---

1 Hayyim Angel, 'Ezekiel: Priest-Prophet', *Jewish Bible Quarterly* 39, no. 1 (2011), 35–45, at 35–6.

and heard in all its variety and unmanageability, and emotional turmoil and spiritual uncertainty.[2]

The role of a priest is to mediate between God and the Church. The power of mediation lies in the fact that it is God who has cleared the space, not in the power of the priest. In this sense, the role and function of a priest is fluid. When one observes a eucharistic celebration taking place one can become attuned to these subtle shifts in role. At one point the priest acts on behalf of the congregation towards God. A moment later, the priest is repeating the actions of Christ towards the congregation. These shifts are powerful. Sarah Coakley argued that these shifts are inseparably connected to gender and that by moving from one role to the other, as indeed it is natural for the priest to do, the

> priest is in an inherently fluid gender role as beater of the liminal bounds between the divine and the human. But in representing *both* 'Christ' *and* 'church' . . . the priest is not simply divine/'masculine' in the first over human/'feminine' in the other, but *both* in *both*.[3]

At first glance it looks as though the liturgy reinforces gender binaries but the net effect of this fluidity and movement is to destabilize and undermine stereotypical gender associations.

This contemplation of the fluidity and transitional nature of the priestly role exemplifies the contemporary understanding of priesthood. But the history of priesthood is a complex one. By the beginning of the third century, those who presided over eucharistic worship within the early Church were beginning to be considered to be priestly ministers, having previously been thought of more as community leaders. For example, Origen

---

2 Rowan Williams, 'Epilogue', in *Praying for England: Priestly Presence in Contemporary Culture*, ed. Samuel Wells and Sarah Coakley (London and New York: Continuum, 2008), 171–82 at 179.

3 Sarah Coakley, 'The Woman at the Altar: Cosmological Disturbance or Gender Subversion?', *The Anglican Theological Review* 86, no. 1 (2004), 75–93, at 76.

referred to bishops as priests and believed that the presbyters exercise an inferior form of priesthood.[4] It was the bishops who celebrated the Eucharist, whereas the presbyters were those who led the communities. Similarly, Cyprian wrote of a high concept of priesthood:

> For if Jesus Christ, our Lord and God, is Himself the chief priest of God the Father, and has first offered Himself a sacrifice to the Father, and has commanded this to be done in commemoration of Himself, certainly that priest truly discharges the office of Christ, who imitates that which Christ did; and he then offers a true and full sacrifice in the church to God the Father, when he proceeds to offer it according to what he sees Christ Himself to have offered.[5]

The history of ordained ministry and the changes it has undergone cannot be separated out from the histories of other sacraments, but most especially the sacrament of the Eucharist. As one considers the changes in the early Church's understanding of the Eucharist so one can similarly see the way in which their understanding of the role of the priest also changed. As the Eucharist came to be understood more specifically as a sacrificial act, so the status and purity of the one presiding over this act became more significant. Indeed, by the early Middle Ages, the role of the priest was almost entirely focused on the priest's power to consecrate and to offer the Eucharist.

The history of the sacraments in the later Middle Ages is marked by significant change in the understanding of the priesthood, as seen particularly in the evolution of the

---

4 See for example Origen, 'Homily 6', trans. Gary Wayne Barkley in *Homilies on Leviticus 1–16* (Washington, DC: The Catholic University of America Press, 1990), 116–28.

5 Cyprian, 'Epistle 62', trans. Robert Ernest Wallis in *Ante-Nicene Christian Library: Translations of The Writings of the Fathers Down to AD 325, Vol VIII, The Writings of Cyprian, Bishop of Carthage*, Part 1 of 2, ed. Alexander Roberts and James Donaldson (Edinburgh: T & T Clark, 1868), paragraph 14. Accessed online at www.newadvent.org/fathers/050662.htm on 09/03/16.

sacerdotal rites for ordination, the attention to ministry in the turn to Scholasticism, and, especially, the influence of Thomas Aquinas. Aquinas argued that the priestly character conferred upon ordination was the character of Christ the high priest who instituted the Eucharist at the Last Supper and sacrificed himself upon the Cross. For Aquinas, this sacramental conferring of character is considered to be an eternal imprinting of the sacramental seal.[6] This Christ was a perfect mediator between humankind and God, just as the priest was to be. Those who made the Eucharist present in the Church brought God to humanity and humanity to God, just as Christ did. Aquinas wrote: '[T]he office proper to a priest is to be a mediator between God and the people.'[7] Christ does this par excellence, but all priests subsequently function as mediators. This idea, while considered authoritative, was not static. Indeed, marginally later scholars such as Duns Scotus and William of Ockham believed that 'the essential power of the priest was to change the bread and wine into the body and blood . . . They preferred to limit the priestly function to offering sacrifice and to speak of the other duties as ministerial functions.'[8]

It is possible to see this intimate connection between the understanding of the Eucharist and the role of the priest further still when one considers the changes wrought in the wake of the Protestant Reformation. Both Luther and Calvin rejected the theology of the Eucharist as a sacrifice. Arguing that the offering of the Body of Jesus Christ once for all was sufficient and no further sacrificial acts were necessary, Luther strongly advocated a 'priesthood of all believers' (1 Pet. 2.5). Luther wrote:

---

6 Thomas Aquinas, *The Summa Theologica*, trans. Fathers of the English Dominican Province (London: Burns, Oates and Washbourne Ltd, 1920), IV, Q. 35, A. 2. All subsequent quotations from *The Summa* are taken from this edition.

7 Ibid., III, Q. 22, A. 1.

8 Joseph Martos, *Doors to the Sacred: A Historical Introduction to Sacraments in the Catholic Church* (Liguori, MO: Liguori Publications, 1991), 436.

[T]he third captivity of this sacrament [the Eucharist] is by far the most wicked abuse of all, in consequence of which there is no opinion more generally held or more firmly believed in the church today than this, that the mass is a good work and a sacrifice . . . Now there is yet a second stumbling block that must be removed, and this is much greater and the most dangerous of all. It is the common belief that the mass is a sacrifice which is offered to God.[9]

While Luther did believe in the Real Presence of Christ in the Eucharist there was, in his opinion, no need to repeat the sacrifice of the Cross in the celebration of the Eucharist. Indeed, it was impossible to repeat this sacrifice and any attempt to do so was in vain. As such, for Luther, and in contrast to official Roman Catholic theologies of priesthood of that time, ordained clergy had no power that did not belong to all Christians, but rather a calling and commissioning to certain functions within the church community.

Calvin, rejecting the concept of Real Presence in the Eucharist, went further than Luther in arguing that the celebration of the Eucharist was not a sacrificial act but an act of memorial. Calvin posited:

[I]t is a most wicked infamy and unbearable blasphemy, both against Christ and against the sacrifice which he made for us through his death on the cross, for anyone to suppose that by repeating the oblation he obtains pardon for sins, appeases God, and acquires righteousness.[10]

While accepting an ordained priesthood, Calvin felt that only those who were called by God should be ordained to serve within the Church. On the surface, this seems to be a statement

---

9 Martin Luther, 'The Babylonian Captivity of the Church', in *Luther's Works*, ed. Helmut Lehmann, Vol. 36 (Philadelphia, PA: Fortress Press, 1520), 11–126, at 35, 51.

10 John Calvin, *Calvin: Institutes of the Christian Religion*, Vol. 2, trans. Ford Lewis Battles, ed. John T. McNeill (Philadelphia, PA: The Westminster Press, 1960), 1442.

Aquinas would agree with, but the difference between the two men is apparent when one considers the nature of this service. For Aquinas, the ordained priest is called to offer the eucharistic sacrifice.[11] For Calvin, the priest (or pastor-teacher) is ordained to preach, teach and administer the sacraments, having been called to advance the kingdom of God.[12] Both Luther and Calvin rejected the notion of the Eucharist as a sacrificial act, and in both cases this rejection was matched by a change in their understanding of the role and function of the priest.

The Catholic response to the Reformation – the Council of Trent – upheld that the Eucharist was a sacrifice initiated by Christ and that the Christian priesthood replaced the priesthood of the Old Testament. In the twenty-second session of the Council of Trent held in September 1562, the Council decreed:

> [T]hat the Sacrifice of the Mass is propitiatory both for the living and the dead. And forasmuch as, in this divine sacrifice which is celebrated in the mass, that same Christ is contained and immolated in an unbloody manner, who once offered Himself in a bloody manner on the altar of the cross; the holy Synod teaches, that this sacrifice is truly propitiatory and that by means thereof this is effected, that we obtain mercy, and find grace in seasonable aid, if we draw nigh unto God, contrite and penitent, with a sincere heart and upright faith, with fear and reverence. For the Lord, appeased by the oblation thereof, and granting the grace and gift of penitence, forgives even heinous crimes and sins. For the victim is one and the same, the same now offering by the ministry of priests, who then offered Himself on the cross, the manner alone of offering being different.[13]

---

11 Aquinas, *The Summa Theologica*, III, Q. 82, ad. 1.

12 See for example Calvin's argument in Part 4, Chapter 3 of 'Institutes of the Christian Religion', in *Institutes of the Christian Religion, 1536 Edition* (Grand Rapids, MI: Eerdmans, 1995).

13 J. Waterworth, *The Canons and Decrees of the Sacred and Oecumenical Council of Trent* (London: Dolman, 1848), 154–5.

Edward Schillebeeckx noted, in his reflections on these statements of the Council of Trent, that they should not be taken as
an accurate barometer of the Catholic Church's perspective on
priesthood at that time, or indeed at any time. Such statements
were written in express response and opposition to the specific challenges of the Reformers and as such were not broad
in their outlook or comprehensive in their summary of extant
doctrine on the topic.

Nevertheless, the proclamations of Trent became authoritative and set the pattern for understanding ordained ministry
thereafter. The priesthood and its relationship to the Eucharist
remained unchanged for the following five hundred years. It
was only with the convening of the Second Vatican Council in
the 1960s that the door was opened for a change in the conception of the priesthood as the liturgical reform of the years
following the Council took shape.

Historical research conducted in the early part of the twentieth century began to raise questions regarding the priesthood
and the nature of priestly ordination. For example, in 1947
Pope Pius XII called for the reinstatement of the laying on of
hands as an essential part of the ordination of priests, due to
the discovery that the handing over of liturgical instruments
upon ordination was a medieval innovation to the sacrament
of ordination.[14]

Twentieth-century theologians and historians have demonstrated that the meaning of ordination changed dramatically in the
twelfth and thirteenth centuries. For example, Vinzenz Fuchs in
1963[15] and Pierre-Marie Gy in 1979[16] both made clear the significant change that ordination undertook in the time period. Prior to
this shift in meaning, ordination (a surprisingly loose term) was of
a man or a woman to a particular role in a particular church. The

---

14 Pope Pius XII, 'Sacramentum Ordinis', www.vatican.va/holy_
father/pius_xii/apost-constitutions/documents/hf_p-xii_apc_19471130_
sacramentum-ordinis_It.html. Accessed 21/11/2014.

15 Vinzenz Fuchs, *Der Ordinationstitel Von Seiner Entstehung Bis
Auf Innozenz III* (Amsterdam: P. Schippers, 1968).

16 Pierre-Marie Gy, 'Ancient Ordination Prayers', *Studia Liturgica*
13 (1979), 70–93.

shift in meaning to a Eucharist-presiding concentration coincided with a more general development of emphasis on the Eucharist in Catholic thinking. Yves Congar identified such a change in meaning in his research on the terms 'ordain' and 'ordination'.

> When the treatment of the sacrament of orders was developed in the second half of the twelfth century, then formulated in the works of the great scholastics of the thirteenth century, it was dominated by reference to the Eucharist, by the power of consecrating it, *potestas conficiendi* (power of confecting [the Eucharist]). This power was given by an indelible and personally possessed character.[17]

The twentieth century was also a period in which established understandings of the Eucharist and its accompanying terminology were revised and reinterpreted. This was accompanied by an increased recognition of the diverse nature of ministries and liturgies in the early Church. Twentieth-century scholars considered anew the liturgies of the early Church and the writings of Church fathers and mothers in an attempt to understand the origins and the development of the Eucharist in particular.

Schillebeeckx, one such theologian who undertook this task and drawing on the works of historians such as Fuchs and Gy, noted that prior to the Middle Ages a minister had to be ordained in order to preside over a church community (*corpus verum*), but in the Middle Ages this shifted, and a minister was now ordained to preside over the *corpus mysticum*. Schillebeeckx felt that this indicated that ordination became less about leading the church community and more about power to celebrate the Eucharist.[18] Thirty-five years previously, Henri de Lubac had suggested that the terminology

---

17 Yves Congar, 'Note Sur Une Valeur Des Termes, «Ordinare, Ordinatio»', *Revue Des Sciences Religieuses* 58 (1984), 7–14, 13, trans. and cited in Gary Macy, *The Hidden History of Women's Ordination: Female Clergy in the Medieval West* (Oxford: Oxford University Press, 2008), 31.

18 Edward Schillebeeckx, *Ministry: A Case for Change* (London: SCM Press, 1980), 57.

of the *corpus mysticum* had itself shifted. De Lubac suggested that the phrase *corpus mysticum* had originally, in the early Church, referred to Christ's eucharistic body and that it was only in the early Middle Ages that the phrase came to be associated with the ecclesial body of the Church.[19] In this frame, the eucharistic language of the Church came to act as a theological black hole which encompasses everything. All theology came to be understood through this eucharistic lens.

Both Schillebeeckx and de Lubac sought to correct what they believed to be interpretative mistakes made in the Middle Ages, and to return to a more 'authentic' understanding of the relationship between the Eucharist and the Church. Both demonstrated the rise of the importance and significance of the Eucharist in relationship to the priestly ministry and the Church. This turn to reception history is a marked feature of twentieth-century approaches to the Eucharist.

The Second Vatican Council's documents on ordained ministries present a more pastoral than doctrinal tone. The Council did little more than to restate a fairly traditional role of the parish priest, such that the impression one is left with is that:

> [T]heir function as priests was first and foremost the celebration of the eucharistic liturgy, but the administration of the other sacraments was also important, and they were to lead the faithful by their preaching and example as well.[20]

However, the broader effect of the Council was felt in the years following when, combined with the socially conscious climate of the late 1960s and 70s, many lay Catholic men and women moved into new roles outside the walls of churches and convents. The Council encouraged the fostering of Christian community within parishes. The practical outworking of this

---

19 Henri de Lubac, *Corpus Mysticum: The Eucharist and the Church in the Middle Ages*, trans. Gemma Simmonds, Richard Price and Christopher Stephens (London: University of Notre Dame Press, 2006), 248.

20 Martos, *Doors to the Sacred*, 447.

meant that lay Catholic men and women became active in communities, often on behalf of the poor and oppressed.

It is no coincidence that, in the years following the council, Liberation Theology became a significant force within the Catholic Church as concern for the poor and justice within communities became increasingly important. Furthermore, the encouragement for the laity to actively participate in the celebration of the liturgy served to decrease the sense of uniqueness and isolation of the priest-celebrant. The Decree on the Apostolate of the Laity[21] emphasized the importance of active participation in the life of the Church. This was accomplished by the regular receiving of communion by the laity, the revitalization and formation of lay societies such as Pax Christi and the Apostolate for Family Consecration, and the establishment of the permanent diaconate. The priest no longer performed a service that was his alone, but rather a service on behalf of, and in union with, the congregation.

In line with this shift in understanding came the decline of the private Mass. Edward Foley noted that there was '[E]vidence of priests saying Mass without a congregation from as early as the seventh century.'[22] In 1963, Pope Paul VI decreed in *Sacrosanctum Concilium* that:

> It is to be stressed that wherever rites, according to their specific nature, make provision for communal celebration involving the presence and active participation of the faithful, this way of celebrating them is to be preferred, so far as possible, to a celebration that is individual and quasi-private.[23]

The strong counsel to proceed via communal celebrations and to avoid where possible individual ones further emphasizes the

---

21 Pope Paul VI, 'Decree on the Apostolate of the Laity', Vatican, www.vatican.va/archive/hist_councils/ii_vatican_council/documents/vat-ii_decree_19651118_apostolicam-actuositatem_en.html. Accessed 24/11/15.

22 Edward Foley, *From Age to Age: How Christians Have Celebrated the Eucharist* (Collegeville, MN: Liturgical Press, 2008), 157.

23 Second Vatican Council, 'Constitution on the Sacred Liturgy'.

change in perception of the role of the priest and their relationship to the Eucharist. These changes all serve to emphasize the role of priest, not as one who performs sacrifices for the sins of the congregation, but rather as one who acts as mediator between the human and the Divine; one who holds open the door for humanity to enter the space cleared by God.

A Changed Understanding of the Eucharist

As we have already seen, the somatic memory of Christianity as exemplified in the core ritual of the Eucharist, and the event(s) that it non-identically repeats, are not as fixed on the traumatic Paschal experience of Christ as one might imagine (certainly not in the early Church). A number of questions arise from this understanding of the Eucharist. What happens, for example, when one considers the Eucharist to be a non-identical repetition of the generative action of the Annunciation-Incarnation event rather than a non-identical repetition of the violence of the sacrificial Cross? And as understanding of the Eucharist moves away from the sacrifice of the death of Christ, are there other understandings of priesthood that can come to the fore? It became apparent in the analysis of early Church understandings of the Eucharist that there were three key modes of eucharistic interpretation: the Annunciation-Incarnation event, the Nativity of Christ, and the Eucharist as breast milk.

If the Eucharist is a non-identical repetition of the Annunciation-Incarnation event, as has previously been suggested, then what role does the priest play? At the beginning of the Annunciation-Incarnation event it is Mary who first offers up the bodily elements that will become the flesh and blood of Christ and it is Mary who gives her *fiat* in agreement with the work of God. The somatic memory of this offering is non-identically repeated through Jesus' own table practices, at the Last Supper when Jesus offers his body and blood to his disciples, and again at each subsequent eucharistic celebration. To follow the logic through, in enacting the Eucharist as a non-identical repetition of the Annunciation-Incarnation event, the priest still represents the congregation to God, but more significantly, the priest acts in the role of Mary (as well as in the role of Christ) before the congregation and before God. The Church is the Bride of Christ (e.g. Eph. 5.25–7 and Rev. 21.2) and traditionally referred to as feminine. To return to Coakley's priest in a 'fluid gender role',[24] the priest who represents the congregation in the celebration of the Eucharist as a non-identical repetition of the Annunciation-Incarnation event, is thus both the feminine Church and the feminine Mary.

Furthermore, if the Eucharist is a non-identical repetition of the Nativity, as some early Church theologians understood it, then what role is the priest playing in such a celebration? In this non-identical repetition, Christ must already be particularly present in the bread and wine, just as he was already particularly present in the womb of Mary. The Incarnation is not, then, confined to the specific person of Christ, but rather is the Divine in all things. The epiclesis is not the transformation of the elements into something else (from the mundane to the Divine), but rather the revelation of something already present. In this understanding of the Eucharist, the priest births the elements as Mary birthed Christ. Once again, it is possible to see Mary as providing the role model for the activities of the priest. While the priest does not contain the eucharistic elements within him as Mary did, this perspective on the Eucharist suggests that we should understand the priest as participating, with the Spirit, in the particular revelation of Christ, already present in the elements, as the Divine is present in all things.

If the Eucharist is intimately associated with milk, and specifically breast milk, then what can one infer about the role of the priest? If the Eucharist is that which nourishes the congregation, as milk nourishes those who drink it, then the priest, who dispenses the eucharistic bread and wine to the church, is a breastfeeding mother, passing on to the church the nourishment of the Son, received from the Father, through the activity of the Holy Spirit. Or perhaps it is possible to argue that

---

24 Coakley, 'The Woman at the Altar', 76.

the priest is more like a wet nurse feeding us in place of the actual mother? In contrast, one might suggest the image of bottle-feeding as more theologically productive. The milk still comes from God, but believers receive it via someone else – not necessarily our mother. The imagery is strikingly maternal and would indicate that our understanding of the priestly role is a maternal one.[25]

What conclusion, then, can we draw? Taking these elements of eucharistic meaning and symbolism together as a whole, in line with a full and extended understanding of the Annunciation-Incarnation event, rather than considering them disparately, one is left with the conclusion that Mary is integral to our understanding of priesthood through this lens. If one considers a multivalent understanding of the Eucharist and takes into account some of the other legitimate interpretations of the Eucharist in the early Church, one comes to the conclusion that, in some aspects of non-identical eucharistic repetition, the priest is acting as a woman, specifically as Mary. A consequence, then, of considering the Annunciation-Incarnation event to be at the core of Christian somatic memory, is that one can look to Mary to offer a new interpretation of the concept of priesthood. The exploration of the consequence of the destabilizing effect of the hermeneutical lens of trauma inevitably leads to the construction of a new narrative.

Mary the Priest

Mary was not a priest: not in the Hebrew Temple sense nor in the contemporary, ordained sense of presbyter. However, if the role of the priest is one who mediates between heaven and earth then Mary is an extraordinary mediator. The very fact of her assent to the Annunciation marks her out as one who mediates between heaven and earth. She is *Theotokos* – the

---

25 Emma Percy has attended to the maternal image of the priest in *Mothering as a Metaphor for Ministry* (Farnham, Surrey: Ashgate, 2014). See 27–8 for her reflection on breastfeeding and ministry.

God-bearer. The title *Mediatrix* has been given to Mary since at least the fifth century and has been reaffirmed in the twentieth century (*Lumen Gentium*[26]) and by various recent Popes. Mary has long been understood as one who especially intercedes on the part of humanity in the salvific redemption accomplished by Jesus.

Despite my assertion that Mary was not a priest, Mary has, at various points in history, been associated with priesthood. In 1873, Pope Pius IX said, '[S]he was so closely united to the sacrifice of her divine Son, from the virginal conception of Jesus Christ to his sorrowful Passion, that she was called by some Fathers of the Church the Virgin Priest.'[27] René Laurentin investigated this claim in his 1953 work on Mary and determined that Pius' statement was not true. There is no evidence to suggest such a title was ever ascribed to Mary, by the Church Fathers or anyone else. Laurentin suspected Pius had drawn this connection from 'poetic allusions used by the Greek homilists'.[28] Sceptical of understanding Mary to be priestly in any sense apart from the priesthood of all believers, Laurentin rejected any concept of Mary as priest in the sacramental or mediatory sense on two grounds: '1) Mary did not receive the sacrament of orders because she was a woman. 2) She is superior to sacramental priests.'[29] Despite the rejection of any tradition of a title of priest given to Mary, there is a strong typological and artistic tradition of understanding Mary in a sacerdotal sense.

---

26 Pope Paul VI, *Lumen Gentium*, Vatican, www.vatican.va/archive/hist_councils/ii_vatican_council/documents/vat-ii_const_19641121_lumen-gentium_en.html. 3. 62. Accessed on 31/08/2017.

27 Cited in Michael O'Carroll (ed.), *Theotokos: A Theological Encyclopedia of the Blessed Virgin Mary* (Collegeville, MN: The Liturgical Press, 1982), 293.

28 Tina Beattie, 'Mary, the Virgin Priest?', *The Month* (December 1996). Accessed online at www.womenpriests.org/mrpriest/beattie/asp on 09/03/16.

29 René Laurentin, *Marie, L'Eglise et le Sacerdoce*, 2 vols, Vol. 2 (Paris: Nouvelles Editions Latines, 1953), 37. Cited in and trans. Beattie, 'Mary, the Virgin Priest?'

Mary as Priest in Typology

Typology is a way of understanding and interpreting the relationship between the Hebrew Bible and the New Testament. A typological interpretation understands events, characters and even language in the Hebrew Bible to be pre-figurative types that are superseded by antitypes found in the New Testament. Erich Auerbach, in his landmark essay 'Figura', wrote of typology, or figural interpretation:

> Figural interpretation establishes a connection between two events or persons, the first of which signifies not only itself but also the second, while the second encompasses and fulfils the first. The two poles of the figure are separate in time, but both, being real events or figures, are within time, within the stream of historical life.[30]

So, for example, the character of Jonah in the Hebrew Bible might be understood as a type of Christ as he emerges from three days in the belly of a whale thus prefiguring the resurrection of Christ. Both characters are real figures, but the figure of the resurrected Christ encompasses and fulfils the figure of Jonah. It is this encompassing and fulfilment that will be essential to our examination of Marian typology.

Typology is usually drawn across tightly constructed gender boundaries. People from the Hebrew Bible understood to be Christ types are almost always male – which means that those Hebrew Bible characters understood to be types of Mary are invariably female. For example, many of the ancestral matriarchs are understood to be pre-figurative Marian types, including Eve, Sarah and Hannah. However, when one considers Mary in connection with a theology of priesthood, one finds that typologies begin to traverse gender boundaries.

Marian typology is extraordinarily complicated and complex. A wide array of people, objects, buildings, plants, animals and

---

30 Erich Auerbach, 'Figura', in *Scenes from the Drama of European Literature* (Manchester: Manchester University Press: 1984), 11–78 at 53.

events are all understood to be pre-figurative Marian types. A useful place to begin our consideration of Mary and priesthood is in the Nativity homily of Proclus of Constantinople. This is a helpful place to begin for two reasons. In the first instance, Proclus was a participant in the Nestorian Controversy we encountered in the previous chapter. Proclus was one of those proclaiming Mary to be *Theotokos* and thus one of the instigators of the conflict. In the second instance, it is in the writings of Proclus that we find an extraordinarily developed, extended and explicit use of Marian typology. Indeed, Proclus drew a specific correlation between the Temple building and the person of Mary.

Proclus understood the Temple of Solomon, the seven-branched lamp stand, the closed sanctuary, the living Temple, and the Daughter of Zion to all be pre-figurative types of Mary.[31] It is significant that he connected her so strongly to both the Temple and the temple objects. Proclus created a clear link between Mary and the place and objects of priestly service and devotion. Cleo McNelly Kearns reflected on this typological association and concluded:

> In this encomium, Mary becomes the temple, enclosing a new kind of priesthood for which she has in a sense woven the garment. It is a priesthood of unique persons, one not without either Old Testament precedents or New Testament warrants, but one specifically abjuring ethnic identity, kinship, genealogical descent, spilled blood, and perhaps even gender as the necessary basis for the sacrificial discourse that carries forth the spiritual patrimony of Israel.[32]

Proclus is not the only ancient source to make such a connection. For example, one could consider the writer of the

---

31 Proclus, 'Homily 1: Encomium on the all-holy Mary, Birthgiver of God', in J. H. Barkhuizen, *Proclus, Bishop of Constantinople: Homilies on the Life of Christ* (Brisbane, Australia: Centre for Early Christian Studies, 2001), 63–70.

32 Cleo McNelly Kearns, *The Virgin Mary, Monotheism, and Sacrifice* (New York: Cambridge University Press, 2008), 249.

Gospel of Luke. This author constructs the whole of the opening two chapters of the Gospel as an extended Marian typology. The Gospel writer uses the term 'overshadow' in the account of how Mary became pregnant. This 'overshadow' is the same word used in the Hebrew Bible to describe the cloud of God's glory over the Tabernacle in the desert (Ex. 40.35; Num. 9.18, 22). It is also the same word used to describe the winged cherubim that overshadowed the Ark in Exodus 25.20 and 1 Chronicles 28.18. These literary references call the reader's (or listener's) mind back to these Hebrew Bible passages, and both the tabernacle and the Ark are objects with which a Marian typological connection has been drawn. As the Ark of the Old Covenant contained the word of God in the form of His Laws, so does Mary, the Ark of the New Covenant, contain the Word of God within her in the form of the Christ-child.

Other writers also draw a pre-figurative typological relationship between the Temple and Mary. For example, Athanasius wrote: 'O [Ark of the New] Covenant, clothed with purity instead of gold! You are the Ark in which is found the golden vessel containing the true manna, that is, the flesh in which divinity resides.'[33] For Jerome, in the early fifth century, the Temple typology supports the doctrine of Mary's Perpetual Virginity. He noted:

Only Christ opened the closed doors of the virginal womb, which continued to remain closed, however. This is the closed eastern gate, through which only the high priest may enter and exit and which nevertheless is always closed.[34]

---

33 Athanasius, 'In Praise of the Blessed Virgin', cited in Luigi Gambero, *Mary and the Fathers of the Church: The Blessed Virgin Mary in Patristic Thought*, trans. Thomas Buffer (San Francisco: Ignatius Press, 1999), 106.

34 Jerome, 'Against the Pelagians 2, 4: PL23, 563', cited in Gambero, *Mary and the Fathers*, 211.

These typological connections to the Hebrew Temple not only establish Mary as the fulfilment of the Temple but also draw a clear relationship between Mary and the priestly realm. In these texts, she is connected to the building, objects within the building, and events surrounding the building. Let us turn our attention, then, to the figures of priests themselves.

Our first consideration is the first person to be identified as a priest in the Hebrew Bible – Melchizedek. The character of Melchizedek is a mysterious one in the Hebrew Bible. Only appearing once in the Genesis narrative, and with a handful of references to him found elsewhere, Melchizedek is the High Priest after whom Jesus' own High Priestly status is modelled. In his only dramatic activity in scriptures (Gen. 14.18–20), Melchizedek, entitled as King of Salem and priest of God Most High, brings out the bread and wine to Abram and his company before blessing them.

While the typological relationship between Melchizedek and Jesus is well established, Melchizedek is also a Marian type. He brings out the earthly elements, with such a clear eucharistic connection, in his priestly activity. He blesses Abram and God Most High. This activity is repeated by Mary. With her *fiat* at the Annunciation, Mary offers herself and her womb as the earthly elements that will bless the people of God. This blessing is articulated in Mary's *Magnificat* (Luke 1.46–55) in which she invokes both Abraham and God, as Melchizedek did.

This Marian typology extends further still. In Hebrews 7.2b–3 the author wrote:

> His name, in the first place, means 'king of righteousness'; next he is king of Salem, that is, 'king of peace'. Without father, without mother, without genealogy, having neither beginning of days nor end of life, but resembling the Son of God, he remains a priest for ever.

Melchizedek is described as being without father and mother. Mary, of course, did have parents. Their names are supplied in the apocryphal literature that surrounds her life, little of which is known from the scriptures. The most significant text, for this exploration, is that of the *Protevangelium of James*.[35] This text is a Marian infancy narrative, offering details of Mary's family, her birth and her early life. Thanks to this text, we know that the early Church understood Mary's parents to be Anna and Joachim and that her birth itself was a miraculous event. What is significant about this text, however, is that throughout the narrative Mary is never referred to as either daughter (*thygatēr*) or wife (*gynē*).[36] She is entirely understood not in relation to her lineage, but rather in terms of her relationship to God. This isolation from family and, one can presume, familial responsibilities, allows Mary a mode of active agency that would have been denied to her in the patriarchal signifiers of being someone's daughter, someone's wife.

This is, perhaps, too generous a reading of the *Protevangelium*. Mary certainly does not seem to brimming with active, self-motivated agency throughout the text. Indeed, she appears to be one without a voice through the whole narrative. Mary rarely speaks in this context, and it is primarily her body and its purity that is of interest to the author and the characters around her. Mary Foskett noted: 'the apocryphal "virgin of the Lord" loses her prophetic voice even as she wins unsurpassed praise and vindication of an unequivocal purity'.[37] The *Protevangelium* does offer an interesting opportunity to understand Melchizedek as a Marian type and to draw some significant conclusions about Mary's status outside familial boundaries. However, the text does not offer us a model of a Marian priest with independent agency.

---

35 Ronald F. Hock, *The Infancy Gospels of James and Thomas* (Santa Rosa, CA: Polebridge Press, 1995). All references to the *Protevangelium* (PJ) are taken from this translation.

36 Mary Foskett, *A Virgin Conceived: Mary and Classical Representations of Virginity* (Bloomington & Indianapolis: Indiana University Press, 2002), 157.

37 Mary Foskett, 'Virginity as Purity in the *Protevangelium of James*', in *A Feminist Companion to Mariology*, ed. Amy-Jill Levine and Maria Mayo Robbins (London: Continuum International Publishing Group Ltd, 2005), 67–76, at 76.

As well as describing Melchizedek as one who has neither father nor mother, the author of Hebrews also commented that the King of Salem has 'neither beginning of days nor end of life'. Here again, Melchizedek functions as a Marian type. Like Melchizedek, Mary has no beginning of days. Mary is chosen from all eternity to be the mother of Jesus by virtue of her Immaculate Conception. She is predestined to be *Theotokos*. Karl Rahner indicated that this is the significance and function of Mary's Immaculate Conception:

> She is different from us not merely through her having become the graced one at a temporally earlier point in her existence. The mystery that really gives the temporal difference between her and us in the mystery of her immaculate conception its proper meaning is, rather, the mystery of her predestination.[38]

Rather than thinking of Mary as simply being placed in the same state of grace that all believers receive, only earlier, Rahner indicates that this is too small a difference to justify her exalted status. Instead, the doctrine of the Immaculate Conception indicates Mary's predestination to be the mother of God. Like Melchizedek, she has no beginning of days.

This typological connection extends to the end of life as well. Mary's life did not end in the way that an ordinary human life tends to end. Pope Pius XII confirmed the doctrine of Mary's Assumption in the 1950 encyclical *Munificentissimus Deus*. The encyclical articulated in the doctrine that Mary:

> By an entirely unique privilege, completely overcame sin by her immaculate conception, and as a result she was not subject to the law of remaining in the corruption of the grace,

---

38 Karl Rahner, 'The Immaculate Conception', in *Theological Investigations, Volume 1* (London: Darton, Longman and Todd, 1954), 210–11.

and she did not have to wait until the end of time for the redemption of the body.[39]

Despite the relatively late twentieth-century date for the confirmation of this belief as orthodox by the Catholic Church, narratives surrounding the ending of Mary's life on earth had been in circulation since the early sixth century in their written form, and certainly earlier still in oral tradition. Like Melchizedek, Mary has no end of life. She keeps her status as *Theotokos* in perpetuity, and remains foremost intercessor (that notably priestly function) between humanity and her Divine Son.

This typology, while not common in the Marian tradition, is reflected in the eighth-century homiletics of Andrew of Crete. Andrew wrote:

> Today from Judah and David comes the young virgin, presenting the face of royalty and of the priesthood of Aaron, who exercised the functions of the priest according to the order of Melchizedek.[40]

This homily was given on the Feast of the Nativity. Here, Mary – the young virgin – presents the face of royalty and priesthood. The term 'face' here is the Greek πρόσωπον meaning 'face' or 'mask'. But this is not a mask of deception or a pretence of royalty and priesthood. Rather, this 'mask' has its origins in Greek theatre where a mask was often used to reveal true character to the audience. Mary's 'face' of royalty and priesthood here exemplifies her true character. Once again, it is Melchizedek who is the Hebraic priest par excellence. Drawing a typological relationship in this way makes Mary's priestly status very clear. If Melchizedek is a type of Mary, then

---

39 Pius XII, *Munificentissimus Deus*, Papal Constitution of 1950, cited in S. J. Shoemaker, *Ancient Traditions of the Virgin Mary's Dormition and Assumption* (Oxford: Oxford University Press, 2004), 9.

40 Andrew of Crete, 'Sermon 1 on the Nativity', PG IXCVI, 812 BC, cited by Kearns, *The Virgin Mary*, 220.

typologically, Mary fulfils and exceeds the High Priest type. It is the priesthood of Melchizedek that informs and shapes the priestly ministry of her Son, and thus Mary's own actions inform the priestly ministry of Jesus. Such a strong typological connection brings the priestly elements of Mary and her activity into sharp relief. When the Eucharist is understood in the light of the Annunciation-Incarnation event, Mary is the model of New Covenant priesthood.

Typological relationships are usually drawn along gender lines and, as such, Mary has been more commonly connected to the figure of Sarah in the Abrahamic narratives. However, Abraham is also a pre-figurative Marian type and a number of events in his life prefigure elements of the Marian discourse. While Abraham functioned in a Hebraic setting that predated the formal arrangements of priests at the Temple, Abraham is a significant model for Israel's priesthood and even paradigmatic for subsequent priests. Therefore, drawing a typological relationship between Mary and Abraham once again connects her with a priestly figure, and interprets her life and actions as a fulfilment of this priestly nature and activity. For example, Abraham's 'Here I am' response to God (Gen. 22.1) prefigures Mary's response to the angel Gabriel at the Annunciation. She replies, 'Behold, I am the servant of the Lord; let it be to me according to your word' (Luke 1.38). Her *Magnificat*, outlined in the subsequent verses (47–55), invokes the promises made to Abraham by God and establishes that the Incarnation of Christ is the fulfilment of these promises.

Kearns highlighted, in her detailed analysis of the connection between these two figures, a depth of typological relationship. Kearns noted that Abraham is a pre-figurative Marian type in the promptness of his obedience to God, his presence at the 'sacrificial' death of his son, and as a founding figure in cultic and sacrificial discourse.[41] Furthermore, Abraham exemplifies a Divine hospitality that is a pre-figurative type of Mary's own hospitality. For example, the same reciprocal relationship between guest and host can be seen in the manner of

---

41 Kearns, *The Virgin Mary*, 146.

Abraham's welcome to the three heavenly visitors in Genesis 18 and in Mary's activity at the Cana wedding in John 2. Both of these events are redolent with a eucharistic flavour offering a taste of heaven on earth. Mary's hospitality, prefigured in Abraham, is the generous welcome of the other.

This typological relationship, evident in word and deed, is further visible in character. Mary is the fulfilment of the progression of purity of God's people. This purity is established under, and prefigured in, the person of Abraham and reaches its pinnacle in the birth of Christ who can be born without being touched by sin. Likewise, Mary's faith, exhibited in her *fiat*, is the perfection of Abraham's faith and the long wait, through generations, for the coming of the Messiah. Pope John Paul II compared Mary's faith to that of Abraham when he noted that 'Abraham's faith constitutes the beginning of the Old Covenant; Mary's faith at the Annunciation inaugurates the New Covenant.'[42]

Much of the narrative of Mary's life, and the theological endeavour that accompanied it, was developed in the period of the early Church. This was matched by a simultaneous development of Talmudic and Midrashic exegesis that tied the person of Abraham with the priesthood of Israel, primarily through the character of Melchizedek. Given the extent of this typological relationship, it is not unreasonable to understand that, as Abraham was an important model for the priests of the Hebrew Bible, so Mary is an important model for the priests of the New Testament (and beyond).

Hannah, mother of Samuel, typologically prefigures Mary. Both bear sons who will be dedicated to the Lord and instrumental in shaping the Hebraic world. Samuel is frequently understood to be a type of Jesus. However, the character of Hannah makes more sense when understood as a pre-figurative type of Anna, Mary's mother, and thus to interpret Samuel as a Marian type. In the case of Anna and Hannah, both are

---

42 Pope John Paul II, *Redemptoris Mater*, accessed online at http://w2.vatican.va/content/john-paul-ii/en/encyclicals/documents/ht_jp-ii_enc_25031987_redemptoris-mater.html on 09/03/16. Paragraph 14.

older, childless women who weep for a child (1 Sam. 1.10–22 and *Protevangelium* (PJ) 2.1). Both women vow to dedicate any future child they bear to the service of the Lord (1 Sam. 1.11 and PJ 4.2). Both women praise God when they become miraculously pregnant (1 Sam. 2.1–10 and PJ 6.11–13), and both take their children to reside in the Temple from an early age – Samuel from the point at which he has been weaned (1 Sam. 1.23–24), and Mary from the age of three (PJ 7.4). Hannah is a pre-figurative type of Mary's mother, Anna.

With regard to the children – Samuel and Mary – the typological relationship continues. Both Samuel and Mary respond to God with a repeat of the Abrahamic 'Here I am' that we have already considered, when they are called into His service. Mary, like Samuel before her, inaugurates a kingdom. For Samuel, this is anointing the king chosen by God (1 Sam. 9). Samuel recognizes and responds to God's choice of king – Saul – and anoints him with oil, imparting kingship upon him. Mary recognizes and responds to the character of her child – Jesus – as she names him as instructed to by the angel (Luke 1.31). Both are mediators between human and Divine. Samuel ushers in an earthly kingdom. This is fulfilled in the person of Mary who, in her response and faithful service to God, ushers in the heavenly kingdom.

Typological connections of the kind I have made so far are rarely, if ever, drawn across gender lines as I have done. A consequence of examining the Eucharist from the perspective of the Annunciation-Incarnation event is that it offers an opportunity to queer the gender boundaries traditionally at play in understandings of the Eucharist (and therefore the priest). Each of these three characters from the Hebrew Bible – Melchizedek, Abraham and Samuel – are significant models for Israel's priesthood. All three of these priestly men are types of Mary, drawing strong typological connections between Mary and the office of priest. The impact of this queer reading is the opening of new models of serving the people of God and new ways of being devoted to Him.

The priesthood is usually understood in terms of the broader patriarchal hierarchy at work in Christian tradition. But the ecclesial Body of Christ – the Church – is always feminine. This contrast is complicated further when one considers that the Temple, the place of God's presence, was a pre-figurative type of Mary. In the person of Mary, the Temple reaches its fulfilment; she is the Temple of Temples.

The Church looks to Mary as an example of faith and service. As such, Mary is the fulcrum of the New Covenant. In this new order, gender is no prohibition to priestly service. Mary's priestly actions fulfil the priesthood of the Hebrew Bible and as such the male priesthood is ruptured: split open to make way for a new kind of priestly mediation. This new mediation is dependent upon maternal love rather than on immolatory sacrifice of a victim.

Mary as Priest in Artistic Tradition

Having explored a literary tradition of connecting Mary to the priesthood, we can now turn our attention to the artistic tradition. Artwork from the time of the early Church to the present day depicts Mary as or like a priest, reflecting a strong, popular sense in which her actions are understood to be sacerdotal. Not all Marian artwork fits this trend but there are two distinct patterns that draw strong connections with the priesthood. In the first instance, there are a significant number of pieces of art that depict Mary wearing priest's or even bishop's clothing. In the second there are a number of pieces of art that show Mary doing priestly things.

Turning first to art that depicts Mary wearing priest's clothing, the sixth-century mosaic that hangs over the archbishop's chapel in Ravenna, clearly shows Mary wearing a pallium and chasuble. The pallium is a great indicator of ecclesial authority, and at that time was a distinctive mark of episcopal office, worn by the Pope or archbishop to denote their union with Rome. It is clear in this piece that the artist considered Mary to exercise sacerdotal authority of the highest order.

Mary is similarly depicted in the twelfth-century title page of the Frowinus Bible. Here one can clearly see Mary standing before Abbot Frowinus. They are both wearing the same chasuble, covered in crosses, but Mary also wears a bishop's mitre and carries a crozier. Again, it is clear that the artist, most likely at the behest of Abbot Frowinus, has depicted Mary exercising not merely priestly but episcopal authority.

A final example of this style of artwork is the fifteenth-century French panel painting commissioned from the Amiens School (now on display in the Louvre) entitled *Sacerdoce de la Vierge* (The Priesthood of the Virgin). This image is the example par excellence of the Marian priest genre. Paul Cardile described the image vividly:

> She is dressed in an elaborate sacerdotal costume, which appears to be based on the type of vestments described in the twenty eighth chapter of Exodus as belonging to the High Priest Aaron. Her undergarments a white tunic or alb, over which is a recreation of Aaron's sacerdotal overgarment, the ephod, and from beneath it projects the ends of a stole. The ephod is made from a richly figured brocade and is jewelled along its borders. As described in Exodus, small bells hang from its hem. Over her breast attached by gold chains suspended from the ephod's two shoulder pieces, the Breastplate of Judgement with the twelve stones for the Tribes of Israel may be seen and around Mary's waist hangs a long sash which probably refers to the biblical ephod . . . The papal tiara and jewelled cross are references, I believe, to Mary's New Covenant priesthood.[43]

Strikingly, not only is she clearly dressed as the High Priest Aaron, Mary is depicted standing in front of an altar with a paten in hand, ready to distribute the Eucharist to those awaiting the sacrament. The typological connections do not end there, however:

---

43 Paul Y. Cardile, 'Mary as Priest: Mary's Sacerdotal Position in the Visual Arts', *Arte Cristiana* 72 (1984), 199–208, at 199.

The liturgically vested Virgin prefigures the New Testament priest, Christ, just as the figures of Abel, Abraham and Melchizedek on the altarpiece behind her foreshadow his inevitable sacrifice. She holds the hand of the youthful Christ as if to encourage his participation in the Mass.[44]

While not all the pieces are as elaborate as this from the Amiens School, there is clearly an artistic tradition, within Christianity, of connecting the actions of Mary to those of a priest and so she is clearly depicted as a sacerdotal actor within these pieces.

The second genre of Marian priest artwork are those where she is depicted performing the actions of the priest. Indeed, the previous piece from Amiens is an example of this as it shows Mary ready to present the Eucharist to the gathered congregation (including her son) as a priest. This is similarly shown in the series of paintings by nineteenth-century French painter Jean-Auguste-Dominique Ingres. This series, usually titled *The Virgin with the Host*, shows Mary standing behind an altar which holds a eucharistic chalice with a host rising from it. Mary is shown in her traditional blue robe with her hands clasped in prayer, flanked by candles, angels and saints. Paintings depicting the adoration of the Blessed Sacrament usually show it encased in a monstrance with the adorers kneeling in front of the altar. The presence of Mary behind the altar, and the open nature of the eucharistic bread and wine, gives a strikingly priestly feel to the painting.

The Ravenna mosaic considered earlier shows Mary not only dressed as a priest but also performing the actions of a priest. She is shown here in the act of prayerful intercession with her hands raised level with her head, a pose commonly known as Virgin Orant. Maurice Vloberg noted:

The orant figure is a common example of this type [images that would have been immediately comprehensible to the initiated]. A Christian transposition of a Hellenistic creation,

---

44 Barbara Lane, *The Altar and The Altarpiece: Sacramental Themes in Early Netherlandish Painting* (New York: Harper & Row, 1984), 71.

it combines the naturalistic and the figurative in order to express either the act or the idea of prayer, *oratio*, and is admirably suited to depict the fervour of the union between Mary and God.[45]

This adoption of a priestly pose is frequently accompanied by the wearing of priestly garments. As well as in the Ravenna mosaic, the same juxtaposition can be seen in the Evangelistery of the Benedictine Monastery of Gengenbach. Dating from around 1150 AD, the image shows Mary again wearing those priestly garments, and adopting the *orans* position of priestly intercession. Significantly, though, this is an image of Mary at the Annunciation. She adopts this position and wears these clothes as the Spirit descends upon her. Berger, in her analysis of this image, wrote: 'The Blessed Virgin, with the angel next to her, is clearly styled analogously to the priest at the moment of consecration.'[46] A clear connection is drawn here between the actions of Mary consenting to the Incarnation and the priest's actions in consecrating the bread and wine to become the body and blood of Christ. Mary is clearly depicted as priest at the Annunciation.

Marian Model of Priesthood

I began this chapter with an examination of the priesthood by Rowan Williams. It is useful to return to this definition as we draw our reflections on the Marian priesthood to a close. He wrote:

> [Priesthood is] crucially to do with the service of the space cleared by God; with the holding open of a door into a place where a damaged and confused humanity is able to move slowly into the room made available, and understand that it

---

45 Maurice Vloberg, 'The Iconographic Types of the Virgin in Western Art', in *Mary: The Complete Resource*, ed. Sarah Jane Boss (Oxford: Oxford University Press, 2007), 537–85, at 542.

46 Berger, *Gender Differences*, 152.

is accompanied and heard in all its variety and unmanage-ability, and emotional turmoil and spiritual uncertainty.[47]

Key to this understanding of priesthood are elements of medi-ation, access and service in the space prepared by God. Having previously established that the Eucharist can be understood to take its referent from the Annunciation-Incarnation event, just as easily as from the Crucifixion, we have examined the rela-tionship between Mary and the priesthood. Reading theology through the lens of trauma is to allow traditional narratives to be ruptured by the traumatic event. In this case, the traditional narrative of priesthood is split open to allow a new narrative to emerge. In this new narrative, Mary is the model of priestly service and activity.

While none of the examples – typological or artistic – I have considered here are designed to *prove* that Mary was an ordained priest in the traditional, ecclesial sense that the term 'priest' is understood, they do demonstrate the presence of a tradition within the Church that made a strong connection between Mary and priesthood, and understood her actions to be sacerdotal. If, as Williams has argued, a priest is a mediator, one who provides access and service in the space prepared by God, then Mary is a priest. Mary serves in the space cleared by God – bearing a child in her very womb – her body *is* the space cleared by God. It is her *fiat* that holds open the door to humanity.

What happens to traditional theological narratives of priest-hood when we understand the trauma of the Body of Christ to be the Annunciation-Incarnation event, non-identically repeated in the celebration of the Eucharist? Such narratives are split wide open and Mary emerges as the model of priest-hood for the New Covenant. To be a priest is to be one in her likeness.

---

47 Williams, 'Epilogue', 176.

5

Sacrifice

The Priestly Sacrifice and the Eucharist

Bearing the symptoms of trauma, we find the Body of Christ repeating the experience of this trauma in each celebration of the Eucharist. Understanding the repeated trauma to be not the crucifixion and death of Christ but rather the traumatic ruptures of the Annunciation-Incarnation event has significant implications for theology. Having already destabilized the traditional narrative of priesthood through the exploration of this trauma, a further theological consequence of this event is the destabilization of the narrative of sacrifice. The rupture such a destabilization creates clears the theological space for the construction of a new narrative.

Sacrifice has featured, and continues to feature, prominently in some areas of ecclesial eucharistic discourse. In the Catholic and Orthodox Church, the bread and wine are believed to be the body and blood of Christ. Similarly, in high Anglican churches there is an understanding of Real Presence. The celebration of the Eucharist is a memorial, even as it is a re-enactment. All non-identical repetition is, at its very essence, memory. This Real Presence of Christ in the eucharistic elements has led to an understanding of eucharistic celebration as sacrifice either in memory of Christ's death on the Cross or in some confidence that the Eucharist is itself a sacrificing of Jesus' body and blood.

In order to explore the Christian notion of sacrifice and its relationship to the Eucharist, it is first important to turn our attention to the current situation. Kilmartin presented a summary of what he calls the 'modern average Catholic theology of the Eucharist':

[I]n the Western tradition, the words of Christ spoken over the bread and wine are [also] understood to be the essential form of the sacrament. These words thus constitute the moment when the sacrament is realized, namely, when the bread and wine are converted into the body and blood of Christ. Thus, while the words are spoken by the presiding minister, they are understood as being spoken by Christ through his minister. This act is one accomplished only by the minister acting *in persona Christi* in the midst of the prayer of faith of the Church . . . The representation of the death of Christ occurs with the act of conversion of the elements. The somatic presence of Christ and the representation of the sacrifice of Christ are simultaneously achieved in the act of the consecration of the elements . . . Nowadays the average Catholic theology of the Mass . . . affirms that the representation of the sacrifice of the cross is a sacramental reactualization of the once-for-all historical engagement of Jesus on the cross. The idea that in the act of consecration a sacramental representation of the sacrifice of the cross is realized in the sense that the historical sacrifice is re-presented or reactualized also seems to be favored by official Catholic theology today.[1]

This 'average' theology of the Eucharist bases an understanding of the Mass on a traditional, Old Testament notion of sacrifice.

The Problems with Sacrifice

This concept of sacrifice holds that sacrifice involves the death of a victim in order to placate a higher power. In the Hebrew Temple the priests performed a variety of sacrifices: the burnt offering, the grain offering, the sacrifice of well-being or fellowship offering, the sin or purification offering, and the guilt

---

1 Edward J. Kilmartin, *The Eucharist in the West: History and Theology* (Collegeville, MN: Liturgical Press, 1998), 294–5.

offering. The average theology of the Eucharist that Kilmartin highlights above, however, draws specifically on the sin or purification sacrifice to the apparent exclusion of the other types of offerings. So, in the Hebrew temple, the priests perform sacrifices that involve the death of an animal in order to achieve purity in the eyes of Yahweh or to atone for sins. This is what is referenced in this understanding of the celebration of the Eucharist. This kind of sacrifice requires the death of the victim.

By elevating the presiding minister to a role in which they are acting in the place of Christ, (re)performing the sacrifice of his body and blood, the Old Testament ideas of ritual priestly purity, necessary for the acceptability of sacrifice, become applicable in the modern Church. Thus, this kind of sacrifice requires a celibate, male priest to perform it.

Nancy Jay considered these tropes of ritual sacrifice in her work on sacrifice and religion and in specific reference to the Catholic celebration of the Eucharist. Here, she argued that the regular practice of the sacrifice of the Eucharist is intimately entwined with the hierarchical structure of the Catholic Church. The priest acts sacrificially and supernaturally in the person of Christ and thus the 'exclusive power to sacrifice'[2] becomes the basis for priestly authority. The power to sacrifice – to enact the central ritual of the Catholic faith – is passed from 'father' to 'son' through the bishop's consecration of priests. This conflation of maternity and priesthood is developed further by Jay. She suggested:

[B]ecause it identifies social and religious descent, rather than biological descent, sacrificing can identify membership in groups with no presumption of actual family descent. This is the case with the sacrifice of the Mass, offered by members of a formally institutionalized 'lineage', the apostolic succession of the clergy in the Roman Church. This social organization is a truly perfect 'eternal line of descent', in

2 Nancy Jay, *Throughout Your Generations Forever: Sacrifice, Religion, and Paternity* (Chicago: University of Chicago Press, 1992), 113.

which authority descends from father to father, through the one 'Son made perfect forever', in a line no longer directly dependent on women's reproductive powers for continuity.[3]

Jay argued that the masculine priesthood, by bestowing the power to sacrifice through the ordination of male priests by male bishops, circumvents the natural female maternity necessary for the creation of lineage. In this sense, the conflation of priesthood with a spiritual maternity serves to further exclude women from the priesthood.

This created perpetual line of masculine authority is entirely separate from women and feminine reproduction. Jay argued that where there is a stronger, blood-sacrificial, material and actual understanding of the presence of Christ in the Eucharist, there is a requirement for a priestly hierarchy with emphasis on ritual practice and the legitimacy of continuity from 'father' to 'son'. Where the understanding of the presence of Christ in the Eucharist is 'weaker', more symbolic or commemorative, one will often find a more egalitarian structure with more relaxed views of ritual purity.[4] If one wants an egalitarian structure, the implication is that one will have to forgo Real Presence in order to achieve it.

Beattie, in her analysis of Laurentin's thesis on the title Virgin Priest that we considered in the previous chapter, noted that Laurentin rejects the term 'Virgin Priest' in favour of a more nuanced understanding of Mary's maternal role. For Laurentin, '[T]he conflation of maternity with priesthood obscures the balance between the unique calling of men to the sacramental priesthood, and the unique calling of women to motherhood.'[5]

Beattie criticized Laurentin's argument as 'deeply flawed'[6] and challenged his identification of God with man and creature with woman. Laurentin drew a distinction between the

---

3 Ibid., 37.
4 Ibid., 112–25.
5 Beattie, 'Mary, the Virgin Priest?', 4.
6 Ibid., 5.

priesthood of all believers, of which Mary is the pre-eminent example, and the ordained priesthood which depends on Christ as its example. So, he wrote: '[I]f one can rigorously affirm that the hierarchical priesthood is by nature manly, the femininity of the communal priesthood calls for a more nuanced approach. While women are excluded from the hierarchical priesthood, men enter into the ranks of the communal priesthood.'[7] Thus Beattie argued that 'we find the maleness of Jesus elevated to an ontological status that by its very nature excludes women from participation in the priesthood'.[8] If these distinctions are pressed too far then one is left with a masculine saviour who only saves men. After all, that which has not been assumed has not been redeemed. Such a perspective leads to a characterization of all other genders as *not* made in the image of God.

Away from implications for understanding theology surrounding the Eucharist, this kind of sacrifice is problematic more widely. Such a concept is alien to contemporary culture unversed in sacrificial tropes and language. It can seem immoral and paint a picture of a God who is vicious and uncaring. This account of sacrifice would seem to glorify suffering and those who suffer, alongside appearing to validate violence as a way of accomplishing things. A new perspective on sacrifice is sorely needed.

Sacrificial Theory

The groundwork for contemporary understanding of sacrifice was laid in the twentieth century by French philosopher and historian René Girard. Girard posited that sacrifice lay at the heart of human culture and ritual. Acknowledging a mimetic desire that caused conflict within a community, he wrote:

Since the power of mimetic attraction multiplies with the number of those polarized, it is inevitable that at one moment

---

7 Laurentin, *Marie, L'Eglise et le Sacerdoce*, 2, 75.
8 Beattie, 'Mary, the Virgin Priest?', 5.

the entire community will find itself unified against a single individual. Conflictual mimesis therefore creates a *de facto* allegiance against a common enemy, such that the conclusion of the crisis is nothing other than the reconciliation of the community.[9]

The community unites against one person, who becomes the victim of scapegoating. The destruction of that victim brings peace to the community and as such that victim is retrospectively understood as 'sacred'. Girard appealed to myth to support this understanding of sacrifice and understood this 'unanimous victimage [to be] the generative mechanism of all religious and cultural institutions'.[10]

Philosophical and anthropological studies on sacrifice typically begin by tracing the development of sacrifice and sacrificial acts throughout time and across cultures. For example, Henri Hubert and Marcel Mauss drew on many different cultures and perspectives in producing their work on sacrifice.[11] Similarly, Jay compared sacrificial systems from across the world, including Hawaiian, Ashanti and Jewish sacrifice, in order to draw her conclusions about sacrifice and the Eucharist. In this sense they are seeking similarities in diverse acts that might help to explain what sacrifice is about. However, looking externally to understand the internal working of a faith or a community is a mistake. It is more helpful to ask what a community thinks it is doing rather than to impose meaning from the outside. Better instead to look inside the community performing the sacrifice and seek to find the meaning there.

---

9 René Girard, *Things Hidden Since the Foundation of the World*, trans. Stephen Bann and Michael Metteer (Stanford, CA: Stanford University Press, 1987), 26.

10 René Girard, *'To Double Business Bound': Essays on Literature, Mimesis, and Anthropology* (Baltimore, MD: The Johns Hopkins University Press, 1978), 199.

11 Henri Hubert and Marcel Mauss, *Sacrifice: Its Nature and Functions* (Chicago: University of Chicago Press, 1981).

A New Understanding of Christian Sacrifice

Looking to the Hebrew Bible or to the sacrificial practices in other cultures to explain the Christian Eucharist is not helpful. To seek to understand Christian sacrifice from any starting point other than from its own faith and practice is to do Christian sacrifice a disservice.

To understand the Christian concept of sacrifice we must begin with the traumatic event remembered in the celebration of the Eucharist – the Annunciation-Incarnation event. If this event is at the heart of each celebration of the Eucharist, then it is also the event that is key to understanding Christian sacrifice. In the Annunciation-Incarnation event it becomes clear that sacrifice is fundamentally Trinitarian as well as Incarnational. Traditional high eucharistic theology insists that the Eucharist must be in continuity with the Christ-event. The Christ-event in this reference is usually considered to be the crucifixion but, as has already been demonstrated, to limit the interpretation and understanding of the Eucharist to only the suffering, death and resurrection of Christ is too small a vision of Christianity. The fuller understanding is found in the Annunciation-Incarnation event. Therefore, it is the Annunciation-Incarnation event that should provide the reference point for our understanding of Christian sacrifice. In this sense, the Girardian concept of mimetic desire can rightly be considered to be at the basis of sacrifice but it is rendered obsolete in the understanding of sacrifice outlined here – mutual self-offering of the Trinity. This self-offering is entirely at odds with the competitive desire that Girard posited and thus opens up the concept of sacrifice to a new interpretation.

Gordon Lathrop, in his work on liturgical theology, has also sought to re-conceptualize Christian understanding of sacrifice in relation to the Eucharist. Lathrop suggested that words such as 'sacrifice', 'offering' and 'priest' are the wrong words to use when talking about the Eucharist but that they become the right words when we allow their meaning to be transformed.

For us to newly criticize the pervasive language of sacrifice, requiring its transformation, will be for us to newly open ourselves to transformations in the meanings of Christian worship, of the death of Christ, of Christian ethics, and of the human relationship with the created world.[12]

Such a fresh, critical approach to the Eucharist is entirely necessary and Christian sacrifice cannot be understood with reference to any other type of sacrifice (except in antithesis). While Lathrop does positively connect this Christian sacrifice to the meal of thanksgiving we call the Eucharist, he does not remove it from the Cross. For Lathrop, the meaning of the meal still comes from the Cross.

Robert Daly, like Lathrop, recognized a need to consider afresh the Christian understanding of sacrifice. In contrast to Lathrop, however, he presented a notion of sacrifice that doesn't begin by looking at other religions to see how sacrifice is done there and what it means there. In contrast, he begins with a Trinitarian understanding of the Annunciation-Incarnation event. By understanding that in this Christ-event, sacrifice, in the 'history of religions' sense of the word, is made obsolete, Daly argued for an understanding of sacrifice based on personal relationship, evidenced par excellence in the Annunciation-Incarnation event. Daly summarized this as the 'three "moments" of Trinitarian Christian sacrifice: the self-offering of the Father; the "response" of the Son, and the responding self-offering of the believers [enabled by the Holy Spirit]'.[13] Coakley outlined this enabling activity of the Spirit as 'the primary means of incorporation into the trinitarian life of God, and as constantly and "reflexively" at work in believers in the circle of response to the Father's call'.[14]

This understanding of sacrifice does not depend on the immolation of the victim. It is not inextricably linked to violence and suffering; in fact these are rejected as key paradigms

---

12 Gordon W. Lathrop, *Holy Things: A Liturgical Theology* (Minneapolis, MN: Fortress Press, 1998), 156.

13 Robert Daly, *Sacrifice Unveiled: The True Meaning of Christian Sacrifice* (London and New York: T & T Clark, 2009), 10.

14 Sarah Coakley, *God, Sexuality, and the Self: An Essay 'On The Trinity'* (Cambridge: Cambridge University Press, 2013), 111.

for considering sacrifice and instead we are offered a paradigm of love. When one considers the purpose of the Eucharist this becomes abundantly clear. If the Eucharist is celebrated in order to bring about the deep and ongoing transformation of the community of believers who receive it, this transformation is facilitated by the transformation of the bread and wine into the body and blood of Christ. In this sense, the transformation of the eucharistic elements is subordinate to the transformation of the community of believers. Not a subordination of superiority but rather of temporarility – the transformation of the eucharistic elements happens prior to the transformation of the community; it happens so that the community transformation might occur. This transformation is not one of violence and suffering but one of love; love of God and love of each other.

To understand the Eucharist as a mutual, Trinitarian self-offering is to release the Eucharist from its focus on the death of Christ as the key paradigm for sacrifice, and instead offer a eucharistic understanding of sacrifice that places the Annunciation-Incarnation event at the centre of this new narrative. This, then, is a consequence of considering the Annunciation-Incarnation event to be at the heart of Christian somatic memory. As our understanding of the Eucharist is re-visioned with regard to the Incarnation in its fullest sense, so are our understandings of priesthood and sacrifice.

While this shift in focus serves to highlight loving self-offering over and above violence and death, it does not detract from the Real Presence at the altar. In contrast to Jay's conclusion that suggested when one removed the destructive, immolatory sacrificial dimension of the Eucharist one was left with a weak notion of the Eucharist that reflected a memorial, symbolic offering only, the removal of this dimension of the Eucharist actually makes way for the Incarnational dimension. The dead Body of Christ is replaced with the living one – the Incarnate Christ – in all its fullness (which includes the death of Christ). Through this understanding of sacrifice Christ is even more Really Present at the altar. The transformation of the elements into the Real Presence is a re-actualization of the Trinitarian self-offering glimpsed in the Annunciation-Incarnation event.

Placing the Annunciation-Incarnation event at the heart of Christian somatic memory allows for an understanding of the Eucharist that embodies the person of Christ at the altar but does not impose unobtainable ritual purity on either the celebrant or the congregation. The trauma of the Cross is relinquished for an equally traumatic, but life-focused, Incarnational event. The priest is not re-sacrificing Christ on the altar, but rather re-birthing (or even re-membering) the Body of Christ in the celebration of the Eucharist. It is in the celebration of the Eucharist that one is born again anew with each participation in the sacrament.

The ritual of the Eucharist is based on a meal that itself is a non-identical repetition of a religious sacrifice – the Passover. However, the Eucharist is not only a backwards-looking remembrance of the Last Supper. To suggest this is to imply that the Last Supper is the model for all subsequent eucharistic celebrations and thus the priest inevitably comes to represent Christ. This meal is not only backwards-looking but also forward-looking. The meal of the Eucharist is celebrated and shared in anticipation of the heavenly banquet in the eschaton. This banquet, characterized as a wedding feast, appears in Matthew 22.1–14 and in Luke 14.15–24. In this sense, the Eucharist is eschatologically focused. Here we receive a morsel and a sip, but in the future we will receive a banqueting table – the full and continued presence of Christ.

To understand the celebration of contemporary Eucharists in this manner is to draw them in line with the full understanding of the Annunciation-Incarnation event proposed here. Just as with the Incarnation we do not need to look back to one specific temporal moment to find our point of reference, so too with the Eucharist. To look back to the Last Supper as the only point of reference is to miss the many meals Jesus shared before this final meal and to allow the centuries of eucharistic celebration that have happened since then to go unacknowledged in our understanding. Furthermore, to only look backwards deprives us of a future hope for the meal that is to come.

In this model of the eucharistic sacrifice, the priest does not act in the person of Christ but rather fully and completely as a representative of the Church. The presider does not consecrate but rather the Holy Spirit does. The eucharistic anaphora should be recognized as petitionary prayers rather than performative ones. Both transformations – that of the bread and wine into the body and blood and also the transformation of the gathered congregation into one corporate body – are accomplished by the work of the Holy Spirit, not by the actions of the priest. The first epiclesis, spoken before the Words of Institution, petitions God to send the Spirit on the eucharistic elements: '[M]ake holy, therefore, these gifts, we pray, by sending down your spirit upon them like the dewfall, so that they may become for us the Body and Blood of our Lord, Jesus Christ.'[15] Similarly, the second epiclesis, spoken after the Words of Institution, petitions God to send the Spirit upon the people, that by 'partaking of the Body and Blood of Christ, we may be gathered into one by the Holy Spirit'.[16] In both cases these prayers, and indeed the whole of the eucharistic liturgy, is spoken in the corporate 'we' and both are petitionary rather than performative. It is the Holy Spirit who accomplishes the transformation of the bread and wine, which in turn accomplishes and facilitates, in the power of the Holy Spirit, the transformation of the self-offered community that receives it. The priest acts as representative of the gathered believers, but has no ontological power to effect any change in the eucharistic elements. Rather, the priest has the authority to call upon the Holy Spirit to effect such change.

I noted in Chapter 3, when considering the eucharistic theology of Ambrose of Milan, the power of human language that reaches its supra-fulfilment in the speaking of the Words of Institution. However, these words have a power that is not dependent on the priest acting *in persona Christi*. Returning to Williams' definition of priesthood as one who serves in the space cleared by God,[17] it is Christ at the Last Supper who clears the

---

15 'Eucharistic Prayer II', The Roman Missal, http://catholic-resources.org/ChurchDocs/RM3-EP1-4.htm, accessed on 15/02/16.

16 Ibid.

17 Williams, 'Epilogue', 176.

space for humanity to enter into communion with him, rather than the power of the priest to accomplish anything. The Words of Institution have become limited to a particular vision of priesthood. As our understanding of the nature of Christian sacrifice shifts, when considered through the lens of trauma, so is there a shift in emphasis from the Words of Institution to those of the epiclesis as the significant words of eucharistic consecration.

A consequence of considering the Annunciation-Incarnation event to lie at the core of Christian somatic memory is a re-envisioning of what is taking place on the altar in a eucharistic celebration. When we view the priest as participating in a non-identical repetition of the Annunciation-Incarnation event, having already established that Mary must be centre-stage in our understanding of priesthood, one can view the priest as a representative of the congregation, calling on the Holy Spirit to overshadow these gifts as Mary was overshadowed by the Spirit. Bodily memory of this event is, therefore, central to celebration of the Eucharist, and thus to our understanding of sacrifice.

Real Presence is essential to somatic memory. As we saw with the theology of Cyril of Alexandria, the unity of the body is imperative to an understanding of the Eucharist. It is, therefore, important that the body offered to us in the Eucharist is a body of unity and not a body that is atomized into disparate parts. The eucharistic body is actual body – not representation of body. The material and actual understanding of the Eucharist is central to a theology that is informed by embodied traumatic experience. The embodied nature matters. However, the egalitarian structure with more relaxed views of ritual purity is essential also. Such an approach to the ecclesial Body of Christ calls us to love all bodies. It does not condemn some bodies as being ritually unclean, or spiritually inferior to others. Rather such an egalitarian structure welcomes all bodies and affirms all have equal roles to play.

The Marian Sacrifice

If Mary is our model of priesthood what, then, does this understanding of eucharistic sacrifice mean for Mary? This model of sacrifice, based on mutual self-offering and love, is highly significant for our understanding of Mary and her relationship to both the Incarnate Christ and the Eucharist. Mary takes part in this sacrificial self-offering in her *fiat* and is responsive in her obedience to the call of God. She models this eucharistic understanding of sacrifice in her participation in the Annunciation-Incarnation event – she is at the heart of Christian somatic memory.

Mary's sacrifice in this sense is both ontological and epistemological. It is ontological in that her sacrificial self-offering makes the sacrificial self-offering of the Father and the self-giving response of the Son really present in her womb. It is at this moment, and through her agreement, that the Incarnate Christ becomes particularly present in the world. Thus her role is also essential in a soteriological sense – through Mary's *fiat* salvation is made available to humankind.

However, Mary's sacrificial self-offering, her self-giving response, is also epistemological. In this sense it reveals to us the Trinitarian model of self-offering that is the intrinsic hinge of Christian sacrifice. Furthermore, it reveals to us the Incarnate Christ. Mary's sacrificial self-offering can, therefore, be considered to be sacramental. Her self-offering makes visible and present the mutual, sacrificial self-giving that is at work within the Trinity.

Mary's participation in this intrinsic revelation of the Trinitarian model of sacrifice, the very model that will become the basis for understanding what happens in the celebration of the Eucharist, is significant for our re-visioning of sacrifice in the light of an Annunciation-Incarnational understanding of the Eucharist. Her specific involvement in this revelation of the Trinity offers her as the priest par excellence. Mary, as type of the Church and as the first Christian, offers the earthly element, her body, as the place in which Christ will be revealed to the world and made particularly present. This *fiat* is sacramental and, as such, makes visible the invisible Trinitarian self-offering – she makes visible the foundation of Christian sacrifice and thus the somatic memory at the core of Christian faith. The memory of Mary's body, in all its fullness, becomes key. It is these actions that the priest at the altar undertakes.

The priest offers the earthly elements of bread and wine as the loci of the revelation of Christ to the world, made particularly present in this celebration of the Mass. Here the self-offering of the Father and the mutually self-giving response of the Son are made manifest. The Eucharist re-members the somatic memory at the heart of the Christian faith; it is a non-identical repetition of the Annunciation-Incarnation event. Through the activity of the Holy Spirit what was invisible is transformed into the visible and the congregation is transformed in their response. Here, the truly Christian idea of sacrifice is enacted, drawing its reference and meaning internally, rather than externally.

The Value of the Mutual Self-Offering Sacrifice

This construction of a new narrative of Eucharist, priesthood and sacrifice is a consequence of considering the Annunciation-Incarnation event to be at the core of Christian somatic memory. Such a narrative has value and currency in contemporary Christian discourse.

From the perspective of one attempting to engage with trauma theory from a theological perspective and exploring the implications of the Annunciation-Incarnation event lying at the centre of Christian faith, there is tremendous value in understanding Christian sacrifice from the perspective of Trinitarian mutual self-offering. When one takes the Crucifixion as the baseline for Christian sacrifice, one inevitably implies that Christian sacrifice is inextricably connected to violence and suffering. The somatic memory at the heart of Christianity becomes, then, the suffering and death of Christ. From this perspective, the Incarnation is merely a lengthy prologue to the Crucifixion. Rather, when one considers Christian sacrifice from the perspective of mutual self-offering, one posits love as the key paradigm for sacrifice. Indeed, it is love at the root of the Annunciation-Incarnation event – maternal love and Divine love – and from this all things flow. Not immolatory, destructive love, but rather mutual, interdependent, self-giving love. In the words of the writer of the Gospel of Matthew:

'You shall love the Lord your God with all your heart, and with all your soul, and with all your mind.' This is the greatest and first commandment. And a second is like it: 'You shall love your neighbour as yourself.' On these two commandments hang all the law and the prophets.[18]

This mutual, interdependent, self-giving love as the key paradigm for understanding sacrifice is a radical departure from the violent, destructive understanding of sacrifice that has played such a prominent part in shaping perceptions of the Eucharist and has been at the core of the trauma of Christianity for centuries. In line with the teachings of Jesus, this loving sacrifice is one of life, not death. This destructive sacrifical love has often been used to give legitimacy to suffering and to encourage believers to remain in suffering. For example, Rita Nakashima Brock and Rebecca Ann Parker argued that when we hold on to the necessity of violence to repay human disobedience to God, then violence becomes theologically justified. Such an understanding of sacrifice comes at too high a personal cost.[19]

A focus on the Cross as the paradigm for sacrifice can lead to a triumphalistic perspective on the resurrection and can 'operate in such a way as to promise a radically new beginning to those who have experienced a devastating event'.[20] Shelly Rambo characterized the potential pitfalls of such a reading of sacrifice as she states that it can 'gloss over the realities of pain and loss, glorify suffering, and justify violence'.[21] For Rambo this is evidence in support of her argument for a theology of 'remaining'. Rambo argued that when love becomes linked exclusively to the Cross event, it can easily reinforce violent ideas of sacrifice.[22] The solution, then, is to find a new rhetoric

---

18 Matthew 22.37–40.

19 Rita Nakashima Brock and Rebecca Ann Parker, *Proverbs of Ashes: Violence, Redemptive Suffering, and the Search for What Saves Us* (Boston, MA: Beacon, 2001).

20 Shelly Rambo, *Spirit and Trauma: A Theology of Remaining* (Louisville, KY: Westminster John Knox Press, 2010), 143.

21 Ibid., 143.

22 Ibid., 131.

of love in the pneumatology of Holy Saturday. Love, Rambo suggested, remains in a mode of witnessing in the place between life and death. While I consider that Rambo's argument still rests almost entirely on the Crucifixion event, albeit in an interpretation that is broadened to include Holy Saturday and the resurrection of Easter Sunday, I do agree that to see love as exclusively linked to the Cross event ultimately results in a glorification of suffering and a justification of violence.

Understanding the somatic memory of Christian sacrifice (and thus the Eucharist) from the starting point of the Annunciation-Incarnation event, through the activity of the Trinity, is far more helpful than trying to find points of comparison in vastly differing ritual systems and sacrificial acts across cultures and across timeframes. This comparative approach has its value and is useful when considering anthropological and psychological perspectives on sacrifice. But this comparative approach is no position from which to construct or explore doctrine. Christian doctrine, particularly for something as intrinsic as the Eucharist, the very place where bodies and memories meet, must begin from the perspective of the Trinitarian God made known to humanity through the revelatory event of the Annunciation-Incarnation.

Furthermore, to attempt to understand Christian sacrifice from the perspective of the mutual self-giving evidenced within the Trinity takes seriously the concept of *lex orandi, lex credendi*. In this context, the nature of the eucharistic prayers, drawn from ancient but varied sources, offers to the theologian a useful glimpse into the purpose of the Eucharist. Taking seriously the petitionary nature of these prayers reveals that the power to consecrate does not lie with the priest, but with the Holy Spirit as the activity of the Trinitarian God. Furthermore, considering the corporate nature of these prayers reveals that the priest does not act *in persona Christi* but rather *ut repraesentativus Ecclesiae*.

When the Words of Institution are included in the eucharistic liturgy the priest is not playing the role of Christ, but is rather narrating the account of the Last Supper. This is not the Last Supper as the first eucharistic celebration upon which all subsequent eucharistic celebrations are modelled, but rather the Last Supper as one meal among many, albeit a very significant meal. The non-identical repetition of the Last Supper in the eucharistic celebrations of the Church bridges the gap between the table practices of Jesus and the future heavenly banquet, offering a taste of the kingdom of God to those who believe.

Finally, what then is the value of this understanding of sacrifice with regard to our discussion of Mary as priestly in the previous chapter? When one considers the Annunciation-Incarnation event to be at the core of somatic memory and thus at the heart of Christian sacrifice, then one cannot separate out Mary from Christian sacrifice, just as one cannot conceive of the Annunciation-Incarnation event without her involvement. Both ontologically and epistemologically, Mary becomes essential to our understanding of what sacrifice means in this new Christian context. In this event, Mary acts as priest par excellence. She is *ut repraesentativus Ecclesiae*, as indeed are all priests who celebrate the Eucharist. Thus we see that Mary performs a sacrifice of mutual self-giving, responsive love. She is both type of the Church and archetypal Christian.

Ut Repraesentativus Ecclesiae

If one considers the Annunciation-Incarnation event to be at the core of Christian somatic memory then one must, necessarily, re-envision one's understanding of sacrifice. The hermeneutical lens of trauma destabilizes traditional narratives and creates a rupture from which a new narrative can be constructed. This narrative challenges both the traditional focus on the suffering and violence of the Cross and the exclusion of women from the priestly function of eucharistic celebration – both traumatic in their own rights. Such a new narrative places Mary centre-stage in both our understanding of priesthood and our conception of sacrifice. Mary becomes the role model for the priest of the New Covenant – representing the people rather than acting in the person of Christ. Mary's self-offering becomes integral to our understanding of sacrifice – drawn, as she is, into the Trinitarian mutual self-offering of the Annunciation-Incarnation event. Thus the destructive, violent, sacrificial Eucharist celebrated by a male priest acting *in persona Christi* can be transformed into an act of mutual self-offering, still full of Real Presence, but an act that can now be undertaken by an ordained celebrant of any gender acting *ut repraesentativus Ecclesiae*. A consequence of placing the Annunciation-Incarnation event at the heart of Christian somatic memory is to flood the Ecclesial Body of Christ with generative and life-giving ritual, focused on nourishment and life rather than suffering and death.

6

The Materiality of the Eucharist

He [the Lord] suffered for us, He left us in this Sacrament His Body and Blood, which He made even as He made us, also. For we have become His Body, and through His mercy we are what we receive.[1]

Body and Memory

When framing theological endeavour through the hermeneutical lens of trauma, one thing becomes extraordinarily clear – bodies, and embodied experience, matter. In this chapter, I will examine the Eucharist and its relationship with somatic memory in the context of its materiality. I will consider how the physicality of the Eucharist and its place as a material substance might be understood. Beginning with a brief tracing of the understanding of the issue of 'presence' in the Eucharist, this chapter posits that bodies matter and examines in detail *how* they matter for a sufficient contemporary account of the Eucharist. An essential precursor to the examination of notions of materiality is an exploration of the concept of *perichorēsis*. This chapter will investigate the concept that the embodied experience of the Eucharist matters and that the feminine body matters in terms of mysticism, motherhood and miscar-

---

1 Augustine, 'Sermon 229', trans. Sister Mary Sarah Muldowney, in *Saint Augustine: Sermons on the Liturgical Seasons* (New York: Fathers of the Church, Inc., 1959). Accessed online at https://archive.org/stream/fathersofthechur00951 2mbp/fathersofthechur00951 2mbp_djvu.txt on 01/03/16.

riage. Throughout this chapter, the twin themes of body and memory will be examined with regard to the materiality of the Eucharist – its celebration and reception.

Real Presence

The doctrine of Real Presence outlined here stems from an understanding of the Eucharist informed by the Annunciation-Incarnation event. This Real Presence is a real body not a metaphysical abstract. With that in mind, it is important to understand the way in which belief in eucharistic presence has developed. Any examination of the materiality of the Eucharist must take into account the various ways in which memory interacts with the Body of Christ in Christian understanding of the presence of God in the Eucharist. By the end of the first century, Christians were beginning to relate the presence of Christ in the Lord's Supper to the bread and wine used in the celebration of the ritual meal. This understanding was developed in the second century and a number of early Christian theologians began to speak in language that is recognizably used with reference to the Real Presence of Christ. For example, Justin Martyr noted:

> the food which is blessed by the prayer of His word from which our blood and flesh by transmutation are nourished, is the flesh and blood of that Jesus who was made flesh.[2]

There was a general acceptance, in the diverse and complex forms of Christianity that existed up until the early medieval period, that, by mysterious power and process, the bread and wine consecrated by the celebrant on the altar were, in truth, the Body and Blood of Christ. With one or two notable exceptions, it is not until the eleventh century that these loose eucharistic formulations become codified and set out clearly as doctrine. Indeed, a precise eucharistic theology and, in particular, the term

---

2 Justin Martyr, 'Apology 1', paragraph 66.

transubstantiation, appear to be one of the lasting influences of Scholastic theologians on the contemporary Church.

The significant earlier discussions of eucharistic theology and Real Presence occur in the writings of the ninth-century abbot, Paschasius Radbertus. Radbertus argued that the very (true) Body of Christ was present in the Eucharist through the operation of the priest's words:

> Imagine, then, whether indeed any corporeal thing could be worthier than the substance of the bread and wine for the purpose of changing internally and in fact into Christ's flesh and blood, so that following the consecration Christ's real flesh and blood is truly created.[3]

Radbertus' clarification of the Real Presence of Christ in the Eucharist is closely linked to his understanding of the Eucharist as a sacrifice. If the bread and wine is not truly the flesh and blood of Christ then the sacrifice of the Eucharist is insufficient and ineffective. I have demonstrated the ways in which an understanding of sacrifice can be shaped in terms of a Trinitarian mutual, loving self-giving rather than in terms of the immolation of a victim that Radbertus clearly had in mind. But in both understandings of sacrifice (Radbertus' and the interpretation suggested here) the Real Presence of Christ in the eucharistic elements is important.

The heretical theology of Berengar of Tours in the early eleventh century led to a prescriptive and closely defined formula of eucharistic faith replacing the loosely identified eucharistic beliefs that had previously held sway. Berengar believed in a spiritual presence of Christ in the Eucharist rather than a physical presence. For Berengar, the eucharistic bread and wine must be a *sign* of Christ's body and blood, not identical with it. This rift between the physical and spiritual realms meant

---

3 Paschasius Radbertus, '*De corpore et sanguine domini*', lib. 8, 42–3, cited in and trans. Miri Rubin, *Corpus Christi: The Eucharist in Late Medieval Culture* (Cambridge: Cambridge University Press, 1991), 15.

that Berengar believed that bread continued to be bread as well as the presence of Christ after the consecration (impanation). Berengar wrote: '[T]hrough the consecration at the altar bread and wine become the Sacrament of faith, not by ceasing to be what they were but by remaining what they were and being changed into something else.'[4] Similarly, this rift between the physical and the spiritual did not allow Christ to be physically present in the Eucharist, but only spiritually present. Berengar argued: '[A] portion of the flesh of Christ cannot be present on the altar . . . unless the body of Christ in heaven is cut up and a particle that has been cut off from it is sent down to the Altar.'[5]

It is no surprise that Berengar's work was considered an assault on eucharistic theology. Instructed to recant, Berengar was made to sign a statement of true belief that would become the building block for the formulation of eucharistic theology in the Middle Ages. The oath stated:

> the bread and wine which are placed on the altar after the consecration are not only the sacrament but also the true body and blood of our Lord Jesus Christ, and that they are palpably handled and broken by the hands of the priest and torn by the teeth of the faithful, not simply as a sacrament but as a true fact.[6]

This specific statement led to an increased sense of realism in the eucharistic elements and also paved the way for the Scholastic development of distinctions between sacrament and reality – *sacramentum et res* – which would shape the next nine hundred years of eucharistic theology.

Arising from the Scholastic explorations of the Eucharist, it is the concept of *transubstantiation* that has had the most influence

---

4 Berengar, 'Opusculum', in Jaroslav Pelikan, *The Christian Tradition: A History of the Development of Doctrine, Vol. 4, Reformation of Church and Dogma (1300–1700)* (Chicago and London: The University of Chicago Press, 1984), 198.

5 Berengar, *On the Holy Supper* 37, in ibid., 194.

6 Cited in and trans. Martos, *Doors to the Sacred*, 237.

in Catholic eucharistic theology. First used by Hildebert of Tours in the early thirteenth century, *transubstantiation* is a term that seeks to give some element of understanding as to how the reality (or substance) of the elements of the eucharistic bread and wine could be changed while their appearances remained that of bread and of wine. The most significant development and detailed exploration of the term is given by Aquinas:

> Christ's body is not in this sacrament in the same way as a body is in a place, which by its dimensions is commensurate with the place; but in a special manner which is proper to this sacrament. Hence we say that Christ's body is upon many altars, not as in different places, but 'sacramentally': and thereby we do not understand that Christ is there only as in a sign, although a sacrament is a kind of sign; but that Christ's body is here after a fashion proper to this sacrament, as stated above.[7]

Understanding the Eucharist in this manner led Aquinas to propose that the manner in which Christ's body became present in the eucharistic bread must be described with a name of its own – this conversion was unlike any other.

> Therefore He can work not only formal conversion, so that diverse forms succeed each other in the same subject; but also the change of all being, so that, to wit, the whole substance of one thing be changed into the whole substance of another. And this is done by Divine power in this sacrament; for the whole substance of the bread is changed into the whole substance of Christ's body, and the whole substance of the wine into the whole substance of Christ's blood. Hence this is not a formal, but a substantial conversion; nor is it a kind of natural movement: but, with a name of its own, it can be called 'transubstantiation.'[8]

---

7 Aquinas, *The Summa Theologica* III, Q. 75, A. 1, ad. 3.
8 Ibid., Q. 75, A. 4, ad. 3.

Transubstantiation became established as doctrine in the Catholic Church in the thirteenth century. However, Gary Macy has clearly demonstrated that the meaning of the term transubstantiation in the Middle Ages was not fixed. Theologians held a variety of positions regarding how any change in substance took place, and what substance was present on the altar post-consecration.

> There was not common understanding of the category of substance, much less agreement on either the use of the term transubstantiation or on what the term might have meant when used. In fact, theologians at the time of the Fourth Lateran Council [1215] fell roughly into three camps in regard to the eucharistic change. 1) Some believed that bread and wine remained present along with the Body and Blood of the Lord; 2) others felt that the substance of the bread and the wine were annihilated, the substance of the Body and Blood alone remaining. Finally, 3) a third group argued that the substance of the bread and wine was changed into the substance of the Body and Blood at the words of consecration. Modern terminology would categorize the first theory as 'consubstantiation', the second as 'annihilation' or 'succession' theory, and the third as 'transubstantiation'.[9]

Nevertheless, the doctrine of *transubstantiation* was later reinforced by the Tridentine pronouncements. The Council of Trent produced three documents on the Eucharist: one on the Blessed Sacrament (1551), one on the reception of communion (1562), and one on the Mass as a sacrifice (1562). The result of these documents was that the scholastic approach to the Eucharist became the definitive word on the matter. This concept of the consecrated Eucharist as transubstantiated elements and thus the invisible, spiritual presence of Christ was the dominant understanding of the Eucharist until the late twentieth century.

---

9 Gary Macy, *Treasures from the Storeroom: Medieval Religion and the Eucharist* (Collegeville, MN: Liturgical Press, 1999), 82–3.

The twentieth century has seen further development of the concept of Real Presence. Rediscovery of ancient sources and the contribution of the Second Vatican Council have led to the consideration of the Eucharist in the wider context of the Mass and Liturgy. The rediscovery of texts from this era indicated that for over a thousand years Christians had been able to talk eloquently and theologically about the Real Presence of Christ in the eucharistic elements without the need for the term *transubstantiation*.

Heaney, in his anti-theology of the Eucharist, challenges us to a broader understanding of the concept of Real Presence, rejecting the metaphysics that had become so attached to discussions of presence in the Eucharist. In his analysis of the notion of presence, Heaney noted that '[T]o be present is to be recognized as being able to be counted or characterized by an observer at a particular moment and in a particular place.'[10] He concluded:

> presence is neither an activity, especially an ongoing one, nor is it any state other than that which allows that which is present to be counted as such, 'Presenting' oneself does not make one any more present than was already the case by reason of being there. References to 'presence' in the Eucharist that imply a state, characterized as 'real', or an activity of being there fall well short on formal terms of telling us anything more than this.[11]

Heaney's critique of Real Presence is useful in encouraging a broader notion of 'presence'; however, I would not want to discard the modifier 'Real' from my narrative of Real Presence in the Eucharist. The real-ness – the materiality – of such a presence is essential.

In the late twentieth century, examination of the concept of presence has moved out of the Church and into a more secular contemplation. For example, George Steiner subtitled his 1989

---

10 Heaney, *Beyond the Body*, 125.
11 Ibid., 126.

work *Real Presences* with the question '[I]s there anything *in* what we say?' This subtitle reveals Steiner's desire for immanence. 'For Steiner, God is the premise upon which speech is based, and the wager on meaning and understanding – which we all undertake in experiencing art – is in fact a wager on transcendence.'[12] Indeed, Steiner opened his examination of presence with the statement that:

> [This essay] proposes that any coherent understanding of what language is and how language performs, that any coherent account of the capacity of human speech to communicate meaning and feeling is, in the final analysis, underwritten by the assumption of God's presence. I will put forward the argument that the experience of aesthetic meaning in particular, that of literature, of the arts, of musical form, infers the necessary possibility of this 'real presence'.[13]

Steiner moved the discussion of presence away from its importance at the altar and instead posited a world in which the presence of God is necessary in all aspects. God's presence does not just give meaning to the celebration of the Eucharist, it also gives meaning to language itself.

Similarly, the performance artist Marina Abramović moved the exploration of presence away from Church, although I argue that, like Steiner, it is significant that even a seemingly secular contemplation of presence is not irreligious. Abramović invited members of the public to sit opposite her for as long as they liked and hold her gaze. Entitled *The Artist is Present*, this piece of art was performed over a period of three months at New York's Museum of Modern Art (MoMA) in 2010.[14] Julie

---

12 Wendy Steiner, 'Silence', *London Review of Books* 11, no. 11 (1989), 10–11, at 10.

13 George Steiner, *Real Presences: Is There Anything in What We Say?* (London and Boston, MA: Faber and Faber, 1989), 3.

14 Marina Abramović, *The Artist is Present*, 2010, Museum of Modern Art, New York.

Hamilton reflected on this performance, noting its relationship with the celebration of the Eucharist:

> [D]ressed in flowing gowns resembling priestly vestments, her performance in MoMA is liturgical, symbolically akin to the Adoration of the Blessed Sacrament. Merleau-Ponty's sacramentality of the flesh is quite vivid in this artistic instance with regards to Eucharistic dimensions of her venerated human flesh, adored as people assemble within the museum, keeping vigil. Masses wait in line to receive the same 'wafer' of her presence, a clear analogy to the Real Presence within the Eucharistic Monstrance.[15]

Abramović's exploration and reflection on the power of presence has distinctly sacramental overtones and even the videos of her performance are exceptionally powerful. This piece of artwork, along with Steiner's identification of the presence of God as that which gives meaning, demonstrate the significance of Real Presence both within Christianity and in the (so-called) secular world. Both Steiner and Abramović explore an understanding of 'presence' that is far bigger than the narrow, metaphysical focus of Aquinas. They challenge us to paint our concept of presence on a big canvas.

The last forty years have seen a move away from the Scholastic insistence on *transubstantiation* and the Mass as a sacrifice in favour of other, equally Catholic, less Scholastic interpretations of the Eucharist.[16] Indeed, Martos concluded that the reach of the Second Vatican Council with regard to the Eucharist should not be underestimated.

> The council broadened the notion of Christ's presence to include not only his sacramental presence in the bread and wine but

---

15 Julie Hamilton, 'Praktognosia and Performance: Phenomenological Epistemology in the Performance Art of Marina Abramović and Lia Chavez', http://civa.org/sitecontent/wp-content/uploads/CIVA-Between-Two-Worlds-2-Hamilton_Praktognosia-Phenomenological-Epistemology-and-Performance-Art_FINAL.pdf. Accessed on 15/12/2015.

16 Martos, *Doors to the Sacred*, 261.

also his presence as the Word of God in the scripture readings of the mass, and indeed his presence as the risen Lord in the assembly of believers.[17]

Exploring the way in which it is possible to understand this presence of Christ both in the bread and wine and in the assembly of believers, through thinking about the Annunciation-Incarnation event, is essential to understanding the materiality of the Eucharist. An emphasis on the physicality and materiality of the Eucharist is one of the implications of considering the Eucharist through the lens of the traumatic somatic memory. When read in the light of the Annunciation-Incarnation event, the Eucharist is not simply a sacrifice, but an exaltation of the material world. Seeing Real Presence through the lens of the Annunciation-Incarnation event leads us to an exploration of mutual, indwelling relationship – *perichorēsis*.

Perichorēsis: The Indwelling God

It might seem counter-intuitive to begin an exploration of the significance of the materiality of the Eucharist with a reflection on the distinctly immaterial concept of the indwelling of God. It is only by reflecting on the relationship between the three Persons of the Trinity, however, that it is possible to understand the way in which the two natures of Christ (human and Divine) are related within his body. Understanding the Trinity and the nature of Christ in this way allows an exploration of the relationship between material elements and the presence of God in the Eucharist. The way in which this indwelling takes place within the Triune God, the person of Christ, and the eucharistic elements provides a model for understanding what happens when believers consume the Eucharist. The memories of indwelling in each of these bodies become the constituent memory celebrated and received in the Eucharist, non-identically repeated in each instantiation.

---

17 Ibid., 263.

The key to understanding all of these relationships is the concept of *perichorēsis* – the mutual interpenetration of the three Persons of the Trinity.[18] Through this concept of indwelling, it becomes impossible to conceive of the Divine Persons as separate from each other. It is *because* the Divine Persons of the Trinity are different from each other that it becomes possible to understand their relationship as being one of *perichorēsis*. Precisely because they are different from each other, they are able to be in relationship with each other. The difference within the Trinity is what enables communion and relationship. As Moltmann noted:

> [T]he doctrine of perichoresis links together in a brilliant way the threeness and the unity, without reducing the threeness to the unity, or dissolving the unity in the threeness. The unity of the triunity lies in the eternal perichoresis of the trinitarian persons. Interpreted perichoretically, the trinitarian persons form their own unity by themselves in the circulation of the divine life.[19]

Without relinquishing either unity or difference, the doctrine of *perichorēsis* allows an insight into how multiplicity can exist in oneness.

The term *perichorēsis* was first used by Gregory of Nazianzus as a way of encapsulating the relationship between the human and Divine in the person of Christ. In his first letter to Cledonius, Gregory used the verb *perichōréō* to address the nature of the hypostasis of Christ. Gregory wrote: 'Just as the natures are blended [*perichōréō*] so too are the titles which mutually transfer by the principle of their natural togetherness.'[20] This image

---

18 Paul S. Fiddes, *Participating in God: A Pastoral Doctrine of the Trinity* (London: Darton, Longman and Todd Ltd, 2000), 47.

19 Jürgen Moltmann, *The Trinity and the Kingdom of God*, trans. Margaret Kohl (London: SCM Press, 1981), 175.

20 Saint Gregory of Nazianzus, 'Letter 101', in *On God and Christ: The Five Theological Orations and Two Letters to Cledonius*, ed. Lionel Wickham (Crestwood, NY: St Vladimir's Seminary Press, 2002), paragraph 5, 158.

of reciprocity and exchange between the two natures of Christ carries with it the qualities of mutuality, equality and exchange that the doctrine of *perichorēsis* offers in an understanding of the Trinity. Indeed, while Gregory was writing about a Christological issue, he was doing so in a Trinitarian context. The letter to Cledonius clearly set the Apollinarian heresy against the backdrop of an orthodox understanding of the Trinity. It is not until the eighth century that one finds the term applied to the Trinity specifically when John Damascene used the term περιχώρησις in his notion of coinherence in chapter 8 of *On the Orthodox Faith*. He used the term to demonstrate that the persons of the Trinity are wholly in one another and that 'their distinct individuality is conceptual, in reality there is no separate individuality, but a complete coinherence between the persons of the Trinity'.[21]

Understanding the way in which neither unity nor difference are relinquished in the multiplicity of the Trinity and the nature of Christ, offers in turn a model for understanding the Real Presence of Christ in the Eucharist. Just as both the human and Divine natures of Christ mutually indwell, becoming inseparable and yet not less distinct, so it becomes possible to understand the Real Presence in the Eucharist in these terms.

The presence of Christ indwells the eucharistic elements fully without negating their materiality and without diminishing the divinity of this Real Presence. Thus, the model of mutual indwelling that is outlined in relation to the Trinity and the person of Christ is the same mutual indwelling in the consecrated eucharistic elements. The two early discussions of the Eucharist – Radbertus' stressing of the corporality of the presence of Christ in the elements and Berengar's heretical insistence on a spiritual presence only – are brought together in this understanding of the Eucharist. Through the model of *perichorēsis*, so richly displayed with regard to the Trinity and the Person of Christ, the eucharistic elements are indwelt by Christ without relinquishing

---

21 Andrew Louth, 'Late Patristic Developments in the East', in *The Oxford Handbook of the Trinity*, ed. Gilles Emery O.P. and Matthew Levering (Oxford: Oxford University Press, 2011), 138–53, at 148.

either unity or difference. They retain their fully material status as bread and wine even as they are indwelt by the Real Presence of Christ that makes them His body and blood.

If one is to take the doctrine of the Triune God seriously, one cannot separate out the Divine Persons of the Trinity, and thus it is the presence of God, not just Christ alone, that indwells these eucharistic elements. It is the presence of God that is found in the eucharistic elements but not the presence of the First Person in isolation. The Second Person of the Trinity is present in the Eucharist along with the First and Third Persons, but the First and Third Persons are not present apart from the presence of God.

These three models of indwelling (the Trinity, the hypostasis of Christ, and the Real Presence in the Eucharist) provide a model for understanding the effects of receiving the Eucharist on the believer. Each body is informed by the memory of the bodies that have gone before it. Just as it is possible to understand the Trinity as a relationship of *perichoretic* mutual interpenetration between the three Divine Persons, so it is possible to understand the hypostasis as a mutual interpenetration of humanity and divinity in Christ. Furthermore, it is possible to understand the Real Presence of Christ in the eucharistic elements as a mutual interpenetration of the Body and Blood of Christ with the bread and wine. If the *perichorēsis* of the Trinity and the Person of Christ provide a model for understanding the Real Presence in the Eucharist, then the indwelling is not one-way. The material elements become part of Christ, even as Christ becomes part of the material. The goodness of the material world is affirmed as the material elements are drawn into mutual indwelling with the presence of Christ. Indeed, Coakley noted, in her exploration of the 'prayer-based' model of the Trinity, that 'the "mystic"/church vision of the Trinity haunted the celebration of the eucharistic mysteries from relatively early years: the *lex orandi* as "incorporation" was ever on offer to the faithful'.[22] She reads the Spirit as the transforming agent of both the eucharistic elements and the

---

22 Coakley, *God, Sexuality, and the Self*, 133.

people of God. Being 'incorporated' into the Body of Christ (the Church) is the activity of the Spirit in the Eucharist.

More recent teachings of the Catholic Church have moved away from a focus on Christ's Real Presence in the eucharistic elements alone and stressed the presence of Christ in the whole celebration of the Eucharist. In this sense, then, the *perichorēsis* at the Eucharist is not just the indwelling of Christ in the elements, but rather the mutual interpenetration between God and the believers gathered in celebration.

Sacraments, then, while being intimately connected to bodies, are access points into this *perichorēsis*. The memory of each *perichorēsis* informs the body of the next *perichoretic* experience. Through participation in the sacraments, believers come to experience and be experienced in this indwelling, for it is through the reception of the sacraments that the believer is drawn into the Body of Christ and known by other believers in that same unity. Paul Fiddes noted:

> [W]e share in death as we share in the broken body of the bread and in the extravagantly poured out wine, and as we are covered with the threat of hostile waters. We share in life as we come out from under the waters (whether immersed in them or affused by them), to take our place in the new community of the body of Christ, and to be filled with the new wine of the Spirit.[23]

This understanding of the concept of relationship in unity and difference enables an exploration of the materiality of the Eucharist and the experiences that are incumbent upon this materiality.

Embodied Eucharistic Experience

While the early Christians actively participated in a frequent eucharistic service, the history of active lay participation in the

---

23 Fiddes, *Participating in God*, 281.

Eucharist is not a consistent one. In the Middle Ages an increasing understanding of the eucharistic elements as Christ's presence, combined with an increasingly disembodied identification of Christ with God, led to a decline in the reception of communion. Fewer Christians felt worthy or willing to risk such direct contact with God and the manipulations of an increasingly clericalized clergy ensured that this sense of inadequacy was keenly felt. The role of the laity in the liturgy changed from one of active participation to one of passive inspiration and adoration, predominantly of the consecrated host – the 'Blessed Sacrament'. What was once a communal prayer and celebration had become a clerical ritual separated from the congregation by barriers of language, architecture and worthiness. Clerics discouraged the laity from receiving communion lest it bring damnation rather than salvation to their souls. Removed from the body, and thus from the somatic memory, communion was distorted. It was no longer an embodied experience, no longer *perichoretic* in a physical sense.

By the thirteenth century, almost all lay people abstained from communion. The experience of the Eucharist was no longer, for most, an embodied one. Rather it was an observed encounter. The Consecration and Elevation of the Host came to be regarded as the high points of the liturgy observed by the congregation. As the Mass was regarded as a sacrifice (performed by the priest, *in persona Christi*, on behalf of the people) the efficacy of the Mass was not dependent on the participation of the people. If present, the laity had only to observe and 'participate by reason of their spiritual devotion'.[24] The Eucharist was a sacrifice performed by the priest on behalf of the people – they had no active role to play. A personal sense of unworthiness (the result of deliberate manipulation on the part of the Church to advance its power) combined with clerical anxiety about a host breaking and dropping to the floor, or a drop of wine spilling from the chalice, made reception of the eucharistic elements by the laity a rare event. Where the Eucharist *was* received by

---

24 Kilmartin, *The Eucharist in the West*, 114.

laity it was in wafer form only. Only the priests drank from the chalice.

However, it is possible to see at this time an intense desire, particularly among women mystics, to receive an embodied experience of Christ in the Eucharist. Caroline Walker Bynum noted that '[M]ystics (especially women mystics) who were denied access to the cup at mass repeatedly experienced both the flooding of ecstasy through their limbs and the taste of the water in their mouths as blood.'[25] For example, Catherine of Siena (d. 1380) reported two miracles in which Christ fed her directly in a vision because she was denied the Eucharist by servers or celebrants.[26] Furthermore, as she was denied the chalice, Catherine experienced blood in her mouth or pouring from it, although what she had actually received was the bread.[27] Similarly, Beatrice of Nazareth (d. 1268) was overwhelmed with the experience of Christ's blood when she received the wafer.[28]

This desire for a physical element to the embodied experience of Christ in the reception of the Eucharist, for some women mystics, went beyond images of food. For example, the thirteenth-century mystic Hadewijch expressed her desire for Christ in the Eucharist to be a physical union. To consume the Eucharist meant, in some instances, to become pregnant with Christ, to have Christ growing within her.[29] One is reminded, in this startling image, of the equally startling declaration made some eight hundred years previously by Pulcheria, who vindicated her presence at the altar with the words, 'Have I not given birth to Christ?' Hadewijch used the language of *perichorēsis* to explain the knowing and experiencing of God. She

25 Caroline Walker Bynum, *Wonderful Blood: Theology and Practice in Late Medieval Northern Germany and Beyond* (Philadelphia: University of Pennsylvania Press, 2007), 4.

26 Caroline Walker Bynum, *Holy Feast and Holy Fast: The Religious Significance of Food to Medieval Women* (Berkeley, Los Angeles and London: University of California Press, 1987), 174.

27 Ibid., 177.

28 Bynum, *Wonderful Blood*, 4.

29 Bynum, *Holy Feast*, 154.

wrote: '[T]hey [the receiver of the Eucharist and Christ] penetrate each other in such a way that neither of the two distinguishes himself from the other. But they abide in one another in fruition, mouth in mouth, heart in heart, body in body, soul in soul.'[30] This mutual interpenetration and dwelling within one another is the mark of the reception of the Eucharist for Hadewijch.

Concerns about the frequency of the reception of communion for the laity are a recurring theme in the pronouncements of the Church Councils. For example, in Canon 21 of the Fourth Lateran Council (1215), the Church decreed:

> [A]ll the faithful of either sex, after they have reached the age of discernment, should individually confess all their sins in a faithful manner to their own priest at least once a year, and let them take care to do what they can to perform the penance imposed on them. Let them reverently receive the sacrament of the eucharist at least at Easter unless they think, for a good reason and on the advice of their own priest, that they should abstain from receiving it for a time.[31]

Similarly, the documents of the Council of Trent, some three hundred years later, indicate that the issues surrounding the reception of the Eucharist had not abated. Thus, in Canon XIII, the Council declared:

> [I]f any one denieth, that all and each of Christ's faithful of both sexes are bound, when they have attained to years of discretion, to communicate every year, at least at Easter, in accordance with the precept of holy Mother Church; let him be anathema.[32]

---

30 Hadewijch, 'Letter 9', in *Hadewijch: Works*, ed. Columba Hart (Mahwah, NJ: Paulist Press), II. 7–11, 66.

31 H. J. Schroeder, *Disciplinary Decrees of the General Councils: Text, Translation and Commentary* (St Louis, MO: B. Herder, 1937), 236–96.

32 Waterworth, *The Canons and Decrees of the Sacred and Oecumenical Council of Trent*, 83.

It is indicative that, three hundred years after the Lateran Council, the Council of Trent felt the need to reaffirm regular (annual) reception of the Eucharist. Perhaps reception of the Eucharist had become even less frequent. The little change in Canon law, the Tridentine Mass, and parochial practice in the subsequent five hundred years indicates that the obligation of one reception of the Eucharist per year had become not the minimum, but the norm. It is important to note that this annual reception of the Eucharist was intimately connected to the practice of penance and can, itself, be seen as the culmination of the period of shriving – Lent. This focus on sin and unworthiness dominated the understanding of the Eucharist, certainly in the minds of those articulating the rubrics of its practice.

It was only with the rise of the Liturgical Movement in the late nineteenth and early twentieth century and its eventual contribution to the Second Vatican Council, that the laity's assigned role of predominantly passive observation of the Mass returned to active participation in the Mass. Papal approval had been given in 1903 for the more frequent reception of communion, and the reception of a person's first communion, aged about seven years, became an important ceremonial occasion from this time onwards. But the Constitution on the Sacred Liturgy in 1963 went much further, establishing the celebration of Mass in the vernacular, allowing congregations to understand all the words of the service. Furthermore, it paved the way for lay readers and eucharistic ministers to assist in the duties of the Mass. The congregation was expected to hear the Mass and to join in with the appropriate responses. Just as significantly, the priest celebrating the Eucharist now faced the congregation – the laity were now able to see, hear and taste the celebration of the Eucharist. The engagement of the senses in communion served to make it an embodied experience, one in which the body and the bodily memory of the Christian faith played an active role.

The tracing of this history of active participation in the Eucharist is significant in that it indicates that merely watching the celebration of a Mass, just adoring the Blessed Sacrament, is insufficient as a reception of the Eucharist. An embodied participation in the celebration of the Eucharist is vital. The reading of the Eucharist through the traumatic lens of the somatic memory of the Annunciation-Incarnation event not only makes Christ Really Present in the Eucharist but demands the real active, embodied presence and participation of the people in the Eucharist. If Christ is Really Present, so must we be.

While the high medieval Church was convinced of the vitality of the Eucharist, the adoration of the Blessed Sacrament was considered to be an appropriate substitute for bodily reception which could only be received once a year. It is the idea of a weekly, if not daily, reception of the Eucharist, recovered in the late nineteenth century and developed throughout the twentieth century, which has shaped the significant liturgical changes seen in the Catholic Church. The implication, then, of considering the Eucharist through the lens of traumatic somatic memory of the Annunciation-Incarnation event is that Real Presence understood through the paradigm of *perichorēsis* demands our real presence in response. One can conclude, therefore, that bodies – the eucharististic Body and Blood of Christ in the bread and wine and the active, embodied participation of the believer – matter. As becomes evident from considering the relationship of bodies to the Eucharist throughout history, as I have done here, it is only through our bodies that the Eucharist is experienced. Furthermore, the way in which our bodies are taught or encouraged to engage with the Eucharist can profoundly influence the way in which we perceive of ourselves. The sinner who dare not receive the bread, let alone the wine, for fear of the presence of God is unlikely to have the most positive of self-images.

Somatic Memory in the Sacramental Body

Bodies are profoundly linked to sacraments. Indeed, the body is the site of all sacramental encounters. As David Power noted: '[P]eople enter into sacrament first through their bodies.'[33] We

---

33 David Power, *Sacrament: The Language of God's Giving* (New York: Crossroad, 1999), 149.

enter into the sacraments through our embodied experience of them. Sacraments do not exist, except in the doing of them, the celebrating of them. Sacramentality, and in particular the sacrament of the Eucharist, must be deeply woven into an understanding of materiality and the materiality of the body. Brannon Hancock, in his anatomy of the sacrament, indicated: 'the Eucharist is a body, given to bodies, creating a body'.[34] It should be unsurprising, therefore, to see that the earliest Christians celebrated their belief in the Incarnation of God, his resurrection, and their own future bodily resurrections with the very material sharing of a meal. It is this eucharistic meal that shapes the eucharistic community that shares it, and food is at the heart of the material. Indeed, food constitutes the material. It is absorbed into our bodies and becomes a very part of us. As the early Christians ate their eucharistic meal, that which they ate came to constitute who they were.

This eucharistic gift in material substance, in a form that can be consumed by each member of a congregation, reaffirms the goodness of the material world. The Incarnation of Jesus reveals, again, the goodness of materiality; that Christ was fully material and corporeal reveals the positive nature of the material world. He did not scorn the material nature of humanity. The Eucharist, in its non-identical repetition of the Annunciation-Incarnation event, affirms the goodness of the body and its senses. The embodied experience of sacraments, their irreducible materiality, helps to right one's perspective on the material world and the uses to which humankind puts material goods. This is echoed in the *Didache*'s account of an early eucharistic celebration. The prayer given for the celebration includes the words, '[E]ven as this broken bread was scattered over the hills, and was gathered together and became one, so let Your Church be gathered together from the ends of

---

34 Brannon Hancock, *The Scandal of Sacramentality: The Eucharist in Literary and Theological Perspectives* (Eugene, OR: Wipf and Stock, 2014), 65.

the earth into Your kingdom'.[35] This emphasis on the goodness of the material in the celebration of the Eucharist is central from the earliest accounts.

It appears to have been customary, until the Middle Ages at least, for the congregation gathered to celebrate the Eucharist to bring with them their own offerings to be made as part of the celebration. For example, writing in the early second century, Justin Martyr noted: '[A]t the conclusion of the prayers we greet one another with a kiss (1 Pet. 5.14). Then bread and a cup containing wine and water are presented to the one presiding over the brothers.'[36] The word used for 'presented' here is προσφέρεται (offered), seeming to indicate that something is brought to the celebrant or offered to him. That it follows a kiss of peace seems to reflect the teaching in Matthew 5.23–4 regarding making peace with a fellow believer before making an offering at the altar. This kiss of peace further indicates the kinship felt by early Christians who exchanged kisses to demonstrate their familial status within the early Christian communities:

> Early Christians constructed the ritual kiss not only as a means to 'talk' about being a family, but also as a way to act it out. The adoption and modification of a typical familiar gesture into a decidedly Christian ritual helped early Christians redefine the concept of family. With the kiss's assistance, Christian communities became families united by faith.[37]

Significantly, the kiss exchanged between these Christians is not a kiss on the cheek but rather a more intimate kiss on

35 'Didache', trans. M. B. Riddle, in *Ante-Nicene Fathers*, Vol. 7, ed. Alexander Roberts, James Donaldson and A. Cleveland Coxe (Buffalo, NY: Christian Literature Publishing Co., 1886), Chapter 9. Accessed online at www.newadvent.org/fathers/0714.htm on 09/02/2015.

36 Justin Martyr, 'Apology 1', Chapter 65.

37 Michael Philip Penn, *Kissing Christians: Ritual and Community in the Late Ancient Church* (Philadelphia: University of Pennsylvania Press, 2005), 31.

the lips – a merging of bodies at the mouth that echoes the interpenetration of *perichorēsis*. The kiss, in this context, is not only a sign of peace but also a radical rejection of the cultural norms that dictated the propriety of relationships between men and women and a ritual reinforcing of a group's strength, unity and cohesion.

It was with Justin Martyr that a reference to the ritual act of offering as part of the eucharistic celebration first appeared. There are similar contemporary references to the congregation presenting an offering as part of the Eucharist. For example, the *Apostolic Tradition* included reference to catechumens celebrating their first Eucharist and bringing with them the gifts for the celebration as their offering.[38] Thus, Joseph Jungmann could note that:

> [S]ince the third century, then, it very quickly became a fixed rule that the faithful should offer their gifts at a common Eucharistic celebration, but because of the close connection with the performance of the sacred mystery it was from the very start recognised as a right restricted to those who were full members of the Church, just like the reception of the Sacrament . . . [and] the gifts of all who openly lived in sin were to be refused.[39]

This offering of gifts by the faithful became almost obsolete by the beginning of the sixteenth century. As ordinary bread began to be replaced with unleavened bread in the early ninth century, people could no longer bring their own bread for use in the celebration. Combined with the increasing clericalism of the Church and the increasing distancing of the laity from the rite of Communion, the offertory reached its lowest point in the Tridentine Mass of 1570. Here the Deacon handed the

---

38 Hippolytus, 'The Apostolic Tradition', trans. Burton Scott Easton, in *The Apostolic Tradition of Hippolytus* (Cambridge: Cambridge University Press, 1934), Chapter 20, at 45.

39 Joseph Jungmann, *The Mass of the Roman Rite: Its Origins and Development*, 2 vols, Vol. 2 (New York: Benziger, 1955), 19f.

Priest the paten with the Host, if it was a solemn Mass. In the case of a private Mass, the Priest merely took the paten with the Host himself. Neither are actions that could adequately be termed an 'offering'. It was not until the reforms of the Second Vatican Council that the Offertory would be restored to its former importance within the celebration of the Eucharist. Pope Paul VI noted at this time of reform that:

> [T]he offertory seems lacking, because the faithful are not allowed any part in it (even though it should be the part of the Mass in which their activity is more direct and obvious) . . . The offertory should be given a special prominence so that the faithful (or their representatives) may exercise their special role as offerers.[40]

It should not, perhaps, be surprising that, during a period of time when the material and the physical was despised as sinful and worthy of disdain, there should be little emphasis on the goodness of the material world and thus a corresponding decline in the offering of material goods as part of the celebration of the Eucharist. This offering of the material serves as a reminder at once of the goodness of creation, but also human abuse of this goodness. It is not possible to overlook the corrupted way in which the material world is put to use, when it is seen in the light of sacramental materiality.

> The church uses physical things to convey God's grace, and this use has a significance for the way Christians look on the natural world. They cannot ignore the fact that the water that is used to incorporate people into the church is the same water that human beings pollute; that bread is denied to many in the world while others are overfed; that countries go to war over oil while Christians use it to anoint.[41]

---

40 Annibale Bugnini, *The Reform of the Liturgy 1948–1975* (Collegeville, MN: The Liturgical Press, 1990), 364.

41 Ben Quash and Samuel Wells, *Introducing Christian Ethics* (Oxford: Wiley-Blackwell, 2010), 354.

The eucharistic meal exposes our own corrupted eating practices even as it reaffirms the goodness of the body.

The embodied experience of the Eucharist is an exposer of difference – both positive and negative. Thus, Angel Méndez-Montoya argued:

> [S]elf and other, human and divine, spiritual and material, the individual parts and the whole, do not collapse into one another, but, rather, they co-exist or mutually indwell in and through this *metaxu*, the in-betweenness that is the [ecclesial and eucharistic] Body of Christ. Difference is not eliminated but is brought into a new harmonious and excessive unity (Christ's Body) that opens up an infinite space for relations of affinity, mutual care (mutual nurturing), and reciprocity.[42]

This understanding of the Eucharist as the place in which difference is not eliminated but brought into unity is significant. It is possible to understand this unity of difference in the Body of Christ with regard to gender. If one considers the concept of *perichorēsis* as offering a model of understanding the way in which difference and unity indwell together, then just as in the Eucharist 'human and divine, spiritual and material' do not eliminate each other, neither do the divisive categories of gender.

In the sense of the eucharistic elements, difference is not eliminated but mutually indwells in the inbetween-ness that is Christ. The eucharistic elements remain fully material even as they are fully indwelled by the presence of Christ, the presence of Christ remains fully Christic even as it fully indwelt the materiality of the bread and wine, and the gathered congregation. Difference is not eliminated for the sake of unity just as unity is not despised in the honouring of difference. Christ's body is in between. In the Eucharist, it is both material and Divine. As Linn Tonstad noted: 'Christ's body moves past even

---

42 Angel Méndez-Montoya, *The Theology of Food: Eating and the Eucharist* (Oxford: Wiley-Blackwell, 2012), 140.

sexual difference and joins itself to the materiality of the whole world.'[43] As the Church – the Body of Christ – it is similarly both material and Divine, existing as a place of both unity and difference.

The implication of considering the Eucharist through the lens of the traumatic somatic memory is to conclude that all genders mutually indwell in the Body of Christ. The Body of Christ can be a place in which unity and difference do not have to eliminate each other, but rather is a place where difference, inbetween-ness, is valued. It matters, therefore, that people of all genders serve the Body of Christ. No body is more or less Christ-like than the other but both adequately and inadequately represent and are represented by the inbetween-ness of the Body of Christ.

This *perichoretic* language of 'indwelling' has significance not just for an understanding of sexual difference in the Body of Christ and the Eucharist, but also for an understanding of the Trinity and the relationship between the Triune God and humankind. Janet Soskice provided the following account of the Trinity:

> The First person, as Unoriginate Origin, begets the Son (and is thus named 'Father' or we could say equally 'Mother'), and from these two proceeds the Spirit. The Son, by being Son, is the one who makes God Father/Mother. The Son gives birth to the Church in the Spirit, represented figuratively in the high tradition of western religious art by the water and the blood flowing from Christ's pierced side on the Cross.[44]

Soskice herself characterized this account of the economy of the Trinity as one of a *perichoretic* outpouring of love and birth[45]

---

43 Linn Tonstad, *God and Difference: The Trinity, Sexuality, and the Transformation of Finitude* (New York and London: Routledge, 2016), 248.

44 Janet Soskice, 'Trinity and "the Feminine Other"', *New Blackfriars* 75, no. 878 (1994), 2–17, at 11.

45 Ibid., 12.

and thus the language of indwelling seems entirely appropriate. As each member of the Trinity is connected by birth to the other, mutually indwelling, so too do the two natures of Christ indwell within him; so do people of all genders find their indwelling in the Body of Christ; so does the presence of Christ, indeed the presence of God, indwell in the eucharistic elements; so does Christ dwell within believers and believers within Him in their reception of the Eucharist.

The embodied experience of the Eucharist matters, then, as it affirms the goodness of the materiality into which Christ was incarnated while simultaneously affirming the goodness of the bodies who receive him. This is a further implication of considering the Eucharist through the lens of the traumatic somatic memory. Looking at the Eucharist through the hermeneutical lens of the Annunciation-Incarnation event – the somatic memory – one recognizes that the embodied experience of the Eucharist is vital. The Real Presence of Christ in the eucharistic elements is made paramount by viewing the Eucharist in the light of the Annunciation-Incarnation event. The presence of Christ is material and physical and therefore it matters that the experience of the Eucharist is a physical act. The embodied experience of the Eucharist helps to create a eucharistic perspective on the natural world in which sacramental materials reflect, in their ritual use, the broken practices of the world. When considered through the hermeneutical lens of the traumatic somatic memory, the Eucharist demonstrates, in material form, the ideal relationship between the material and the Divine. As the bread is distributed to all who come to receive it, so Christians are urged to take action on hunger. As the same cup of wine is lifted to each pair of lips, Christians are reminded of what it really means to love those different from us. As within the Eucharist, as in the Incarnate Body of Christ, two natures, human and Divine, exist side by side, without eliminating each other and without holding one in preference to the other, so it is possible to see a model for priesthood that does not exclude participation based on difference – whether gender or sexual orientation.

We Are What We Eat

This chapter could be subtitled 'we are what we eat' in reference to Augustine's comment on the effect of the Eucharist upon Christians. Augustine's understanding of the Eucharist is not without ambiguity. However, so powerful is this declaration ('we are what we receive') that it is worth examining his understanding of the Eucharist in detail. While some have suggested[46] that Augustine believed the eucharistic elements to be only representative of the Body and Blood of Christ, it is possible to demonstrate that Augustine did believe in the Real Presence of Christ in the Eucharist and that his understandings of the implications of this Real Presence have significant consequences for an exploration of the materiality of the Eucharist.

Considerations of Augustine's perspective on bodies and materiality more broadly have been of recent interest to theologians. For example, Meredith Minister concluded her reflection on Augustine's theology of the Trinity by noting that Augustine has, somewhat reluctantly, affirmed the necessity of the material body for knowing God. She determined that he fails in his attempt to find an interior way, one that excises the body, of knowing God and thus one must conclude that knowledge, apart from bodies, is impossible.[47]

For Augustine, Christian sacraments contained what they signified. As visible elements, they bear a certain similarity to those things of which they are sacrament. There is a distinction to be made between the reality (the *res*) and the power (the *virtus*) of the sacrament. The reality and power don't exist apart from the sacrament (*sacramentum*). For example, when considering the Eucharist, the *res* is the image and likeness of

---

46 See, for example, the discussion in James T. O'Connor, *The Hidden Manna: A Theology of the Eucharist* (San Francisco, CA: Ignatius Press, 2005), 51–2.

47 Meredith Minister, 'Knowing the Trinity: Augustine's Material Epistemology in *The Trinity*', in *Trinitarian Theology and Power Relations: God Embodied* (New York: Palgrave Macmillan, 2014), 39–62.

Christ in the material elements. However, the *virtus* of the Eucharist is almost always connected by Augustine to grace.

Therefore, Augustine could declare that '[T]hat Bread which you see on the altar, consecrated by the word of God, is the Body of Christ. That chalice, or rather, what the chalice holds, consecrated by the word of God, is the Blood of Christ.'[48] Furthermore, '[H]e took earth from earth, because flesh is from the earth, and he took Flesh of the flesh of Mary. He walked on earth in that same Flesh, and gave that same Flesh to us to be eaten for our salvation.'[49] It seems clear that the physicality of the Eucharist mattered to Augustine. Jesus is truly Flesh, and the consecrated elements offered to believers are truly his Flesh.

The truth of this physicality and materiality is borne out in the effects of the consumption of the consecrated elements on those who receive them. The sacrament of the Eucharist is that which produces and symbolizes the unity of the Church as the Body of Christ. The Eucharist produces a transformation in those faithful who receive it. Augustine wrote:

> so if it is you that are the body of Christ and its members, it is the mystery meaning you that has been placed on the Lord's table; what you receive is the mystery that means you . . . Be what you can see and receive what you are.[50]

Most significantly, he argued that '[H]e who suffered for us has entrusted to us in this sacrament his Body and Blood, which

---

48 Augustine, 'Sermon 227: On Easter Sunday', trans. Sister Mary Sarah Muldowney, in *Saint Augustine: Sermons on the Liturgical Seasons* (New York: Fathers of the Church, Inc., 1959), 96.

49 Augustine, 'Exposition on Psalm 98', trans. J. E. Tweed, in *Nicene and Post-Nicene Fathers*, Vol. 8, ed. Philip Schaff (Buffalo, NY: Christian Literature Publishing Co., 1888), Chapter 8. Accessed online at www.newadvent.org/fathers/1801099.htm on 01/03/16.

50 Augustine, 'Sermon 272', in *Sermons*, Part 3, Vol. 7, trans. Edmund Hill (New Rochelle, NY: New City Press, 1993), 300–1.

indeed he has even made us. For we have been made his Body, and, by his mercy, we are that which we receive.'[51]

'We are that which we receive' or, to put it another way, 'we are what we eat'. If we are the Body of Christ, then we are present on the altar in the eucharistic elements. We are what we eat and we become what we receive. In this respect, the materiality and Real Presence of Christ matters not just to Augustine and the early Church but to the contemporary Church as well. If the presence of Christ is only *represented* in the Eucharist, then those who consume the Eucharist will only *represent* the Body of Christ in the world. If, however, the presence of Christ in the Eucharist *is* spiritual, symbolic, real, fleshly, physical and material, then this is what those who consume the eucharistic bread and wine will become: not merely representatives of the presence of Christ in the World but real members of the Body of Christ who *are* spiritually Christ in the world as well as physically Christ in the world. When it comes to extending this eucharistic presence beyond the doorways of the Church, then the physical, fleshly presence matters. It is this physical, fleshly presence that has real effect on the world. It is the Real Presence of Christ in Christians that rolls up its sleeves and gets its hands dirty in the filth of poverty, death and disease.

That Christ instructs those who believe to consume his body as food is significant. After all, humankind can be filled with the presence of God in other ways besides eating. For example, Jesus could say, 'This is the Spirit of truth, whom the world cannot receive, because it neither sees him nor knows him. You know him, because he abides with you, and he will be in you' (John. 14.17). Similarly, Paul could write, 'you are in the Spirit, since the Spirit of God dwells in you' (Rom. 8.9). In his first letter to the church at Corinth Paul also noted that it is through Baptism that believers are incorporated into the body. He wrote: '[F]or in the one Spirit we were all baptized into one body – Jews or Greeks, slaves or free – and we were all made to drink of one Spirit' (1 Cor. 12.13). No eating is required

---

51 Augustine, 'Sermon 229'.

in order to be filled with the third person of the Triune God or to be made part of the Body of Christ. But eating matters because bodies matter, and The Body matters pre-eminently. Food is a material sign of relationality, interdependence and sharing in the life eternal. Eating is a primordial function of humankind. And indeed, it is through eating that God makes himself known. Not all can hear the Gospel, not all will understand it, but all can receive the presence of God in the bread and wine. The need for food motivates human action in the form of labour. So, in the Eucharist, the urgency of hunger and the satisfaction of eating forcefully combine in the reception of eucharistic food.

Throughout scripture God repeatedly calls people into relationship and community with him by the sharing of food and drink. Thus, God provides manna for the Hebrews throughout their time in the desert. Jesus establishes his solidarity with the outcast of society through his radical table practices.[52] He eats with the disciples in his resurrection body, both on the road to Emmaus and subsequently with them in Jerusalem. In each case those who share in this eating are brought into closer relationship with the Divine. Méndez-Montoya imagined Divine sharing as the spatial and temporal locus of 'holy communion' with one another and with God. He suggested that '[T]he political dimension of divine sharing speaks about alimentation as incorporation into Christ's Body.'[53]

Graham Ward offered an image of 'co-abiding' in which the Father co-abides with the Spirit in the Son, Christ co-abides in the eucharistic elements and in the partaker, and the material elements as well as the partakers co-abide in Christ and the Holy Spirit.[54] This co-abiding bears marked similarities with the understanding of sacrifice as a mutual self-giving we considered earlier. This mutual, Trinitarian, self-offering offers

---

52 See Mitchell's discussion of table practices in Mitchell, *Eucharist as Sacrament of Initiation*.

53 Méndez-Montoya, *Theology of Food*, 114.

54 Graham Ward, *Christ and Culture* (Oxford: Wiley-Blackwell, 2005).

a profound basis for understanding the mutual reciprocity in the Triune God. For Ward, then, in his reflection on the Johannine Bread of Life discourse, co-abiding between Christ and humanity and the notion of mutual reciprocity become the essential elements of the Eucharist and thus the constitution of the ecclesia.[55] Thus, the *perichoretic* principle outlined at the start of this chapter takes its full form in the flesh of Christ. How we understand the material of Christ's offer of his flesh to eat matters. Drawing on the co-abiding imagery developed by Ward, Méndez-Montoya argued that:

> [W]hat is suggested by this corporal feeding is not simply absorption, and this is significant. There is an 'abiding' *in* Christ, but there is also an abiding *of* Christ (in the one who eats). This co-abiding is complex and richly suggestive. It is, I suggest, the chiasmic heart of an *ekklesia* performed and constituted through the eucharist. Why chiasmic? Because observe the curious manner of the reciprocal relation. I eat the flesh of Christ. I take his body into my own. Yet in this act I place myself *in* Christ – rather than simply placing Christ within me. I consume but do not absorb Christ without being absorbed into Christ.[56]

This placing of the self within Christ draws on the concept of mutual interpenetration that lies at the heart of *perichoretic* imagery and echoes Paul's words to the Colossians in which he wrote:

> So if you have been raised with Christ, seek the things that are above, where Christ is, seated at the right hand of God. Set your mind on things that are above, not on things that are on earth, for you have died, and your life is hidden with Christ in God. When Christ who is your life is revealed, then you also will be revealed with him in glory. (Col. 3.1–4)

---

55 Ibid., 105.
56 Méndez-Montoya, *Theology of Food*, 133.

Through faith the believer is called to place themselves in God. This placing of the self within God can itself be the cause of faith. For example, Thomas placed himself in Christ when he touched His wounds and believed in the resurrection (John 20.24–8). Similarly Salome had to touch the virgin flesh of Mary in order to believe that 'a virgin has given birth' (PJ 19.19). Her hand was destroyed because of her lack of faith, but restored when she cradled the infant Jesus in her arms. The embodied experience of Christ is powerful.

This gift of food is broken apart by one's teeth, consumed and taken into one's very flesh. Dale Martin noted, with respect to Paul's discourse on the Corinthian body that:

> when they [Christians] share in the table of the Lord, the Eucharist, they are integrated into the being of Christ (1 Cor. 10.14–22). The bodily ingestion of idol-meat could mean the dangerous ingestion of the daimonic realm; the parallel with the Eucharist is simply assumed by Paul: normally it would constitute the ingestion of the body of Christ, which would of course be positive, even soteriological.[57]

Once part of the flesh, this food is further transformed into energy, word and activity. Thus, the recipient becomes the Real Body of Christ in our presence in the world. We are what we eat. This Real Body of Christ is, as has already been established, a location in which difference is celebrated and brought into unity. The theological implication of considering the Eucharist through the lens of the traumatic somatic memory of the Annunciation-Incarnation event is one of profound (re)connection with society. If Christians are to be in the world what they have received in the Eucharist, then the Church cannot be a place where difference is rejected. This acceptance of difference has a profound effect when it comes to the acceptance of difference of opinion within the Church. To accept and celebrate difference within the Church is not to

---

57 Martin, *Corinthian Body*, 191.

draw any distinction in difference. To truly become what one has received is to accept difference in all its forms.

Female Body Matters: Motherhood and Miscarriage

With regard to the Eucharist it is the *difference* of the female body that has historically posed the most difficulties for the theologian. The relationship between the female body and the Eucharist is a complex one. The female body defies easy classification, changeable as it is, and frequently circumvents proscribed authority. While officially prohibited from the altar in many Christian traditions, women have often been intimately connected to the Eucharist in ways that men have not necessarily been. Furthermore, understanding the relationship of the female body to the materiality of the Eucharist is a fruitful avenue for the exploration of eucharistic theology.

Exploring the biological materiality of the Eucharist and its relationship to the female body is a reflective exercise in theology. The biological or scientific processes of the Annunciation-Incarnation event are as mysterious to the contemporary theologian as they were to the Gospel writers of the first century. However, this section of the chapter will engage in reflections on natural science and the ways in which they resonate with Christian theology. One implication of considering the Eucharist through the lens of the traumatic somatic memory of the Annunciation-Incarnation event is that it allows one to speculate on *how* Jesus became Incarnate. What actually happened at the moment of Incarnation? For example, in the beginning of the fourth Gospel, John declared that

In the beginning was the Word,
and the Word was with God,
and the Word was God.
He was in the beginning with God
(John 1.1–2)

159

Later in that same Gospel, Jesus echoed this declaration of his eternal nature when speaking to the Jews in Jerusalem: 'I tell you, before Abraham was, I am' (John 8.58). The creeds reflect this concept when they declare that Jesus is 'true God from true God, begotten, not made'.[58] All this seems to support the idea that Mary served as a surrogate mother. These pronouncements of Jesus and the theology of the early creed seem to imply that Christ is not formed within the womb of Mary but rather that he already existed. It seems logical to conclude, therefore, that Jesus is implanted as a fully formed foetus in her womb, nourished by her placenta – 'the fully divine cell made fully human through the gestation process, and then nurtured by Mary's human milk'.[59]

However, it is wrong to think of the Annunciation-Incarnation event as a surrogacy experience. If one does take the surrogacy approach then one is left with a Christ figure who is not like us, a Christ who bears no relation to humanity except in appearance. Such an approach edges towards a form of Docetism. It is essential to Christian theology that Christ was fully human as well as being fully Divine. Indeed, the writer of the Letter to the Hebrews pointed out that 'he had to become like his brothers and sisters in every respect, so that he might be a merciful and faithful high priest in the service of God, to make a sacrifice of atonement for the sins of the people' (Heb. 2.17). A surrogate 'fully divine cell' made human only through the food of Mary's breast milk is not 'like his brothers and sisters in every respect'.

A further consequence of this contemplation of the Eucharist is that this very Real Presence also offers a rich reflection on the issue of miscarriage. As I noted in the opening chapter, Jones has written a beautiful and powerful theological contemplation on the issues of stillbirth, infertility and miscarriage. In it she reflected that, while there is no explanation of such loss

---

58 'The Order of Mass', in *Catholic Bishops' Conference of England and Wales*, ed. Liturgy Office England and Wales.

59 Mary Lee Wile, 'Surrogacy or Human DNA: What Happened When Mary Said Yes?', *Daughters of Sarah* 18, no. 4 (1992), 14–15, at 14.

to offer a grieving woman, there is an image of Divine support. Jones, in a lengthy quote that is worth reading in full, indicated that:

> [I]n contemporary as well as classical discussions of the Trinity, theologians have been hard pressed to give an account of what happens in the Godhead when Christ, as part of this Godhead, dies. What transpires in the Godhead when one of its members bleeds away? Theologians like Moltmann and Luther have urged us to affirm that on the cross, God takes this death into the depths of Godself. The Trinity thus holds it. First person holds the Second, in its death, united with it by the power of the Spirit . . . what we find in this space of silence is the image of the woman who, in the grips of a stillbirth [or miscarriage] has death inside her, and yet does not die . . . because the God who bears this loss will not turn away from God's people, God is in a sense rendered helpless in the face of this dying. God cannot stop it; and yet by letting it happen, God also bears the guilt for it. In this dying, the borders of divine identity are also confused and made fluid as the One who is the source of life eternal bears now the stamp of complete, full death . . . this is a death that happens deep within God, not outside of God but in the very heart – perhaps the womb – of God.[60]

Jones draws on both Luther and Moltmann in constructing her theology. Luther is one of the few theologians to have written theologically about miscarriage with his *Comfort for Women who have had a Miscarriage*,[61] although it is not to that text that Jones points us. Luther assumed the concept of *perichorēsis* – he preached on it in his Sermon on John 14 given in 1522 with particular reference to verse 11: '[B]elieve me that I am in the Father

---

60 Jones, 'Hope Deferred', 16.

61 Martin Luther, 'Comfort for Women who have had a Miscarriage, 1542', in *Luther's Works*, ed. Jaroslav Pelikan and Helmut T. Lehmann (Philadelphia, PA: Fortress, 1958–86), 243–50.

and the Father is in me . . .'[62] For Luther, then, '[I]f God is in Christ, then whatever God the Son suffers becomes the suffering of God by the union of the Persons of the Trinity.'[63] Indeed, Luther's Trinitarian theology was such that both the Incarnation and the death of Christ are not merely additions to the Trinity but are ontologically constitutive of the Triune God.[64]

In *The Crucified God* Moltmann, drawing on Luther's theology in exploring the passibility of God and the relationship of God to suffering, suggested that 'He [God] humbles himself and takes upon himself the eternal death of the godless and the godforsaken, so that all the godless and the godforsaken can experience communion with him.'[65] This taking within the Godself the eternal death of human experience through the person of Christ places God firmly on the side of the abandoned and the desolate. Such abandonment and desolation are irrevocably drawn into the life of the Trinity.

Both Moltmann and Jones paint an extraordinary picture of death in the very heart of the Trinitarian God. Wisely, Jones did not attempt to offer a theological explanation of miscarriage and stillbirth – what explanation can there be? Instead she offered the image of a God who is familiar not just with the experience of the loss of a child in the death of his Son on the Cross, but also with the wrenching helplessness and responsibility of miscarriage. This image is one of comfort. There is also a sense of solidarity in this image: a sense in which God is Emmanuel – God with us.

Jones' theological reflection on the issue of miscarriage and stillbirth opens the way for a eucharistic reflection on the issues. When one takes the Body of Christ within oneself in the

---

62 Martin Luther, 'A Sermon on Pentecost, Second Sermon John 14.23–31, 1522' in *Sermons of Martin Luther*, vol. 3, ed. and trans. John Nicholas Lenker (Minneapolis, MN: Lutherans in All Lands, 1907), 259–68.

63 Dennis Ngien, 'Trinity and Divine Passibility in Martin Luther's "*Theologia Crucis*"', *Scottish Bulletin of Evangelical Theology* 19, no. 1 (2001), 31–64, at 51.

64 Ibid., 51.

65 Moltmann, *The Crucified God*, 276.

reception of the consecrated elements of bread and wine, one takes within the whole Incarnation of Christ. That is to say, the doctrine of concomitance is extended beyond the presence of God in both the elements. We consume his Real Presence which encompasses his birth, his living body, his dead body, and his resurrected body. All bodies then become paradoxical loci of both life and death. The living, resurrected Christ, inseparable from the Christ who died (indeed, how can one be resurrected without first having lived and died?), is consumed in the nourishment of the communion.

Women's bodies, uniquely, have the capacity to bear life within some of them but they are also uniquely placed to bear death within them. The experiences of miscarriage and stillbirth are intimately connected to pain: the physical pain of unexpected and sudden bleeding, of invasive treatments, of giving birth; the emotional and psychological pain of the loss of a child, of having to give birth to a baby that is already dead, of feeling the hopes and dreams of a pregnancy disappear. Those who study pain are struck by its inexpressibility and its incommunicability. Those in great pain are reduced to inarticulate screams and moans. Elaine Scarry, in her study of the body and its relationship to pain, noted: '[P]hysical pain does not simply resist language but actively destroys it, bringing about an immediate reversion to a state anterior to language, to sounds and cries a human being makes before language is learned.'[66] Pain destroys language and in doing so destroys the world of the sufferer, for it is through language that a person's world is constructed. It has a temporal dimension as well. In the case of miscarriage and stillbirth, the temporal destruction experienced through pain is crucial. Past attachments and future hopes are destroyed by the immediacy of the pain experienced. This inability to articulate combined with a destruction of a personal world and temporal dislocation are, unsurprisingly, features of trauma as well as features of pain.

---

66 Elaine Scarry, *The Body in Pain: The Making and Unmaking of the World* (New York: Oxford University Press, 1985), 3.

The pain of a miscarriage is indescribable and incomprehensible to those outside of the pain. Grief combines and intensifies with a physical pain that is exacerbated by the feeling of death slipping between the thighs. Language fails. But this experience of the Eucharist as a locus of life and death offers an intensely intimate communion with the Triune God, in whom death dwells, at a time when words fail. It is not just, as Jones so descriptively portrayed, a comforting image, but rather, for the miscarrying woman, the embodied experience of the God of life and death within her. It is affirmation that her embodied experience, of miscarriage and of communion, matters. The paradox of life and death, the pain and grief she experiences, the silence of her language are all profoundly part of who the Triune God is and what it means to receive and be part of the Body of Christ.

If one is to take women's embodied experiences seriously, then there is an awful, tragic and wrenching sense in which, through miscarriage, women's bodies become revelatory of the Triune God. As women made in the image of God they have the profound ability to image within their own bodies the death experienced at the very heart of the Trinity. The grief of the miscarrying woman offers a glimpse into the grief of God at the Cross. While she will eventually shed all the tissue that had once formed a child, her body will remain forever the (often only) grave site of the baby. She may go on to bear new life within her, but as a site of memory and mourning, her body remains a grave. If one draws on the image of the indwelling, mutually interpenetrative, Trinitarian God posited earlier then just as each Person of the Trinity indwells in the birthing action of the Incarnation, so too does each Person of the Trinity indwell the death of the Second Person. When searching for an image that enables theologians to begin to comprehend what happens within the Triune God when the Second Person of the Trinity dies, the image of the miscarrying mother is a powerful one. If the image of woman-with-child can enable theologians to understand something of *perichoretic* indwelling, then equally the image of woman-losing-child can enable theologians to understand something of *perichoretic* indwelling and relationship within the Trinity and what occurs within the Trinity at the Cross.

I do not suggest that there is any spiritual value in losing a child. The death of a baby, longed for or not, cannot be a good thing. Nor do I wish to promote a triumphalist image of resurrection – not all situations are redeemed and not all women who experience miscarriage or stillbirth will go on to have a healthy child of their own. There is no 'but' at the end of the sentence. Like Jones, I cannot offer a theology of miscarriage that makes sense of the experience; I can only argue that a consequence of considering the Eucharist through the hermeneutical lens of the traumatic somatic memory of the Annunciation-Incarnation event is that such consideration reveals the experience of the miscarrying woman as part and revelatory of the Triune God and that in the reception of the Eucharist there is a sense of comfort from Emmanuel – God truly with us.

When it comes to the Eucharist, and indeed to the theology and faith in general, women's bodies matter a lot. Not because they are superior to other bodies, but precisely because they have, for so long, been considered to be inferior and subsequently marginalized. This marginalization has been not only the denial of priestly ordination to women, but also the historical denial of the Eucharist to birthing and bleeding women. The natural functions of the female body have traditionally been an obstacle for receiving the body. Women's bodies matter as I seek to offer a vision of the Eucharist, and indeed theology, which is truly holistic and inclusive.

B/body Matters

This chapter has demonstrated that there are two consequences that arise when considering the Eucharist through the lens of the traumatic somatic memory of the Annunciation-Incarnation event. Such a consideration gives emphasis to the physicality of the Eucharist and the variety of ways in which the significance of the materiality of the Eucharist can be understood. As I demonstrated at the outset of this chapter, an exploration of the concept of *perichorēsis* is an essential precursor to examining the notions of materiality embedded in the Eucharist and in eucharistic ritual.

By demonstrating that the embodied experience of participation in the celebration of the Eucharist is an essential part of the Eucharist, it is clear that the materiality of the Eucharist holds within it a model for priesthood that welcomes all genders. The very in-between-ness of Christ's body, in which difference is not eliminated but mutually co-abides, is the *exemplar par excellence* of the ecclesial body. The Church has, as its model, a place in which difference is welcomed and celebrated. The physicality of the eucharistic body matters. We are what we eat and thus the Church must be a place in which difference, gender and all other differences, do not discount people. To become what we have received in the Eucharist is to become a Church that does not discount anyone, including women, from priesthood on the grounds of their 'differentness'. In celebrating the Eucharist, the priest does not act *in persona Christi* but rather *ut repraesentativus Ecclesiae*. Thus, as representative of the Church the priesthood is a model of the Church – welcoming of difference and celebrating it in the celebration of the Eucharist. An implication of seeing the Eucharist through the lens of somatic memory is that the difference within Christ's body becomes our model for valuing diversity, both within the priesthood and within the wider ecclesial body.

A further consequence of considering the Eucharist through the lens of the traumatic somatic memory of the Annunciation-Incarnation event is the highlighting of the special significance the Incarnate Christ has for women. The exploration of a hypothetical biology of the Annunciation-Incarnation event reveals the significance of Mary's biological contribution to the Incarnate Body of Christ – she is more than simply a surrogate mother. Furthermore, an understanding of the eucharistic body as fully Incarnate, fully living, fully dead, and fully resurrected, again reflecting the inbetween-ness of Christ's body, provides us with a powerful reflection on miscarriage and stillbirth. Women's bodies matter when it comes to the Eucharist and thus it matters that, behind the altar, difference is not eliminated but brought into excessive harmony and unity.

7

Trauma and Sacrament

Reading the Eucharist through the traumatic lens of somatic memory locates Mary's body, as we have seen, in a place of significance in Christian theology. The emphasis of the Eucharist rests, in this reading, on the Annunciation-Incarnation event and, in particular, on Mary's experience of it. I have, in previous chapters, demonstrated the way in which trauma acts as a destabilizing lens when applied to the foundational eucharistic narratives of priesthood, sacrifice and presence. This destabilizing lens has caused ruptures from which new narratives can be constructed. Having drawn the traumatic connections clearly between the Annunciation-Incarnation event and the Eucharist in the previous chapters, I will now read the Annunciation-Incarnation event itself through the lens of trauma and examine the implications for the celebration of the Eucharist, our understanding of Mary, and our own recovery from trauma.

The Annunciation-Incarnation Event as Trauma

While Christians generally reflect on Mary's experiences at the Annunciation with a sense of wonder, or as a prelude to a nativity celebration, the Annunciation-Incarnation event was a traumatic one for Mary. As a young girl, not yet married, experiencing an angelic visitation and a subsequent miraculous pregnancy, Mary must have been shocked and overwhelmed by her experience. Mardi Horowitz defined traumatic events as 'those that cannot be assimilated with the victim's "inner schemata" of self in relation to the world'.[1] For all her faith in God and acceptance of what happened to her, it is no stretch of the imagination to understand these events as being traumatic, as requiring a redefinition of self in their aftermath, something we will witness Mary do in her Magnificat. In fact, when we compare the experience of Mary, as sparsely told in the Gospels, to the experiences of both trauma and trauma recovery, it is clear that Mary has a traumatic experience and recovers from it in the same way that those who are symptomatic of PTSD do.

For example, Mary suddenly becomes pregnant. In this sense, her bodily integrity is ruptured, though not in the sense of a rape, for she does not experience sexual intercourse, and she offers her own assent to the events happening to her (Luke 1.38). Rather, her bodily integrity is ruptured by the sudden presence of another life, another being, inside her. The enfleshing of the Divine Son in her womb is a physical rupturing of her flesh to make way for the flesh of another.

Her experience of time is ruptured in the same way. A pregnancy usually follows intercourse. Becoming a mother usually happens after losing one's virginity; cause follows event. The linear notion of time and the usual timescales and patterns of life are disrupted by this sudden, miraculous pregnancy. Mary's flesh is ruptured but the very fabric of time and substance of humanity are also ruptured in the Annunciation-Incarnation event. Beattie characterized this event as 'a moment of radical discontinuity in the history of humankind'.[2] Marcus Pound drew the distinction further still, highlighting the qualitative difference between eternity and time. The Incarnation is an event where the eternal constitutes a dramatic disturbance in the temporal order – this break is so significant that it leads to an impotency of language: words fail.[3]

---

1 Herman, *Trauma and Recovery*, 33.

2 Tina Beattie, *Rediscovering Mary: Insights from the Gospels* (Tunbridge Wells, Kent: Burns & Oates, 1995), 28.

3 Marcus Pound, 'The Assumption of Desire: Kierkegaard, Lacan, and the Trauma of the Eucharist', *Journal for Cultural and Religious Theory* 9, no. 1 (2008), 67–78, at 73.

Words do, indeed, fail. Mary's experience of the Annunciation-Incarnation event ruptures her cognition and language. This event escapes accessibility. She does not understand what has happened to her. She asks, 'How can this be for I am a virgin?' (Luke 1.34). Jones noted that 'Mary is immediately "perplexed" and for good reason. What could an angel want with her, a poor girl with nothing to offer?'[4] The event makes no sense and her cognition cannot keep pace with her experience. Her ability to articulate what has happened to her has failed.

The Annunciation-Incarnation event *is* traumatic for Mary. Whether one considers her to have given consent to what happens to her or not, Mary experiences the three classic ruptures of trauma: body, time and cognition. If the Eucharist is the non-identical repetition of this traumatic event, then the Eucharist must be traumatic as well.

Traumatic Sacraments

The Annunciation-Incarnation event is traumatic in the particular for Mary, but is traumatic in general for each Christian as they participate not only in the celebration of the Eucharist but in all sacramental rituals. All sacramental experiences cause ruptures. For example, Chauvet affirmed that symbolic death and regeneration are at work in all rites of initiation.[5] It is only through a breach (we could easily substitute the word 'breach' for 'rupture' here) that a subject comes to birth. Trauma, therefore, is constitutive of being and a necessary feature of sacraments. In the celebration of the Eucharist, this traumatic rupture is at work, but this rupture, or breach, is visible in other sacraments too.

All sacraments are traumatic in the sense that experiencing any of them causes a rupture within the individual recipient – they cause a breach or disturbance in the individual's concept of self.

---

4 Serene Jones, *Trauma and Grace: Theology in a Ruptured World* (Louisville, KY: Westminster John Knox Press, 2009), 115.

5 Chauvet, *Symbol and Sacrament*, 98.

Our inability to explain what happens in a sacrament (and thus the reliance on faith to know it has been accomplished) is testimony to the rupture in cognition and impotency of language that all sacraments cause. This rupture in cognition is inherent in all sacraments (and here I am referring to the seven sacraments acknowledged by the Catholic and Orthodox Churches) and each sacrament causes a rupture in understanding and is fundamentally inexplicable. As events that both rupture identity and help to reconstruct identity, the sacraments also cause ruptures – breaches or disturbances – in time. Let us consider, briefly, the traumatic nature of each of these seven sacraments.

In the experience of Baptism, the believer is called to share in the death and resurrection of Christ, marking them out as Christian and constituting them as part of the Body of Christ. An indelible sacramental character is conferred in Baptism and therefore it is a sacrament that needs only to be received once. Baptism has long been associated with death. For example, Robin Jensen, in her analysis of baptism imagery in early Christianity, noted that:

> Many freestanding baptisteries were centralized and vaulted structures, often built as round or octagonal buildings. From the outside they would have looked like mausolea or martyrs' shrines. In addition to the mausoleum-like appearance of some of the baptistery buildings, many fonts were made to look like tombs or crosses.[6]

Jensen concluded that both baptisteries and mausolea were 'shelters for transitional rites: one that moved from death to afterlife'.[7] In a full immersion Baptism, the person being baptized is laid down in the grave, going under the ground, before they are physically raised up out of the death they have experienced by their fellow believers. They are raised up out of the

---

6 Robin Jensen, *Baptismal Imagery in Early Christianity: Ritual, Visual, and Theological Dimensions* (Grand Rapids, MI: Baker Academic, 2012), 160–1.

7 Ibid., 161.

water to new life, sharing in the resurrection of Christ. The baptized person is considered to *be* something new when they are raised out of the water and thus the rupture in identity is clear. Time is also ruptured in the experiencing of death within the timescape of life as opposed to at the end of life. The future is brought into the presence.

The sacrament of Confirmation also confers upon the recipient an indelible sacramental character and thus it too is only experienced once. The catechism of the Catholic Church indicates that Confirmation 'imprints on the soul an *indelible spiritual mark*, the "character", which is the sign that Jesus Christ has marked a Christian with the seal of his Spirit'.[8] Once again, this conferring of character – the character of Christ himself – causes a rupture in the sacramental recipient. They are, now, marked out as a Christian in a way that they were not marked out before. Their identity has been ruptured, breached, or disturbed.

The Eucharist is the most traumatic of sacraments. It is the only sacrament in which the believer's body is physically ruptured by the consumption of the Body and Blood of Christ. In the reception of the Eucharist the believer experiences all three of the ruptures characteristic of trauma (body, cognition and time). In consuming the Real Presence of Christ in the bread and wine the believer's physical body is ruptured by the Body of Christ. Participation in the Eucharist constitutes the Body of Christ and thus the believer is drawn into a new identity, that of Christ's. The sharing of the sacramental meal is a foretaste of the eschatological banquet to be shared by all in heaven and thus time is ruptured as the future is brought into being in the present. As with all sacraments, the Eucharist defies understanding and the believer has to rely on faith to be assured of the effects of their participation.

In the sacrament of Reconciliation, the penitent is at once the accuser, the accused and the witness. The experience of this sacrament is traumatic in all three senses of rupture. The

---

8 *Catechism of the Catholic Church with Modifications from the Editio Typica* (New York: Doubleday, 1995), 364. Italics in original.

catechism indicates that in the experience of the sacrament God brings about a 'spiritual resurrection' – once again, death/life imagery is essential in understanding the sacrament. This imagery is reinforced in the catechism through the suggestion that 'in converting to Christ through penance and faith, the sinner passes from death to life'.[9] It is clear that there is a need for reconstruction of identity after a rupture of self in this sacrament. Unlike other sacraments, the sacrament of Reconciliation is not usually received in a corporate setting but rather in a vertical (God to person) dimension that results in a horizontal (person to Church) outworking.

The vertical nature of this sacrament has been challenged in the development of whole-congregation rites of reconciliation and general absolution. Reconciliation has implications for the corporate Body of Christ. Furthermore, the sacrament of Reconciliation causes a rupture in time. The sacrament anticipates the judgement that all will face at the end of their earthly lives and brings a taste of that judgement into the present day as the penitent repents and is forgiven for their sins. The empirical notion of time is ruptured as the future is brought into the present.

Memory plays an important role in the sacrament of Reconciliation. It is the memory of an event or action that triggers the believer's realization of their need for the sacrament. The confession of the believer forms the construction of a trauma narrative that includes the reliving of the trauma and enables a modification of memory. The idea is not to forget – forgetting sin is not the point of the sacrament – but to put the memory into its right perspective, one that will allow the penitent to move forward. The memory of the event collides with the sacramental memory of the ecclesial body; the believer must choose the life offered by Christ over the destructive memory of sin.

The sacrament of Marriage is a traumatic rupturing of identity that sees two individuals become one new unit. They, as a couple, must seek to reconfigure their identity after the

---

9 Ibid., 410.

experience of this rupture. Very often a celebration of marriage will include reference to this verse: 'Therefore a man leaves his father and his mother and clings to his wife, and they become one flesh' (Gen. 2.24). As a couple become one flesh so do they construct a new identity out of the rupturing of their old identities. This sacrament serves to reinforce the idea that trauma does not necessarily have to be couched in solely negative terms. Some traumatic ruptures may not be experienced as negative events and even some of those that are experienced negatively at first might come to have positive effects in the aftermath of recovery, a process known as post-traumatic growth.

The sacrament of the Anointing of the Sick is difficult to couch in terms of a traumatic theme. Like the sacrament of Reconciliation, it has more of a vertical nature than a corporate one, but again, like Reconciliation, the effects and outworking of the sacrament seem to extend beyond the individual's relationship with God and into the corporate Body of Christ. The Constitutions on the Sacred Liturgy affirms that all liturgical services, including the administration of the sacraments, are corporate in nature. This has 'led to public liturgies of anointing for many sick people in the presence of a full congregation; often now practised for example during parish visitations by diocesan bishops'.[10] Indeed, Bruce Morrill, in his work on pastoral care of the sick, repeatedly noted the communal dimension of this sacrament, arguing that it affects those who are committed to the sick person, and the church community as a whole when it is celebrated.[11] This sacrament seems to be designed entirely to bring relief from trauma rather than to affect trauma in some way. However, the sacrament of the Anointing of the Sick, at least as it is understood in the Catholic Church, unites the sick person with the suffering of Christ.

---

10 Archbishops' Council, *A Time to Heal: A Contribution Towards the Ministry of Healing* (London: Church House Publishing, 2000), 66.

11 Bruce T. Morrill, *Divine Worship and Human Healing: Liturgical Theology at the Margins of Life and Death* (Collegeville, MN: Liturgical Press, 2009), 181.

By the grace of this sacrament the sick person receives strength and gift of uniting himself more closely to Christ's Passion: in a certain way he is *consecrated* to bear fruit by configuration to the Saviour's redemption Passion.[12]

Such uniting with Christ serves again to rupture the identity of the sick person receiving the sacrament as well as rupturing the experience of time. In this case, the past event of Christ's Passion is made present in the contemporary suffering of the sick person. The notion of time is ruptured further when the sacrament is conferred in anticipation of the person's death, bringing the future judgement of that person into their present reality.

The Sacrament of Ordination is one of the three sacraments (alongside Baptism and Confirmation) that confers an indelible sacramental character and thus does not need to be received more than once. Once again, this sacrament is a rupture in identity. The recipient has a new identity as a member of a Holy Order after ordination. They have to reconfigure their sense of self in the aftermath of this traumatic sacrament.

All sacraments are traumatic. They rupture the ontological identity of the recipient – the recipient must reconstruct their identity in the aftermath of their sacramental experience. Sacraments both require and facilitate the reconstruction of identity as one who is a member of the Body of Christ. This identity construction is ongoing as each formation of the Body of Christ is newly constituted and different in each experience of the sacrament. Furthermore, all sacraments are traumatic in that they constitute a rupture of cognition and lead to an impotency of language because they are mysterious by their very nature. All sacraments are understood and experienced through faith.

Chauvet focused in particular on the Eucharist as the paradigmatic sacramental event. Indeed, it is the celebration that has become a significant focal point in Christian tradition. If this is the case, then the rupture in Mary's created being, the

---

12 *Catechism*, 422.

ontological rupture, becomes both paradigmatic and constitutive of all the sacramental ruptures experienced by the believer. The Eucharist is a traumatic event. Like Mary, we receive the Body of Christ within us and our bodily integrity is ruptured. This reception within us shatters our sense of self. It requires assembly of self and reorientation of person in line with Divine.

Mary's Recovery from Trauma

Mary's experience of the Annunciation-Incarnation event is traumatic but the narratives that follow that event in the Gospel of Luke make it clear that Mary begins to experience recovery from trauma. Judith Herman, the grand dame of trauma theory, highlighted recovery from trauma as the empowerment of the survivor and the creation of new connections. Such a recovery has to happen in the context of relationship, and cannot happen in isolation.[13] In the first instance, Mary finds a place of safety. She goes to her cousin Elizabeth's house and stays there for three months. Beattie wrote:

> I imagine Mary setting out with wings on her heels to seek the companionship of the one person in all the world who would understand the uniqueness of her situation, and who would share in the delight of her pregnancy. In going to stay with Elizabeth, she found refuge away from the gossiping women of Nazareth in the presence of a woman who was in every sense her soulmate.[14]

In this place of refuge Mary reclaims her bodily integrity and identity as one who is not a victim. She is transformed into a new person. Jones, in her analysis of Mary in relation to sin, creativity and the Christian life, noted that '[A]s a creative agent in relation to the incarnational event, Mary claims

---

13 Herman, *Trauma and Recovery: From Domestic Abuse to Political Terror*, 133.

14 Beattie, *Rediscovering Mary*, 43.

permission to be someone she has not been socialized to be, someone who is not a victim in relationship to the systems that claim her.'[15] This is an image of Mary establishing her own bodily integrity – refusing to be a victim but being transformed into a new person.

> Scripture encourages us to imagine that Mary emerges from that encounter a changed woman. She is pregnant with new life, and she begins making traveling plans. She envisions a new world in which sinful power structures have been over-turned. And she who was voiceless lifts high her eyes, fills her lungs tight with air, and opens her mouth to proclaim this great, redeeming reversal.[16]

Jones is referring here to the Magnificat and it is this great song of Mary that forms a significant part of her trauma recovery. Here it is in full.

> My soul magnifies the Lord, and my spirit rejoices in God my Saviour, for he has looked with favour on the lowliness of his servant. Surely, from now on all generations will call me blessed; for the Mighty One has done great things for me, and holy is his name. His mercy is for those who fear him from generation to generation. He has shown strength with his arm; he has scattered the proud in the thoughts of their hearts. He has brought down the powerful from their thrones, and lifted up the lowly; he has filled the hungry with good things, and sent the rich away empty. He has helped his servant Israel, in remembrance of his mercy, according to the promise he made to our ancestors, to Abraham and to his descendants for ever. (Luke 1.46–55)

The second phase of trauma recovery is the phase in which the trauma survivor constructs a narrative of the trauma event that allows her to move forward. Herman has understood this

---

15 Jones, *Trauma and Grace*, 117–18.
16 Ibid., 116.

as a 'systematic review of the meaning of the event'.[17] Mary's Magnificat is such a review of the Annunciation-Incarnation event. She identifies herself as one who has received the favour of God and gives thanks to God as one who is blessed. In her Magnificat, Mary identifies the situation for what it is in all its complexity. Agger and Jensen, who have researched the telling of trauma narratives among refugees, noted that in the telling of the story, the trauma becomes a testimony.[18] The second half of Mary's Magnificat takes on the political and juridicial flavour of public testimony; Mary reframes her trauma as an experience in which the justice of God is being made known. Joel Green outlined a powerful summary of this aspect of the Magnificat:

> It is difficult to imagine a more powerful reflection on the significance of the coming of Jesus than Mary's prophetic words in Luke 1.46–55, the Magnificat or Mary's Song. Images of the divine warrior and gracious God coalesce in this celebration of the advent of salvation in Jesus. Here, Mary identifies the shape of Israel's restoration as it will be narrated in the words and deeds of Jesus in subsequent chapters, and invites others, her audience in and outside the narrative, to make their home in this redemptive vision.[19]

This shaping of Israel's restoration is the program of God's coming action in the world. The meaning of this traumatic event is, therefore, reframed into public, political and judicial terms. Ivone Gebara and Maria Clara Bingemer wrote:

---

17 Herman, *Trauma and Recovery: From Domestic Abuse to Political Terror*, 178.

18 Inger Agger and Soren B. Jensen, 'Testimony as Ritual and Evidence in Psychotherapy for Political Refugees', *Journal of Traumatic Stress* 3 (1990), 115–40.

19 Joel B. Green, 'Blessed is She Who Believed: Mary, Curious Exemplar in Luke's Narrative', in *Blessed One: Protestant Perspectives on Mary*, ed. Beverly Roberts Gaventa and Cynthia L. Rigby (Louisville, KY: John Knox Press, 2002), 9–20, at 16.

The decisive event of the incarnation of the Word of God is both paradoxical and subversive. Occurring in the body and life of Mary of Nazareth, woman and symbol of the whole people [Israel], this event is filled with social, ethical, and religious implications, despite what is exceptional and unique about it.[20]

We can clearly see the public dimension to Mary's review of the meaning of the story and her testimony, which sits in both the private, confessional sphere and the public, political realm. Beattie concluded: '[T]he *Magnificat* is astonishing in its scope. It is the realization of Mary's role as Mother of God and mother of the poor. It is a hymn that soars up to heaven and extends to the ends of the earth.'[21]

The final phase of trauma recovery is the phase in which the trauma survivor reclaims her world and reconnects with society. Herman noted that many of those who recover from trauma feel called in some way to engage in the wider world:

[the trauma survivor] recognize[s] a political or religious dimension in their misfortune and discover[s] that they can transform the meaning of their personal tragedy by making it the basis for social action. While there is no way to compensate for such an atrocity, there is a way to transcend it, by making it a gift to others. The trauma is redeemed only when it becomes the source of a survivor mission.[22]

This survivor mission is evident in the Magnificat as Mary outlines a social action project that will propel her forward. She will make a gift of the consequences of this trauma (the child Jesus) to the world. Christ in her womb will become a gift of renewal for all people. In this Mary foreshadows the reception of the

20 Ivone Gebara and Maria Clara Bingemer, *Mary, Mother of God, Mother of the Poor*, trans. Phillip Berryman (Maryknoll, NY: Orbis Books, 1989), 165.

21 Beattie, *Rediscovering Mary*, 44.

22 Herman, *Trauma and Recovery: From Domestic Abuse to Political Terror*, 207.

Body of Christ by believers in the Eucharist. Indeed, a particular connection might be drawn with the experience of the medieval mystic Hadjewich, who felt pregnant with Christ upon the reception of the Eucharist! Mary's reconnection is made complete when she does not stay in her place of safety but rather chooses to return home. Significantly, she is about three months pregnant at this point. Perhaps her morning sickness had died down. Perhaps she was confident she would not miscarry. Perhaps she was beginning to show a little in her stomach. Imagine the courage she had to display to leave her cousin's home and return to her town, pregnant and unwed. It would have been easier to stay hidden for another six months, until the baby was born. But she reconnects and bravely faces the world head on.

Trauma and Liturgy

As the celebration of the Eucharist is a non-identical repetition of the traumatic Annunciation-Incarnation event, so too is the liturgy haunted by the memory of trauma. The traditional pattern of liturgical celebration, repeated in so many different ways in Christian celebrations around the world, has a flavour of trauma recovery that reflects an instinct among ancient liturgists. Knowing nothing of the theory of trauma that would be shaped in the twentieth century, these ancient liturgists, nonetheless, constructed liturgy that follows the modes of recovery from trauma.

The first key to recovery from trauma is being in a safe place and restoring bodily integrity. In this instance, it is the gathering together as a Body of Christ that is the safe place, perhaps in a church building but not necessarily so. This bodily integrity is reinforced by an act of repentance that traditionally takes place early in the liturgical rite. Here, the individual has the opportunity to confess their sins and receive forgiveness.

This gathering in safety and forgiveness that reinforces bodily integrity is followed by a construction of a narrative that makes sense of the experiences. In the case of the liturgy this is the celebration of the liturgies of the Word and the Eucharist that construct the narrative. Here the gathered congregation hear the stories of God's interaction with humanity and, in the Gospels, accounts of God's presence here on earth. This is followed by the Eucharist in which a narrative that makes sense of the experience of receiving the bread and wine is articulated, often in the context of Jesus' death and resurrection.

The final stage of trauma recovery is that reconnection with society that enables the survivor to move on, to make their experience a gift to the world. This is mirrored in liturgy in the dismissal. In traditional Christian celebrations the priest or deacon might exhort the people to 'Go in the peace of Christ' or to 'Go in the name of the Lord' or to 'Go in peace to love and serve the Lord.' The emphasis is on the word 'Go!' The gathered congregation is sent out into the world to share what they have heard and experienced in the church, for the good of those who have not experienced it.

Mary as Mode of Recovery

Mary's trauma at the Annunciation-Incarnation event is non-identically repeated in each celebration and reception of the Eucharist. But even as this celebration is traumatic, it is also non-identically repeating the recovery from trauma exemplified for us in the person of Mary. However, Mary does more than simply exemplify *how* to recover from this trauma. Mary, herself, *is* a mode of our recovery from trauma. The Body of Christ is a traumatized body because it is formed of bodies that are, themselves, traumatized. As well as these traumatized bodies, there are also the twin traumatic ruptures I highlighted earlier that make their presence felt in each body. The first rupture is that gulf between the human and Divine. The second is that theological abstraction of the real, physical body. Both of these ruptures are healed in the reception of the Eucharist. The consumption of the Divine Body bridges that rupture between human and Divine and the gap between the theological body and the real. All these bodies are brought into one real body in the reception of the Eucharist.

This healing of ruptures is made possible through the embodied person of Mary. All four of the traditional Marian doctrines are concerned with her real, physical body and its intimate connection with Divine, theological bodies. In the Immaculate Conception Mary's body is established as a place of safety (sin-free) for the Incarnation of the Christ-child. Her participation in salvation history is determined long before the actual Annunciation-Incarnation event takes place. As *Theotokos*, she is Mother of God. This establishes Mary as truly bearing the flesh of God as baby within her womb, even as it establishes the truly human bodily integrity of the Christ Child. The doctrine of Mary's Perpetual Virginity is similarly concerned with maintaining her bodily integrity throughout her life. Assumed into heaven, Mary's body is preserved from the decay of death for all eternity.

As mode of our recovery, Mary's body helps to construct the narrative of this trauma. Through Incarnation in a Jewish woman, Jesus is placed within the line of Jewish matrilineal descent. Born of Mary, Jesus exists within the context and tradition of the Hebrew scriptures and history. Through Mary, Jesus is Jewish. He is the long-awaited Messiah, born in Bethlehem, of the house of David. It is Mary's body that gives this context.

Finally, Mary's life itself is a survivor's gift to the world, to us. She has a continued role as mediator and intercessor on behalf of believers before her Son. The 'Hail Mary' prayer, ancient in its construct and usage, is common to many Christian traditions. Many Christians ask for her intercession. Her Assumption into heaven ensures that she has ears to hear their prayers.

Trauma and Sacrament

Understanding the events of the Annunciation and the Incarnation as inseparable and inextricably linked to the person of Mary, even as they are a traumatic experience for her, brings our understanding of the Eucharist into the same hermeneutical space and allows for consideration through the lens of trauma theory. The Eucharist is a liturgical celebration of sacrament as a ritual repeating of *the* traumatic event – the Annunciation-Incarnation event. Pound noted that 'the Eucharist repeats the trauma of the Incarnation'[23] in which the eternal ruptures time and enters into that which is human and earthly. Pound went further, noting: '[T]he point of transubstantiation amounts to the traumatic intervention of the *real*, which shatters existing symbolic determinates and makes time matter in new ways.'[24] This is witnessed in the eucharistic celebration as the continual return of something not understood. The Annunciation-Incarnation event is part of the Divine mystery and thus beyond the accessibility of humanity.

The Cross has become the pervasive meaning of the Eucharist. But we have already seen that this has not always been the case. Theological discourse does not have to begin at Easter. Theological discourse begins prior to Easter, prior even to the Annunciation-Incarnation event. Theological discourse begins with the creative acts of God in the Genesis narratives. God's relationship with humanity is fundamentally one of creative transformation, not one of suffering and death.

In considering the sacraments, Chauvet wrote: '[T]o theologically affirm sacramental grace is to affirm, in faith, that the risen Christ continues to take flesh in the world and in history and that God continues to come into human corporality.'[25] This statement isn't about death or about the Cross, but rather it is a statement about life. To affirm that, in sacrament, 'God continues to come into human corporality' is to place repetition of the Annunciation-Incarnation event, God's original coming into human corporality, at the heart of sacraments. It is an affirmation of the creative, transformative power of God at the heart of God's revelation and relation to humankind. This returns us to the second account of the creation of

---

23 Pound, 'The Assumption of Desire', 75.

24 Marcus Pound, 'Eucharist and Trauma', *New Blackfriars* 88, no. 1014 (2007), 187–94, at 193. Italics in original.

25 Chauvet, *Symbol and Sacrament*, 212.

humankind in Genesis 2. It is here that we see God creatively transforming matter (the dust of the ground, Gen. 2.7) by filling it with Divine breath. This is the model for God's interaction with humanity – creative transformation of corporality, re-affirmed in the Annunciation-Incarnation and re-enacted in the liturgy of the Eucharist. What a positive and life-giving image of unity!

What, then, does it mean to be Christ-like? Perhaps to be Christ-like, to be Christian, is not to be subsumed into the death and resurrection of Christ (after all, not all events are redeemed). Rather, to be Christ-like is to be born again (and again) in the celebration of the Eucharist as God's mode of revelation and relation to humankind. As the material, the corporeal, is brought into communication with the Divine, so sacrament is connected to action. This becoming Christ-like, through the repetition of the Annunciation-Incarnation event in the celebration of the Eucharist, will affect the lifestyle and mission of the believer. The sacrament, therefore, directs and releases believers to mission as a recovery from trauma.

A Trinitarian Approach to Sacramentality

In his later, shorter treatise on the sacraments, Chauvet posited that the sacraments are 'the ecclesial mediations of the exchange between humanity and God'.[26] Having outlined his theory of symbolic exchange, Chauvet suggested that the sacraments are the language of the Church; they function as language does in mediating between the body speaking and the body spoken to. In this sense, the sacraments are an exchange between two subjects – between divinity and humanity.

In Chapter 5 I posited a new notion of sacrifice, that of a reciprocal self-offering. I argued that this is the understanding of sacrifice demonstrated to us in the Triune God and seen,

---

26 Louis-Marie Chauvet, *The Sacraments: The Word of God at the Mercy of the Body* (Bangalore, India: Claretian Publications, 2002), 123.

paradigmatically, in the Annunciation-Incarnation event. In Chapter 6 I proposed that we can understand the Trinity in terms of *perichorēsis* – mutual, indwelling interrelationship. I will draw both of these ideas together in contemplation of the sacraments and offer a Trinitarian sacramental theology that goes beyond Chauvet's 'mediations of the exchange between humanity and God'.

If sacrifice is, in the model I have offered, a reciprocal self-offering, fundamentally Trinitarian in its nature, then we can view all sacrifice through the paradigm of *the* Trinitarian sacrifice. This is not the death of Christ on the Cross but rather the Annunciation-Incarnation event. As Kilmartin noted:

> sacrifice is not, in the first place, an activity of human beings directed to God and, in the second place, something that reaches its goal in the response of divine acceptance and bestowal of divine blessing on the cultic community. Rather, sacrifice in the New Testament understanding – and thus in its Christian understanding – is, in the first place, the self-offering of the Father in the gift of his Son, and in the second place the unique response of the Son in his humanity to the Father, and in the third place, the self-offering of believers in union with Christ [through the power of the Holy Spirit] by which they share in his covenant relation with the Father.[27]

This connection between Trinity, Incarnation and sacrifice is drawn more sharply still in the work of Kathryn Tanner. Tanner, in her short systematic theology, notes that one should not associate the Incarnation with only one moment of Jesus' life – his birth. Rather, the Incarnation is 'the underlying given that makes all that Jesus does and suffers purifying, healing and elevating'.[28] She follows, as I do, the thinking of Cyril of Alexandria when she concluded that the sacrifice of the Cross

---

27 Kilmartin, *The Eucharist in the West*, 381–2.
28 Kathryn Tanner, *Jesus, Humanity and the Trinity: A Brief Systematic Theology* (Minneapolis, MN: Fortress Press, 2001), 28.

is 'a sacrifice of incarnation'.[29] Her subsequent analysis of the relationship between the three Persons of the Trinity indicated that this action, this death of Christ, is, as all Trinitarian actions are, the action of the three Persons together.[30]

This paradigm of Trinitarian sacrifice then becomes the model for understanding the interrelationship present within the Trinity as well as the way in which the Triune God is in relationship with humanity. It becomes the paradigm for understanding the sacraments. A *perichoretic* approach to sacramental theology cannot be separated from the concept of mutual and reciprocal self-offering at the heart of the Trinity.

Sacraments are, as Chauvet has proposed, an exchange between divinity and humanity – we see this exchange modelled in the Trinity, beginning first with the Annunciation-Incarnation event. Here we see a *perichoretic*, self-offering, reciprocal, loving sacrifice. It is this event that allows us to understand the Pasch. Christ offers himself as the Father has done, in the power of the Spirit – made possible only because of the Trinitarian sacrifice of the Annunciation-Incarnation event. Our response, made available to us (mediated) through the sacraments, is to give ourselves back to the Triune God – a reciprocal self-offering modelled on the paradigmatic Trinitarian sacrifice. Just as in the Annunciation-Incarnation event bodies are the modes of mediation – both Mary's and Christ's as the Incarnate Word – so too in sacraments are our bodies mediatory. Our bodies are the only way of experiencing, participating in and receiving the sacraments. It is in our bodies that memory occurs. The offering we make back to the Triune God is of our own embodied being. The language of the sacraments is, therefore, always Trinitarian, couched in this understanding of sacrifice. If sacraments are an exchange between humanity and divinity, then they are both the places where we lose ourselves and the places where we find ourselves – they are sites of both trauma and trauma recovery.

---

29 Ibid., 29, referencing Cyril of Alexandria, 'On the Unity of Christ', 58.
30 Ibid., 40.

In the initiatory sacraments of Baptism, Confirmation and Eucharist, we are united with Jesus Christ and incorporated into the very life of God.[31] In these sacraments we are drawn into the *perichoretic* relationship of the Trinity. Baptized in the name of the Father, the Son and the Holy Spirit, confirmed by God in the Body of Christ through the power of the Spirit, participating in the eucharistic self-offering of Christ, through the Spirit, to the Father, our experience of these sacraments is, at its very heart, Trinitarian. These sacraments are not Christological experiences to which the Spirit is added on as an optional extra. By their very nature, these sacraments are embodied. We can have no experience of the Triune God that is not mediated through our own bodies.

All the sacraments can be understood as fluid movements of mutual self-offering. All sacraments are Spirit-enabled self-offering responses to the self-offering of the Triune God. As 'ecclesial mediations of the exchange between humanity and God'[32] we can use the metaphor of a kiss to understand the embodied nature of sacraments more fully. A kiss is driven by the desire each participant has for the other. Initiated by one lover, the kiss draws the other in. The kiss is mutual – it flows back and forth between the two lovers, each responding to the other, each offering themselves within the kiss, each penetrating the other. The kiss, in this sense, is both a celebration of love and a declaration of love. It is both giving and receiving. So, too, is the sacrament. Initiated by the Lover God, it draws us into intimate union but we cannot be passive. We must celebrate this sacrament and be actively responsive. As we receive the gift of the Triune God, so we must offer ourselves back in reciprocal, mutual giving. To be 'sealed with a kiss', then, is to be sealed in the mutual interpenetration, participating in the exchange between humanity and the Triune God.

What, then, is the value of such a Trinitarian sacramental theology? The consequence of considering the Annunciation-Incarnation event to be at the core of Christian somatic memory

---

31 Catherine Mowry LaCugna, *God for Us: The Trinity and Christian Life* (San Francisco: Harper, 1991), 297.

32 Chauvet, *The Sacraments*, 123.

is to open up a Trinitarian, holistic approach to sacramental theology. I have shown that, by going beyond Chauvet's somewhat atomistic approach to sacramentality, we arrive at a sacramental theology that is holistic in its approach to both the human and the Divine bodies. Such an approach is truly Trinitarian in that it understands the relationship and mediation within the Trinitarian life to be paradigmatic for all relationships and mediations, both horizontal and vertical. More than making the welcome move of allowing space for the Spirit alongside Christ, such a theology takes the expression of relationship within the persons of the Triune God, exemplified in the Annunciation-Incarnation event, as the model for understanding *how* the sacraments are mediations between God and humanity.

Moving beyond Chauvet into a holistic, Trinitarian understanding of the sacraments allows us to understand the sacraments as a loving expression of relationship and mediation of the *perichoretic*, interpenetrative, mutually self-giving Triune God with humankind. Drawing believers in as the Lover draws the beloved into a kiss, sacraments are, therefore, both a declaration and a celebration of Divine love.

Creative Transformations

Celebration of the Eucharist and indeed all sacramental celebrations are focused upon the Christ-event. But what if the Christ-event that is at their heart is not the death of Christ on the cross, but rather the coming of God into the world – the Incarnation? What if, instead, the Christ-event is the continued and creative transformation of the corporeal? That is the perspective I've highlighted and explored here. This move away from death and towards life is one that examines the implications of such a shift in understanding. In this sense, the embodied experience and person of Mary becomes important to theology. Mary both exemplifies and *is* (in an ontological sense) our mode of recovery from the trauma that impacts us. This might be the personal trauma of rape, death, war, or loss. But it might also be the more general traumas of being part of a traumatized Body of Christ, experiencing the rupture between the Divine and the human, and the theological abstraction of the real, physical body from theology. Mary's body ends up taking a central position in eucharistic theology alongside the Body of Christ and the bodies of the believers. It is bodies that are central to liturgy – ours, hers, Christ's – and through these bodies, liturgy and sacrament are both constructed and experienced, known and felt.

8

Body: A Love Story

The cup of blessing that we bless, is it not a sharing in the blood of Christ? The bread that we break, is it not a sharing in the body of Christ? Because there is one bread, we who are many are one body, for we all partake of the one bread.[1]

We thank Thee, our Father, for the life and knowledge which You made known to us through Jesus Thy Servant; to Thee be glory for ever. Even as this broken bread was scattered over the hills, and was gathered together and became one, so let Thy Church be gathered together from the ends of the earth into Thy kingdom; for Thine is the glory and the power through Jesus Christ for ever.[2]

Hating My Body

I hated my body. It fundamentally let me down. The trauma of miscarriage, reproductive loss and infertility changed who I was, changed my whole life, and I blamed my body. My body had failed to do the one thing I felt, as a woman, it ought to be able to do. Months after my last ectopic pregnancy, one that cost me a fallopian tube and almost cost me my life, I lay, face down, on the cold wooden floor of the hallway of my home and screamed. I beat my fists on the floor, I bashed my knees. I made inhuman and unearthly noises. I threw things. I was

---

1 1 Corinthians 10.16–17.
2 'Didache', Chapter 9.

so incredibly angry. Not at God. But at my body. I hated my body. It had let me down.

As I calmed down, I felt numb. I felt disconnected from my horrible body. I felt disconnected from the ecclesial body that had asked me repeatedly when I was going to have a baby. I felt disconnected from the ecclesial body that had prophesied over me, telling me I would have a living baby in my arms by next Mother's Day. I felt disconnected from the ecclesial body that could stand up and sing: 'You give and take away, my heart will choose to say – blessed be your name.'[3] I hated that body too.

I withdrew from this ecclesial body. I could not attend church services without crying and I could not bear hearing about any more pregnant women. I avoided them. I could not bear the pressure to reproduce and the incomprehension from this body that my body could not do so. I lost my faith. Why did God let this happen to me? The theology I knew gave me no answers.

I can see, now, that my experience of repeated reproductive loss was traumatic. In hindsight, I can see that the last few years have been a process of trauma recovery. I had to establish who I was. The collapse of my future – the dreamt of and longed for family – the collapse of my relationship, and the collapse of my faith meant I was no longer the same person. Far from a gradual, natural process of growing up, this trauma ruptured my identity in an unexpected and unnatural way. I mourned. I mourned the loss of my babies, I mourned the loss of my relationship, and I mourned the loss of my younger self.

This period of mourning gave me space to think about what had happened. I began to construct my narrative. This new narrative said that it was okay to not be okay. It said that healing and recovery did not mean a drive to unrealistic perfection but a coming to terms with reality. It said that the theology I knew was lacking in the language of trauma. This narrative knew that theology was still working out what to do with women's bodies. It wondered about the relationship between bodies,

---

3 Matt Redman, 'Blessed Be Your Name', on *Where Angels Fear to Tread* (Survivor, 2002).

memory and trauma. It recognized that Christian liturgy holds within it an unclaimed memory and experience of trauma, and an instinct for trauma recovery. This narrative took the Annunciation-Incarnation event as its beginning point and paradigm – recognizing it as a traumatic event and wondering what that might mean.

This book is my reconnection with society. It is my survivor's gift that is offered as both a comfort and a challenge. It has been the place in which I worked out the beginnings of my trauma narrative and it is offered as a gift not only to trauma survivors but to all those who have encountered and will encounter trauma; it is my gift to the Church. It is a contribution to the theological language of trauma. It is a contribution to the understanding of the relationship between trauma and theology. It is an exploration of the unexamined traumatic somatic memory at the centre of the Christian faith. More than anything, it is a call to love the body: my body and the bodies I encounter.

Loving the Re-Membered Body

This is a call to learn to love the re-membered body. What do I mean by the oddly hyphenated 're-membered' body? I mean the Body of Christ – the Church – that is assembled afresh in each celebration of the Eucharist. I mean the body that is constituted when believers share in one bread to become one body. I mean the body that is brought into presence and to mind with each celebration of the Eucharist. This body is the bodies of both Mary and Christ remembered in the Annunciation-Incarnation event. Learning to love the re-membered body is learning to love the bodies of the Annunciation-Incarnation event. Loving these bodies is taking them into oneself in the reception of the Eucharist.

Loving the re-membered body has meant affirming that in the early Church there was a multivalent understanding of the meaning of the Eucharist[4] and that the loss of this multiplicity

---

4 Paul Bradshaw, *Eucharistic Origins* (London: SPCK, 2004), 32.

has led to the rise in a type of eucharistic theology that seemed to glorify suffering and death. It has meant recognizing that in the early Church the celebration of the Eucharist was as much a celebration of unity (both vertical and horizontal) as it was about the memory of Christ's death on the Cross.

The re-membered body is the body that is re-constituted in each new celebration of the Eucharist. Made up of those believers present who receive the Incarnate Body of Christ in their consumption of the bread and wine, re-membering the Annunciation-Incarnation event that draws in both Mary and Christ's Body, this re-membered body is born again in each new eucharistic celebration. Learning to love it has meant learning to see it for what it really is and being challenged to allow a new narrative to form the framework for this re-membering.

Loving the Whole Body

This is a call to learn to love the whole body. It has been a call for unity and wholeness in our approach to bodies. Recognizing the way in which theologians sometimes abstract the body from its context offers a challenge to love the contextualized body in its fullness. Learning to love the whole body has meant examining what happens to our theology when we atomize the body. When we view the Eucharist as a Christ-focused sacrament we forget the wholeness of the Triune God. Understanding the Eucharist as an event focused only on the Pasch of Christ atomizes the life and person of Jesus Christ. Similarly, love, when exclusively focused on the event of the Cross, can easily reinforce notions of sacrifice and violence. Learning to love the whole body has meant allowing the fullness of the Annunciation-Incarnation event to come to the forefront of our theology, bringing with it not only the Annunciation and the Incarnation but the whole life of Jesus as our somatic memory, our reference point in the celebration of the Eucharist. Learning to love the whole body has meant bringing whole bodies – the whole Trinitarian body, the whole embodied life of Christ – into places of prominence within our theology. It has meant acknowledging that our celebration of the Eucharist is about how Jesus lived his whole life rather than just being about how he suffered, died and was resurrected.

Learning to love the whole body has meant re-examining the relationship between the Incarnate and the eucharistic Body of Christ. It has meant understanding, along with Cyril of Alexandria, that Christ is One. There is precise unity of humanity and divinity in the person of Christ – 'unabridged unity of God and Man, Spirit and body'.[5] Learning to love the whole body is to recognize that this whole, eucharistic Body of Christ creates both vertical and horizontal unity in the believers who celebrate the Eucharist. Receiving the whole Body of Christ, always *perichoretically* united to the Triune God, is to be drawn into a vertical unity with the Divine, even as the sharing of this one bread, one body, draws believers into a horizontal unity with each other. This body is re-membered in the celebration of the Eucharist.

Learning to love the whole body has meant seeing the Trinitarian body as a whole. It has meant recognizing that the sacrament of the Eucharist is a holistic sacrament of unity with the Triune God. It has meant recognizing that Christ's body is never out of unity or relationship with the Trinity. Even in Christ's suffering and death on the Cross, he is always within the wholeness and unity of the Trinity. The death of Christ puts death within the Trinity; the death of Christ does not put the dead Christ outside or beyond the Triune God. It is, as Jones reflected, 'a death that happens deep within God, not outside of God but in the very heart – perhaps the very womb – of God. It is a death that consumes God, that God holds, making a grave of the Trinity.'[6] Learning to love the whole body has meant not shying away from this difficult image and instead acknowledging that the body of the miscarrying woman is uniquely placed to reveal the Trinity at this moment. Learning to love the whole body has meant learning to love the miscarrying womb as revelatory of the death of Christ within the Trinity. There is no

---

5 Gebremedhin, *Life-Giving Blessing*, 110.
6 Jones, *Trauma and Grace*, 148.

theological value in a miscarriage. A miscarrying womb does, in all its horror and sadness, however, reveal what it means to hold a place of death within oneself, even as one lives. To love the whole body is to love even those parts of it that cause us pain and sorrow; even those parts can reveal something of the nature of the Divine.

Loving the Priestly Body

Learning to love the priestly body has meant allowing the lens of trauma to trouble the narrative of priesthood. Such troubling of narrative has allowed the ruptured space for the construction of a new narrative of priesthood to arise. Learning to love the priestly body has meant thinking again about what it means to be a priest. Taking Williams' description of the priest as the one who holds open the door for humanity to enter into the space cleared by God,[7] learning to love this body has meant recognizing that it is Mary who provides the model for priesthood in this new narrative. Recognizing that understanding Mary as priest is neither new nor even a vaguely feminist turn, learning to love this body has meant exploring the historical, typological and artistic traditions that depict Mary as a priest.

In acknowledging the Annunciation-Incarnation event to be at the heart of Christian somatic memory, one cannot escape the consequences – Mary and her role in this event become paradigmatic for theology, and in this case, specifically for the theology of priesthood. Allowing the Annunciation-Incarnation event to shape our understanding of the Eucharist and the body that is re-membered in this celebration has consequences for our understanding of the actions of the priest at the altar. To love the priestly body is to recognize that it is not a body that must be exclusively male but rather a body that must model itself on the Annunciation-Incarnation event; the priestly body must be an inclusive one.

---

7 Williams, 'Epilogue', 176.

Loving the Sacrificial Body

This is a call to learn to love the sacrificial body. Learning to love this body has meant learning anew the meaning of sacrifice from a Christian perspective. It has meant allowing the lens of trauma to unsettle the traditional Christian narrative of sacrifice. From the rupture caused by such an unsettlement a new narrative of sacrifice has come forth.

Learning to love the sacrificial body has meant coming to realize that Christian sacrifice is best understood from the core of somatic memory – the Annunciation-Incarnation event. This sacrifice is mutual, Trinitarian and self-offering. It is not based on the breaking open of a body in death but rather in the generative opening of a body in life. This sacrificial body is removed from the violence of the Cross but does not detract from the Real Presence of Christ in the eucharistic body. In the celebration of the Eucharist, the broken, dead body of Christ is replaced with the Incarnate Christ in all his embodied fullness.

Learning to love this body means offering oneself to be made new in each celebration of the Eucharist. It means recognizing the true nature of sacrifice based on a personal relationship, evidenced par excellence in the Annunciation-Incarnation event; the 'three "moments" of Trinitarian Christian sacrifice: the self-offering of the Father; the "response" of the Son, and the responding self-offering of the believers [enabled by the Holy Spirit]'.[8] It means loving the living Body of Christ. It means recognizing that none of us are more or less worthy to offer ourselves to God. It means recognizing that the priest holds no mystical power but rather opens the door for humanity to enter into the space already cleared by the living God.

Loving the Material Body

This is a call to learn to love the material body. Loving the material body is, I have argued, a consequence of learning to love the

---

8 Daly, *Sacrifice Unveiled*, 10.

re-membered, whole, priestly and sacrificial body. Learning to love the material body has meant affirming the Real Presence of the Divine in the eucharistic elements. It has meant recognizing the goodness of the material world and the goodness of the body and its senses.[9] Loving the material body is learning to love difference. It means recognizing that in the materiality of the Eucharist difference and unity exist together, neither one eliminating the other. Tonstad goes even further in arguing that 'Christ's body moves past even sexual difference and joins itself to the materiality of the whole world'.[10] For Tonstad, the materiality of Christ's body is more significant than any sexual difference it may embody. Learning to love the material body is recognizing that the materiality of the Eucharist offers us a model of how to negotiate unity and difference within the body.

Learning to love the material body has meant exploring the physicality and materiality of the eucharistic body. It has meant learning to love the female body, recognizing that it is the body of Mary that unites Jesus to humanity. Loving the material body means the Real Presence of Christ in the eucharistic bread and wine is very real indeed. Such Real Presence makes us, the recipients of the Eucharist, not merely representatives of the Body of Christ, but the actual Body of Christ in our communities.

Loving Mary's Body

Did the woman say,
When she held him for the first time in the dark of a stable,
After the pain and the bleeding and the crying,
'This is my body, this is my blood'?

Did the woman say,
When she held him for the last time in the dark rain on a hilltop,

---

9 Méndez-Montoya, *Theology of Food*, 148.
10 Tonstad, *God and Difference*, 248.

After the pain and the bleeding and the dying,
'This is my body, this is my blood'?

Well that she said it to him then,
For dry old men,
Brocaded robes belying barrenness,
Ordain that she not say it for him now.
Frances Croake Franke[11]

This research has been a process of learning to love Mary's body. I was raised Roman Catholic, and so one could be forgiven for thinking that I began this thesis in a position of loving Mary's body already. I didn't. I began in a position of venerating her, of idealizing her, and of abstracting her beyond all recognition. I was untroubled by questions about Mary's personality, what her life had been like, what she had been like. I had very little regard for the physical, traumatized body of Mary, even as the abstract Mary Mediatrix, my intercessor, was present in my prayers. Learning to love Mary's body meant not relegating her to a walk-on part in the nativity or the role of silent, weeping mother at the Cross. It meant learning to love her as a woman in the fullness of her embodied experience. Learning to love Mary's body in this way is a lesson in learning to love the bodies of all women as women – bleeding, birthing, infertile, erotic women. It is learning to love the bodies of women in the fullness of their embodied experiences.

Learning to love Mary's body meant recognizing that her body was traumatized even as, and indeed because, her body bore the presence, the physical materiality, of the Triune God. Learning to love Mary's body meant recognizing that acknowledging her material, biological connection to Christ's eucharistic body did not detract from the Eucharist but rather opened up a beautiful, generative, historically embodied experience of the Eucharist.

---

11 Poem by Frances Croake Franke in Susan Ross, 'God's Embodiment and Women: Sacraments', in *Freeing Theology: The Essentials of Theology in Feminist Perspective*, ed. Catherine LaCugna (New York: HarperCollins Publishers, 1993), 185–210, at 185–6.

Mary's body made Jesus entirely human even as her *perichoretic* relationship with the Triune God – her *fiat* – made him entirely Divine.

Learning to love Mary's body has meant learning anew how to value the body of Mary and Mary's embodied experience within the narrative of theology. It has meant thinking physically and materially about her experience. It has meant naming her experience 'trauma'. To become suddenly and unexpectedly pregnant as Mary did was surely a traumatic experience – frightening and puzzling.[12] To name such an event as 'trauma' does not imply that this was rape. Rather, to name Mary's experience as trauma is to recognize the somatic effect of her experience, even as one acknowledges the positive nature of this experience for future believers. To love Mary's body is to respect it and to not de-humanize it in our attempt to preserve the goodness of God.

Loving All Bodies: The Future

This work has begun to explore what it means to love all bodies equally. It is offered as my survivor's gift but it is both a comfort and a challenge. Loving all bodies means rejoicing that any ordained body – regardless of gender, sex, sexual orientation, physical ability – can celebrate the Eucharist. All bodies are gathered into the One Body in the sharing of the Eucharist, thus all bodies can represent the ecclesial body of which they are a member.

There is much still to be examined in considering what it means to love all bodies. What does it mean to love all bodies when issues of class, race and global location are considered? What happens when one considers the power dynamics at play in both corporate and individual bodies? How are these bodies to be loved? I have reflected on trauma and the body from the perspective of my own dysfunctional but not, in my opinion, disabled body. What does it mean to love one's body if that body is disabled? What does it mean to love the disabled bodies of

---

12 Jones, *Trauma and Grace*, 115.

others? If the ecclesial body is traumatized because the bodies that constitute it are traumatized, then is the ecclesial body also disabled, also gay, also intersex? When we learn to love the body, we love the whole body and resist the temptation to atomize these members as 'only' individual parts. If the narrative of trauma theology I have offered here is a call to love the body, there is much still to be considered in the outworking of such love.

Having established the somatic memory at the heart of Christian faith – the Annunciation-Incarnation event – what now? Bodies are traumatized in very different ways. Some are traumatized through their experience of warfare, some through their experience of violence, some through their experience of loss. Considering these experiences of trauma through the somatic memory of the Annunciation-Incarnation event – the trauma at the heart of the Christian faith – will yield practical, pastoral out-workings of such a conclusion. Recognizing the somatic memory that is being repeated in our embodied experience of 'being Christian' opens up new pathways for considering what it means to be healed, to be redeemed, to be saved.

I have referred to the two ruptures I argue are common to all humankind – a rupture between the Divine and the human and a rupture between body and theology caused by the theological abstraction of the body. I have not had the opportunity to explore these ruptures in great detail in this book (although the work I have done in this project has served to begin to address these two ruptures). Learning to love the body in the future will require reading these ruptures through the hermeneutical lens of the somatic memory of the Annunciation-Incarnation event and examining the consequences of such a reading for embodied theology.

Learning to Love My Body

This has been, for me, a lesson in learning to love my body. In part, it has been coming to terms with the body I have – an incomplete, dysfunctional, unpredictable, imperfect body. It has been a lesson in reshaping how I perceive my female body;

this body of mine is more than just a vehicle for reproduction. It is eucharistic, it is ecclesial, and it is ecstatic. My body is loved.

Trauma is written into the liturgy of my flesh because it is part of who I am. I will always be a trauma survivor. Trauma is permanently etched upon my body. The public worship performed by my body is traumatic because my body is a traumatized body. To say that my body is eucharistic is to acknowledge that when I receive the eucharistic bread and wine, I take the Triune God into my body even as my body is drawn into intimate relationship with the Triune God. To say that my body is eucharistic is to recognize that my body is the presence of God in my community. The materiality of the Eucharist makes me materially eucharistic. It is through my body that I enter into the sacramental encounter with God.[13] The full knowledge of God is an engagement and affirmation of all the senses[14] – a fully embodied experience. My body is eucharistic as it offers an embodied thanksgiving to God.

When my body enters into *perichoretic* intimacy with the Body of the Triune God through my consumption of the Eucharist, I share in the trauma of Christ and Mary. As Fiddes so vividly demonstrated:

> [W]e share in death as we share in the broken body of the bread and in the extravagantly poured out wine, and as we are covered with the threat of hostile waters. We share in life as we come out from under the waters (whether immersed in them or affused by them), to take our place in the new community of the body of Christ, and to be filled with the new wine of the Spirit.[15]

My body, with all its trauma, is drawn into their bodies as we, the Church, non-identically repeat the trauma of the Annunciation-Incarnation event. My trauma-marked body becomes then part of the ecclesial body formed anew in each celebration of the Eucharist. The ecclesial body – the Church – is a traumatized

---

13 Power, *Sacrament*, 149.
14 Méndez-Montoya, *Theology of Food*, 148.
15 Fiddes, *Participating in God*, 281.

body because it is constituted of traumatized bodies. The liturgy of the flesh of this body is the liturgy of a traumatized body. Recognizing this requires a theology of trauma, an understanding of the traumatic somatic memory at the heart of the Christian faith; it means we have to learn how to love the traumatized body that is both ours and others'. We have to learn to witness to and walk in the traumatized body. This is the challenge Rambo presents in her work on Spirit and trauma. She offers a vision of the Spirit that remains and witnesses in the depths of human suffering. The witness of this Spirit is the persistence of Divine love.[16] To witness to and walk in the traumatized body is to be drawn into the Divine love by loving the body.

Rambo has been a significant dialogue partner in the development of this thesis. Through her work on the relationship between trauma and the Spirit, Rambo demonstrated how to allow trauma to constitute the hermeneutical lens through which theology can be constructed. It is through engaging with her work on trauma that I have been urged to challenge the eucharistic focus on the Cross. Rambo argued that when considering the death and resurrection of Jesus we approach the narrative in an atomized fashion.[17] Our reading of this narrative doesn't tell the whole story because we so often skip over Holy Saturday. It is by recovering the whole story that Rambo is able to offer such a powerful call to 'remaining' and 'witnessing'.

This challenge, to tell the whole narrative, is one evident here. Like Rambo, I recognize that when one only tells part of the story, when one focuses on the bits that are 'easier', one loses something from the narrative. Building on Rambo, I have sought to present the Annunciation-Incarnation event – the whole story of Christ from Annunciation to Resurrection – as the somatic memory at the heart of the Christian faith. Looking at the whole story doesn't just make room for the Spirit, as it does in Rambo's work;[18] rather, a consequence of

---

16 Rambo, *Spirit and Trauma*, 172.
17 Ibid., 46–7.
18 Ibid., 82.

such a perspective is that it helps us see what it really means to be Trinitarian in our theology.

By looking at the Annunciation-Incarnation event, which includes Good Friday, Holy Saturday and Easter Sunday, we can see what it means to be a trauma survivor. Mary becomes our model for trauma recovery. We can move away from death/grave imagery and instead find afresh imagery that is nourishing and generative. The persistence of Divine love is found in the witness of the Spirit and, as I have demonstrated, is shared, *perichoretically*, in each new celebration of the Eucharist.

Constructing this narrative from the rupture of my own trauma has shown me not just how to love my body, but that my body – as it is – is worth loving. It has demonstrated to me that to persist in hating my body serves to damage not only myself but also the bodies of those around me. To love my body is to acknowledge that it is only through my body that I can know God and come into *perichoretic* relationship with the Divine. And so I can say, along with Hadewijch, that:

> [T]hey [the receiver of the Eucharist and Christ] penetrate each other in such a way that neither of the two distinguishes himself from the other. But they abide in one another in fruition, mouth in mouth, heart in heart, body in body, soul in soul.[19]

In this, my body is ecstatic. To enter into this *perichoretic* relationship with the Divine is to dwell in God as God dwells in me.

> Beloved, let us love one another, because love is from God; everyone who loves is born of God and knows God. Whoever does not love does not know God, for God is love. God's love was revealed among us in this way: God sent his only Son into the world so that we might live through him. In this is love, not that we loved God but that he loved us and sent his Son to be the atoning sacrifice for our sins. Beloved, since God loved us so much, we also ought to love one another.

---

19 Hadewijch, 'Letter 9', II, 7–11, 66.

No one has ever seen God; *if we love one another, God lives in us, and his love is perfected in us. By this we know that we abide in him and he in us,* because he has given us of his Spirit. And we have seen and do testify that the Father has sent his Son as the Saviour of the world. God abides in those who confess that Jesus is the Son of God, and they abide in God. So we have known and believe the love that God has for us. God is love, and those who abide in love abide in God, and God abides in them. (1 John 4.7–16)

We see in this Johannine letter that the response to being loved by God is to love one another – to love the bodies around us. Loving others is what draws us into intimate union with the Divine. When we love the bodies around us we abide in God, and God abides in us – we enter into that mutual, self-giving *perichoretic* relationship. Learning to love our own bodies, and the bodies of others, is a response to being loved by God. Learning to love in this way allows us to dwell in the Divine and gives permission for the Divine to dwell in us.

Learning to love my body has both flowed from and flowed into learning to love the Eucharist and the Church. This love, too, is *perichoretic*. It dwells in the eucharistic body and the body of the Church, as it dwells in me. These loves feed each other. Being loved by the Triune God and by the Church enables me to love God and the Church. Loving and being loved brings me into vertical unity with the Triune God and horizontal unity with the ecclesial body of the Church of which I am a member.

To love my body is not to despise its role in my traumatic experiences but to marvel at its capacity to survive and seek connection with the other. The process of learning to love my body is redemptive. This love is part of God's work of love in restoring all things. Loving my body, despite its role in my trauma, is to resist the temptation of isolation and detachment as modes of self-preservation. Loving my body is loving and being in communion with other bodies, made possible by and as a response to the love of God.

Further Reading

Trauma and Trauma Theology

Arel, Stephanie N. and Shelly Rambo, eds, *Post-Traumatic Public Theology*, Cham, Switzerland: Palgrave Macmillan, 2016.

Beste, Jennifer Erin, *God and the Victim: Traumatic Intrusions on Grace and Freedom*, Oxford: Oxford University Press, 2008.

Bridgers, Lynn, 'The Resurrected Life: Roman Catholic Resources in Posttraumatic Pastoral Care', *International Journal of Practical Theology* 15, no. 1, 2011, 38–56.

Brison, Susan J., *Aftermath: Violence and the Remaking of a Self*, New Jersey: Princeton University Press, 2002.

Caruth, Cathy, 'Trauma and Experience: Introduction', in *Trauma: Explorations in Memory*, ed. Cathy Caruth, Baltimore, MD and London: The Johns Hopkins University Press, 1995, 3–12.

___ 'Unclaimed Experience: Trauma and the Possibility of History', *Yale French Studies* 79, Literature and the Ethical Question, 1991, 181–92.

___ *Unclaimed Experience: Trauma, Narrative, and History*, Baltimore, MD: The Johns Hopkins University Press, 1996.

Cooper-White, Pamela, *The Cry of Tamar: Violence against Women and the Church's Response*, 2nd ed., Minneapolis: Augsburg Fortress, 2012.

Crumpton, Stephanie M., *A Womanist Pastoral Theology against Intimate and Cultural Violence*, New York: Palgrave Macmillan, 2014.

DeMeester, Karen, 'Trauma and Recovery in Virginia Woolf's Mrs Dalloway', *Modern Fiction Studies* 44, no. 3, 1998, 649–73.

Doehring, Carrie, *Internal Desecration: Traumatization and Representations of God*, Lanham, MD: University Press of America, 1993.

Frantz, Nadine Pence and Mary T. Stimming, eds, *Hope Deferred: Heart-Healing Reflections on Reproductive Loss*, Eugene, OR: Resource Publications, 2005.

Ganzeboort, R. Ruard, 'All Things Work Together for Good? Theodicy and Post-Traumatic Spirituality', in *Secularization Theories, Religious Identity, and Practical Theology*, ed. W. Gräb and L. Charbonnier, Münster: LIT Verlag, 2009, 183–92.

___ 'Scars and Stigmata: Trauma, Identity and Theology', *Practical Theology* 1, no. 1, 2008, 19–31.

___ 'Teaching That Matters: A Course on Trauma and Theology', *Journal of Adult Theological Education* 5, no. 1, 2008, 8–19.

Gillespie, C. Kevin, 'Terror, Trauma and Transcendence: Pastoral Ministry after 9/11', *The New Theological Review*, Feb. 2004, 16–25.

Grundy, Christopher, 'Basic Retraining: The Role of Congregational Ritual in the Care of Returning Veterans', *Liturgy* 27, no. 4, 2012, 27–36.

___ 'The Grace of Resilience: Eucharistic Origins, Trauma Theory, and Implications for Contemporary Practice', paper presented at the Proceedings of the North American Academy of Liturgy, 2006, 147–59.

Herman, Judith, *Trauma and Recovery*, New York: Basic Books, 1992.

___ *Trauma and Recovery: From Domestic Abuse to Political Terror*, London: Pandora, 2001.

Hess, Cynthia, *Sites of Violence, Sites of Grace: Christian Nonviolence and the Traumatized Self*, Plymouth: Lexington Books, 2009.

Horowitz, Mardi, *Stress Response Syndromes*, 2nd ed., New York: Aronson, 1986.

Jones, Serene, 'Emmaus Witnessing: Trauma and the Disordering of the Theological Mind', *Union Seminary Quarterly Review*, Fall 2002, 113–28.

___ *Feminist Theory and Christian Theology: Cartographies of Grace*, Minneapolis, MN: Augsburg Fortress Press, 2000.

___ 'Hope Deferred: Theological Reflections on Reproductive Loss (Infertility, Miscarriage, Stillbirth)', *Modern Theology* 17, no. 2, 2001, 227–45.

___ 'Rupture', in *Hope Deferred: Heart Healing Reflections on Reproductive Loss*, ed. Nadine Pence Frantz and Mary T. Stimming, Eugene, OR: Resources Publications, 2005.

___ 'Trauma and Grace', *Reflections*, 2004, 47–66.

___ *Trauma and Grace: Theology in a Ruptured World*, Louisville, KY: Westminster John Knox Press, 2009.

Keshgegian, Flora, *Redeeming Memories: A Theology of Healing and Transformation*, Nashville, TN: Abingdon Press, 2000.

___ *Time for Hope: Practices for Living in Today's World*, New York: Continuum, 2006.

Lange, Dirk G., *Trauma Recalled: Liturgy, Disruption, and Theology*, Minneapolis, MN: Fortress Press, 2010.

Lepore, S. J. and T. A. Revenson, 'Resilience and Posttraumatic Growth: Recovery, Resistance, and Reconfiguration', in *Handbook of Posttraumatic Growth: Research and Practice*, ed. L. G. Calhoun and R. G. Tedeschi, Mahwah, NJ: Erlbaum, 2006, 24–36.

McFarlane, Alexander and Bessel van der Kolk, 'Trauma and Its Challenge to Society', in *Traumatic Stress*, ed. Bessel van der Kolk,

Alexander McFarlane and Lars Weisaeth, New York: Guilford Press, 1996, 24–46.

Moore, Darnell L., 'Theorizing the "Black Body" as a Site of Trauma: Implications for Theologies of Embodiment', *Theology and Sexuality* 15, no. 2, 2009, 175–88.

O'Donnell, Karen, 'Help for Heroes: PTSD, Warrior Recovery, and the Liturgy', *Journal of Religion and Health* 54, no. 2, 2015, 2389–97.

Pound, Marcus, 'The Assumption of Desire: Kierkegaard, Lacan, and the Trauma of the Eucharist', *Journal for Cultural and Religious Theory* 9, no. 1, 2008, 67–78.

_ _ _ 'Eucharist and Trauma', *New Blackfriars* 88, no. 1014, 2007, 187–94.

_ _ _ *Theology, Psychoanalysis and Trauma*, London: SCM Press, 2007.

Rambo, Shelly, 'Between Death and Life: Trauma, Divine Love, and the Witness of Mary Magdalene', *Studies in Christian Ethics* 18, 2005, 7–21.

_ _ _ 'Beyond Redemption?: Reading Cormac McCarthy's *The Road* after the End of the World', *Studies in the Literary Imagination* 41, no. 1, 2008, 99–119.

_ _ _ 'Haunted (by the) Gospel: Theology, Trauma, and Literary Theory in the 21st Century', *PMLA* 125, no. 4, 2010, 936–41.

_ _ _ 'Review of *God and the Victim: Traumatic Intrusions on Grace and Freedom*', *Modern Theology* 25, no. 3, 2009, 526–8.

_ _ _ 'Saturday in New Orleans: Rethinking Spirit in the Aftermath of Trauma', *Review and Expositor* 105, no. 2, 2008, 229–44.

_ _ _ *Spirit and Trauma: A Theology of Remaining*, Louisville, KY: Westminster John Knox Press, 2010.

_ _ _ 'Trauma and Faith: Reading the Narrative of the Hemorrhaging Woman', *International Journal of Practical Theology* 13, no. 2, 2010, 1–25.

Shay, Jonathan, *Odysseus in America: Combat Trauma and the Trials of Homecoming*, New York: Scribner Book Company, 2003.

van der Kolk, Bessel, 'The Body Keeps the Score: Memory and the Evolving Psychobiology of Post Traumatic Stress', *Harvard Review of Psychiatry* 1, no. 5, 1994, 253–65.

van der Kolk, Bessel and Alexander McFarlane, 'The Black Hole of Trauma', in *Traumatic Stress*, ed. Bessel van der Kolk, Alexander McFarlane and Lars Weisaeth, New York: Guilford Press, 1996, 3–23.

van der Kolk, Bessel and Onno van der Hart, 'The Intrusive Past: The Flexibility of Memory and the Engraving of Trauma', in *Trauma: Explorations in Memory*, ed. Cathy Caruth, Baltimore, MD and London: The Johns Hopkins University Press, 1995, 158–82.

Wylie, Mary Sykes, 'The Limits of Talk: Bessel van der Kolk Wants to Transform the Treatment of Trauma', *Psychotherapy Networker* 28, no. 1, 2004, 1–11.

Bibliography

Scripture quotations are from the New Revised Standard Version of the Bible, Anglicized Edition, copyright © 1989, 1995 by the Division of Christian Education of the National Council of the Churches of Christ in the USA. Used by permission. All rights reserved.

Pre-Modern Texts

Ambrose, 'Homily on Psalm 118', in *Patrologiae Cursis Completus: Series Latina*, ed. Jacques-Paul Mignes, Paris: Migne, 1844–1891.

___ 'On the Mysteries', trans. H. de Romestin, E. de Romestin and H. T. F. Duckworth, in *Nicene and Post-Nicene Fathers, Second Series*, ed. Philip Schaff and Henry Wace, Buffalo, NY: Christian Literature Publishing Co., 1896.

___ *Saint Ambrose: Theological and Dogmatic Works*, trans. and ed. Roy J. Deferrari, Washington, DC: The Catholic University of America Press, 1963.

___ Aquinas, Thomas, *The Summa Theologica*, trans. the Fathers of the English Dominican Province, London: Burns, Oates and Washbourne Ltd, 1920.

Aristotle, *Generation of Animals*, trans. A. L. Peck, Cambridge, MA: Harvard University Press, 1943.

Athanasius, 'On the Incarnation of the Word', trans. Archibald Robertson, in *Nicene and Post-Nicene Fathers*, Vol. 4, ed. Philip Schaff and Henry Wace, Buffalo, NY: Christian Literature Publishing Co., 1892.

Augustine, 'Exposition of Psalm 98', trans. J. E. Tweed, in *Nicene and Post-Nicene Fathers*, Vol. 8, ed. Philip Schaff, Buffalo, NY: Christian Literature Publishing Co., 1888.

___ 'Sermon 227', trans. Sister Mary Sarah Muldowney, in *Saint Augustine: Sermons on the Liturgical Seasons*, New York: Fathers of the Church, Inc., 1959.

___ 'Sermon 229', trans. Sister Mary Sarah Muldowney, in *Saint Augustine: Sermons on the Liturgical Seasons*, New York: Fathers of the Church, Inc., 1959.

_ _ _'Sermon 272', trans. Edmund Hill, in *Sermons*, Part 3, Vol. 7, New Rochelle, NY: New City Press, 1993.

_ _ _'Tractate 27 (John 6.60–72)', trans. John Gibb, in *A Select Library of the Nicene and Post-Nicene Fathers*, Vol. 7, ed. Philip Schaff, Buffalo, NY: Christian Literature Publishing Co., 1888.

Calvin, John, *Calvin: Institutes of the Christian Religion*, Vol. 2, trans. Ford Lewis Battles, ed. John T. McNeill, Philadelphia: The Westminster Press, 1960.

_ _ _*Commentary on John*, 2 vols, Vol. 1, trans. William Pringle, Grand Rapids, MI: Christian Classics Ethereal Library, 1847.

Clement of Alexandria, 'The Instructor Book I', trans. Revd William Wilson, in *Clement of Alexandria, Vol. IV, Ante-Nicene Christian Library: Translations of the Writings of the Fathers Down to AD 325*, ed. Alexander Roberts and James Donaldson, Buffalo, NY: Christian Literature Publishing Co., 1885.

Cyprian, 'Epistle 62', trans. Robert Ernest Wallis, in *Ante-Nicene Christian Library: Translations of the Writings of the Fathers Down to AD 325, Vol VIII, The Writings of Cyprian, Bishop of Carthage*, Part 1 of 2, ed. Alexander Roberts and James Donaldson, Edinburgh: T & T Clark, 1868.

Cyril of Alexandria, 'Commentary on the Gospel According to S. John', trans. P. E. Pusey, in *A Library of the Fathers of the Holy Catholic Church*, 2 vols, Vol. 1, Oxford: James Parker & Co., 1874.

_ _ _*Five Tomes Against Nestorius*, trans. P. E. Pusey, in *A Library of the Fathers of the Holy Catholic Church*, Oxford: James Parker & Co., 1881.

'Didache', trans. M. B. Riddle, in *Ante-Nicene Fathers*, Vol. 7, eds. Alexander Roberts, James Donaldson and A. Cleveland Coxe, Buffalo, NY: Christian Literature Publishing Co., 1886.

Epiphanius of Salamis, 'The Panarion of Epiphanius of Salamis Books 2 and 3', trans. Frank Williams, in *The Panarion of Epiphanius of Salamis Books 2 and 3: De Fide*, ed. Johannes van Oort and Einar Thomassen, Leiden and Boston, MA: Brill, 2013.

Gregory of Nazianzus, 'Letter 101', in *On God and Christ: The Five Theological Orations and Two Letters to Cledonius*, ed. Lionel Wickham, Crestwood, NY: St Vladimir's Seminary Press, 2002.

Hadewijch, 'Letter 9', in *Hadewijch: Works*, ed. Columba Hart, Mahwah, NJ: Paulist Press, 1980.

Hippolytus, 'The Apostolic Tradition', trans. Burton Scott Easton, in *The Apostolic Tradition of Hippolytus*, Cambridge: Cambridge University Press, 1934.

Irenaeus, 'Against Heresies', trans. Alexander Roberts and William Rambaut, in *Ante-Nicene Fathers*, Vol. 1, ed. Alexander Roberts and James Donaldson. Buffalo, NY: Christian Literature Publishing Co., 1885.

Jerome, 'Against the Pelagians', in *Nicene and Post-Nicene Fathers, Second Series*, ed. Philip Schaff and Henry Wace, Buffalo, NY: Christian Literature Publishing Co., 1893.

John Chrysostom, 'On the Birthday of Our Savior Jesus Christ a Sermon', www.tertullian.org/fathers/chrysostom_homily_2_on_christmas.htm.

John Damascene, 'An Exposition of the Orthodox Faith, Book 4', trans. E. W. Watson and L. Pullann, in *Nicene and Post-Nicene Fathers, Second Series*, ed. Philip Schaff and Henry Wace, Buffalo, NY: Christian Literature Publishing Co., 1899.

Justin Martyr, 'Apology 1', trans. Marcus Dods and George Reith, in *Ante-Nicene Fathers*, Vol. 1, ed. Alexander Roberts, James Donaldson and A. Cleveland Coxe, Buffalo, NY: Christian Literature Publishing Co., 1885.

Luther, Martin, 'The Babylonian Captivity of the Church', in *Luther's Works*, ed. Helmut Lehmann, Vol. 36, Philadelphia, PA: Fortress Press, 1520.

___ 'Comfort for Women who have had a Miscarriage, 1542', in *Luther's Works*, ed. Jaroslav Pelikan and Helmut T. Lehmann, Philadelphia, PA: Fortress, 1958–86, 243–50.

___ 'A Sermon on Pentecost, Second Sermon John 14.23–31, 1522', in *Sermons of Martin Luther*, Vol. 3, ed. and trans. John Nicholas Lenker, Minneapolis, MN: Lutherans in All Lands, 1907, 259–68.

Origen, 'Homily 6', trans. Gary Wayne Barkley, in *Homilies on Leviticus 1–16*, Washington, DC: The Catholic University of America Press, 1990.

Proclus, *Proclus, Bishop of Constantinople: Homilies on the Life of Christ*, ed. Jan H. Barkhuizen, Brisbane, Australia: Centre for Early Christian Studies, 2001.

Tertullian, 'On the Flesh of Christ', trans. Peter Holmes, in *Ante-Nicene Fathers*, Vol. 3, ed. Alexander Roberts, James Donaldson and A. Cleveland Coxe, Buffalo, NY: Christian Literature Publishing Co., 1885.

Ecclesial Documents

Archbishops' Council, *A Time to Heal: A Contribution Towards the Ministry of Healing*, London: Church House Publishing, 2000.

Catechism of the Catholic Church with Modifications from the Editio Typica, New York: Doubleday, 1995.

'Code of Canon Law', http://vatican.va/archive/ENG1104/_P39.HTM.

'Eucharistic Prayer II', The Roman Missal, http://catholic-resources.org/ChurchDocs/RM3-EP1-4.htm.

'The Order of Mass', in *Catholic Bishops' Conference of England and Wales*, ed. Liturgy Office England and Wales.

Pope John Paul II, 'Redemptoris Mater', Vatican, http://w2.vatican.va/content/john-paul-ii/en/encyclicals/documents/hf_jp-ii_enc_25031987_redemptoris-mater.html.

Pope Paul VI, 'Decree on the Apostolate of the Laity', Vatican, www.vatican.va/archive/hist_councils/ii_vatican_council/documents/vat-ii_decree_19651118_apostolicam-actuositatem_en.html.

___ 'Lumen Gentium', Vatican, www.vatican.va/archive/hist_councils/ii_vatican_council/documents/vat-ii_const_19641121_lumen-gentium_en.html.

Pope Pius XII, 'Munificentissimus Deus' http://w2.vatican.va/content/pius-xii/en/apost_constitutions/documents/hf_p-xii_apc_19501101_munificentissimus-deus.html.

Pope Pius XII, 'Sacramentum Ordinis', www.vatican.va/holy_father/pius_xii/apost_constitutions/documents/hf_p-xii_apc_19471130_sacramentum-ordinis_lt.html.

Second Vatican Council, 'Constitution on the Sacred Liturgy', www.vatican.va/archive/hist_councils/ii_vatican_council/documents/vat-ii_const_19631204_sacrosanctum-concilium_en.html.

'The Canons of the Church of England', www.churchofengland.org/media/35588/complete.pdf.

Modern Texts

Oxford English Dictionary, Oxford: Oxford University Press, 2015.

Abramović, Marina, 'The Artist is Present', New York: Museum of Modern Art, 2010.

Agger, Inger and Soren B. Jensen, 'Testimony as Ritual and Evidence in Psychotherapy for Political Refugees', *Journal of Traumatic Stress* 3, 1990, 115–40.

American Psychiatric Association, *Diagnostic and Statistical Manual of Psychiatric Disorders*, Vol. 3, Washington, DC: American Psychiatric Association, 1980.

Angel, Hayyim, 'Ezekiel: Priest-Prophet', *Jewish Bible Quarterly* 39, no. 1, 2011, 35–45.

Auerbach, Erich, 'Figura', in *Scenes from the Drama of European Literature*, Manchester: Manchester University Press, 1984, 11–78.

Beattie, Tina, 'Mary, the Virgin Priest?', *The Month*, December 1996.

___ *Rediscovering Mary: Insights from the Gospels*, Tunbridge Wells, Kent: Burns & Oates, 1995.

Benko, Stephen, *The Virgin Goddess: Studies in the Pagan and Christian Roots of Mariology*, Leiden and Boston, MA: Brill, 1994.

Berger, Teresa, *Gender Differences and the Making of Liturgical History: Lifting a Veil on Liturgy's Past*, Farnham, Surrey: Ashgate, 2011.

Bradshaw, Paul, *Eucharistic Origins*, London: SPCK, 2004.

Bradshaw, Paul and Maxwell E. Johnson, *The Eucharistic Liturgies: Their Evolution and Interpretation*, London: SPCK, 2012.

Brock, Rita Nakashima and Rebecca Ann Parker, *Proverbs of Ashes: Violence, Redemptive Suffering, and the Search for What Saves Us*, Boston, MA: Beacon, 2001.

Brown, Peter, *The Cult of the Saints: Its Rise and Function in Latin Christianity*, Chicago: University of Chicago Press, 1981.

Bugnini, Annibale, *The Reform of the Liturgy 1948–1975*, Collegeville, MN: The Liturgical Press, 1990.

Bynum, Caroline Walker, *Holy Feast and Holy Fast: The Religious Significance of Food to Medieval Women*, Berkeley, LA and London: University of California Press, 1987.

_ _ _*Wonderful Blood: Theology and Practice in Late Medieval Northern Germany and Beyond*, Philadelphia: University of Pennsylvania Press, 2007.

Cameron, Averil, 'The Cult of the Virgin in Late Antiquity: Religious Development and Myth-Making', in *The Church and Mary: Papers Read at the 2001 Summer Meeting and the 2002 Winter Meeting of the Ecclesiastical History Society*, ed. R. N. Swanson, Suffolk: The Boydell Press, 2004, 1–21.

Cardile, Paul Y., 'Mary as Priest: Mary's Sacerdotal Position in the Visual Arts', *Arte Cristiana* 72, 1984, 199–208.

Caruth, Cathy, *Unclaimed Experience: Trauma, Narrative, and History*, Baltimore, MD: The Johns Hopkins University Press, 1996.

Chadwick, Henry, 'Eucharist and Christology in the Nestorian Controversy', *Journal of Theological Studies* 2, no. 2, 1951, 145–64.

Chapman, Cynthia R., '"Oh That You Were Like a Brother to Me, One Who Had Nursed at My Mother's Breasts": Breast Milk as a Kinship-Forging Substance', *Journal of Hebrew Scriptures* 12, 2012, 1–41.

Chauvet, Louis-Marie, *The Sacraments: The Word of God at the Mercy of the Body*, Bangalore, India: Claretian Publications, 2002.

_ _ _*Symbol and Sacrament: A Sacramental Reinterpretation of Christian Existence*, trans. Patrick Madigan and Madeleine Beaumont, Collegeville, MN: A Pueblo Book published by The Liturgical Press, 1995.

Clancy, Finbarr G., 'The Eucharist in St Ambrose's Commentaries on the *Psalms*', in *Studia Patristica*, ed. Markus Vinzent, Leuven, Paris, Walpole, MA: Peeters, 2011, 35–44.

Coakley, Sarah, *God, Sexuality, and the Self: An Essay 'On The Trinity'*, Cambridge: Cambridge University Press, 2013.

___ 'The Woman at the Altar: Cosmological Disturbance or Gender Subversion?', *The Anglican Theological Review* 86, no. 1, 2004, 75–93.

Concannon, Ellen, 'The Eucharist as Source of St Cyril of Alexandria's Christology', *Pro Ecclesia* 18, no. 3, 2009, 318–36.

Congar, Yves, 'Note Sur Une Valeur Des Termes, «Ordinare, Ordinatio»', *Revue des Sciences Religieuses* 58, 1984, 7–14.

Corrington, Gail Paterson, 'The Milk of Salvation: Redemption by the Mother in Late Antiquity and Early Christianity', *The Harvard Theological Review* 82, no. 4, 1989, 393–420.

Creamer, Deborah, 'Toward a Theology That Includes the Human Experience of Disability', *Journal of Religion, Disability and Health* 7, no. 3, 2008, 57–67.

Cunningham, Mary, *Wider Than Heaven: Eighth Century Homilies on the Mother of God*, New York: St Vladimir's Seminary Press, 2008.

Daly, Robert, *Sacrifice Unveiled: The True Meaning of Christian Sacrifice*, London and New York: T & T Clark, 2009.

de Lubac, Henri, *Corpus Mysticum: The Eucharist and the Church in the Middle Ages*, trans. Gemma Simmonds, Richard Price and Christopher Stephens, London: University of Notre Dame Press, 2006.

Dix, Gregory, ed., *The Treatise on the Apostolic Tradition of St Hippolytus of Rome, Bishop and Martyr*, London: SPCK, 1937.

Engelbrecht, Edward, 'God's Milk: An Orthodox Confession of the Eucharist', *Journal of Early Christian Studies* 7, no. 4, 1999, 509–26.

Fiddes, Paul S., *Participating in God: A Pastoral Doctrine of the Trinity*, London: Darton, Longman and Todd Ltd, 2000.

Foley, Edward, *From Age to Age: How Christians Have Celebrated the Eucharist*, Collegeville, MN: Liturgical Press, 2008.

Ford, David F., *Self and Salvation: Being Transformed*, Cambridge: Cambridge University Press, 1999.

___ 'What Happens in the Eucharist?', *Scottish Journal of Theology* 48, no. 3, 1995, 359–81.

Foskett, Mary, *A Virgin Conceived: Mary and Classical Representations of Virginity*, Bloomington & Indianapolis: Indiana University Press 2002.

___ 'Virginity as Purity in the *Protevangelium of James*', in *A Feminist Companion to Mariology*, ed. Amy-Jill Levine and Maria Mayo Robbins, London: Continuum International Publishing Group Ltd, 2005, 67–76.

Frantz, Nadine Pence and Mary T. Stimming, eds, *Hope Deferred: Heart-Healing Reflections on Reproductive Loss*, Eugene, OR: Resource Publications, 2005.

Fuchs, Vinzenz, *Der Ordinationstitel Von Seiner Entstehung Bis Auf Innozenz III*, Amsterdam: P. Schippers, 1968.

Gambero, Luigi, *Mary and the Fathers of the Church: The Blessed Virgin Mary in Patristic Thought*, trans. Thomas Buffer, San Francisco, CA: Ignatius Press, 1999.

Gebara, Ivone and Maria Clara Bingemer, *Mary, Mother of God, Mother of the Poor*, trans. Phillip Berryman, Liberation and Theology Series, Maryknoll, NY: Orbis Books, 1989.

Gebremedhin, Ezra, *Life-Giving Blessing: An Inquiry into the Eucharistic Doctrine of Cyril of Alexandria*, Uppsala: Uppsala University Press, 1977.

Girard, René, *Things Hidden Since the Foundation of the World*, trans. Stephen Bann and Michael Metteer, Stanford, CA: Stanford University Press, 1987.

___ *'To Double Business Bound': Essays on Literature, Mimesis, and Anthropology*, Baltimore, MD: The Johns Hopkins University Press, 1978.

Glancy, Jennifer A., *Corporal Knowledge: Early Christian Bodies*, Oxford: Oxford University Press, 2010.

Gray, Patrick T. R., 'From Eucharist to Christology: The Life-Giving Body of Christ in Cyril of Alexandria, Eutyches and Julian of Halicarnassus', in *The Eucharist in Theology and Philosophy: Issues of Doctrinal History in East and West from the Patristic Ages to the Reformation*, ed. Istvan Percvel, Reka Forrai and Gyorgy Gereby, Leuven: Leuven University Press, 2005, 23–36.

Green, Joel B., 'Blessed is She Who Believed: Mary, Curious Exemplar in Luke's Narrative', in *Blessed One: Protestant Perspectives on Mary*, ed. Beverly Roberts Gaventa and Cynthia L. Rigby, Louisville, KY: John Knox Press, 2002, 9–20.

Grillmeier, Aloys, *Christ in Christian Tradition: From the Apostolic Age to Chalcedon (451)*, trans. J. S. Bowden, London: A. R. Mowbray & Co. Ltd, 1965.

Gy, Pierre-Marie, 'Ancient Ordination Prayers', *Studia Liturgica* 13, 1979, 70–93.

Hamilton, Julie, 'Praktognosia and Performance: Phenomenological Epistemology in the Performance Art of Marina Abramović and Lia Chavez', http://civa.org/sitecontent/wp-content/uploads/CIVA-Between-Two-Worlds-2-Hamilton_Praktognosia-Phenomenological-Epistemology-and-Performance-Art_FINAL.pdf.

Hancock, Brannon, *The Scandal of Sacramentality: The Eucharist in Literary and Theological Perspectives*, Eugene, OR: Wipf and Stock, 2014.

Harris, James Rendel and Alphonse Mingana, *The Odes and Psalms of Solomon*, Vol. 2, California: The University Press, 1916.

Harvey, Susan Ashbrook, 'Feminine Imagery for the Divine: The Holy Spirit, the Odes of Solomon, and Early Syriac Tradition', *St Vladimir's Theological Quarterly* 37, 1993, 111–39.

Heaney, James, *Beyond the Body: An Antitheology of the Eucharist*, Eugene, OR: Pickwick Publications, 2014.

Herman, Judith, *Trauma and Recovery: From Domestic Abuse to Political Terror*, London: Pandora, 2001.

Hock, Ronald F., *The Infancy Gospels of James and Thomas*, The Scholars Bible, Santa Rosa, CA: Polebridge Press, 1995.

Holum, Kenneth, *Theodosian Empresses: Women and Imperial Dominion in Late Antiquity*, Berkeley, Los Angeles and London: University of California Press, 1982.

Horowitz, Mardi, *Stress Response Syndromes*, 2nd ed., New York: Aronson, 1986.

Hubert, Henri and Marcel Mauss, *Sacrifice: Its Nature and Functions*, Chicago: University of Chicago Press, 1981.

Jay, Nancy, *Throughout Your Generations Forever: Sacrifice, Religion, and Paternity*, Chicago: University of Chicago Press, 1992.

Jensen, Robin, *Baptismal Imagery in Early Christianity: Ritual, Visual, and Theological Dimensions*, Grand Rapids, MI: Baker Academic, 2012.

Jobes, Karen H., 'Got Milk? Septuagint Psalm 33 and the Interpretation of 1 Peter 2.1–3', *Westminster Theological Journal* 64, no. 1, 2002, 1–14.

Johnson, Maxwell E., 'Sub Tuum Praesidium: The Theotokos in Christian Life and Worship before Ephesus', in *The Place of Christ in Liturgical Prayer: Trinity, Christology, and Liturgical Theology*, ed. Bryan D. Spinks, Collegeville, MN: Liturgical Press, 2008, 243–67.

Jones, Serene, *Feminist Theory and Christian Theology: Cartographies of Grace*, Minneapolis, MN: Augsburg Fortress Press, 2000.

— — —'Rupture', in *Hope Deferred: Heart Healing Reflections on Reproductive Loss*, ed. Nadine Pence Frantz and Mary T. Stimming, Eugene, OR: Resources Publications, 2005.

— — —*Trauma and Grace: Theology in a Ruptured World*, Louisville, KY: Westminster John Knox Press, 2009.

Jungmann, Joseph, *The Mass of the Roman Rite: Its Origins and Development*, 2 vols, Vol. 2, New York: Benziger, 1955.

Kearns, Cleo McNelly, *The Virgin Mary, Monotheism and Sacrifice*, New York: Cambridge University Press, 2008.

Kilmartin, Edward J., *The Eucharist in the West: History and Theology*, Collegeville, MN: Liturgical Press, 1998.

Kilmartin, Edward J. and Robert J. Daly, 'The Eucharistic Theology of Pope Gelasius I: A Nontridentic View', in *Studia Patristica*, ed. Elizabeth A. Livingstone, Leuven: Peeters, 1997, 283–89.

LaCugna, Catherine Mowry, *God for Us: The Trinity and Christian Life*, San Francisco: Harper, 1991.

Lane, Barbara, *The Altar and the Altarpiece: Sacramental Themes in Early Netherlandish Painting*, New York: Harper & Row, 1984.

Lathrop, Gordon W., *Holy Things: A Liturgical Theology*, Minneapolis, MN: Fortress Press, 1998.

Lattke, Michael, *Odes of Solomon: A Commentary*, Minneapolis, MN: Fortress Press, 2009.

Laurentin, René, *Marie, L'Eglise et le Sacerdoce*, 2 vols, Vol. 2, Paris: Nouvelles Editions Latines, 1953.

Louth, Andrew, 'Late Patristic Developments in the East', in *The Oxford Handbook of the Trinity*, ed. Gilles Emery O.P. and Matthew Levering, Oxford: Oxford University Press, 2011, 138–53.

Macy, Gary, *Treasures from the Storeroom: Medieval Religion and the Eucharist*, Collegeville, MN: Liturgical Press, 1999.

___ *The Hidden History of Women's Ordination: Female Clergy in the Medieval West*, Oxford: Oxford University Pres, 2008.

Martin, Dale B., *The Corinthian Body*, New Haven, CT and London: Yale University Press, 1995.

Martos, Joseph, *Doors to the Sacred: A Historical Introduction to Sacraments in the Catholic Church*, Liguori, MO: Liguori Publications, 1991.

McGowan, Andrew, *Ascetic Eucharists: Food and Drink in Early Christian Ritual Meals*, Oxford: Clarendon Press, 1999.

McGuckin, John, 'The Paradox of the Virgin Theotokos: Evangelism and Imperial Politics in the Fifth Century Byzantine World', *Maria* 2, 2001, 8–25.

McKenna, John, *The Eucharistic Epiclesis: A Detailed History from the Patristic to the Modern Era*, Chicago: Hillenbrand Books, 2009.

Méndez-Montoya, Angel F., *The Theology of Food: Eating and the Eucharist*, Oxford: Wiley-Blackwell, 2012.

Minister, Meredith, *Trinitarian Theology and Power Relations: God Embodied*, New York: Palgrave Macmillan, 2014.

Mitchell, Nathan D., *Eucharist as Sacrament of Initiation*, Archdiocese of Chicago: Liturgy Training Publications, 1994.

Moloney, Raymond, *The Eucharist*, Collegeville, MN: The Liturgical Press, 1995.

Moltmann, Jürgen, *The Crucified God: The Cross of Christ as the Foundation and Criticism of Christian Theology*, London: SCM Press, 1974.

___ *The Trinity and the Kingdom of God*, trans. Margaret Kohl, London: SCM Press, 1981.

Morrill, Bruce T., *Divine Worship and Human Healing: Liturgical Theology at the Margins of Life and Death*, Collegeville, MN: Liturgical Press, 2009.

Myers, Alicia D., '"In the Father's Bosom": Breastfeeding and Identity Formation in John's Gospel', *The Catholic Biblical Quarterly* 76, 2013, 481–97.

Ngien, Dennis, 'Trinity and Divine Passibility in Martin Luther's "*Theologia Crucis*", *Scottish Bulletin of Evangelical Theology* 19, no. 1, 2001, 31–64.

O'Carroll, Michael, *Theotokos: A Theological Encyclopedia of the Blessed Virgin Mary*, Collegeville, MN: The Liturgical Press, 1982.

O'Connor, James T., *The Hidden Manna: A Theology of the Eucharist*, San Francisco, CA: Ignatius Press, 2005.

Pelikan, Jaroslav, *The Christian Tradition: A History of the Development of Doctrine*, Vol. 4, *Reformation of Church and Dogma (1300–1700)*, Chicago and London: University of Chicago Press, 1984.

Penn, Michael Philip, *Kissing Christians: Ritual and Community in the Late Ancient Church*, Philadelphia: University of Pennsylvania Press, 2005.

Percy, Emma, *Mothering as a Metaphor for Ministry*, Farnham, Surrey: Ashgate, 2014.

Pickstock, Catherine, *After Writing: On the Liturgical Consummation of Philosophy*, Oxford: Blackwell, 1998.

___ *Repetition and Identity*, Oxford: Oxford University Press, 2013.

Pound, Marcus, 'The Assumption of Desire: Kierkegaard, Lacan, and the Trauma of the Eucharist', *Journal for Cultural and Religious Theory* 9, no. 1, 2008, 67–78.

___ 'Eucharist and Trauma', *New Blackfriars* 88, no. 1014, 2007, 187–94.

Power, David, *Sacrament: The Language of God's Giving*, New York: Crossroad, 1999.

Purtle, Carol J., *The Marian Paintings of Jan Van Eyck*, Princeton, NJ: Princeton University Press, 1992.

Quash, Ben and Samuel Wells, *Introducing Christian Ethics*, Oxford: Wiley-Blackwell, 2010.

Rahner, Karl, 'The Immaculate Conception', trans. Cornelius Ernst, in *Theological Investigations*, Vol. 1, London: Darton, Longman and Todd, 1954.

Rambo, Shelly, *Spirit and Trauma: A Theology of Remaining*, Louisville, KY: Westminster John Knox Press, 2010.

Redman, Matt, 'Blessed Be Your Name', on *Where Angels Fear to Tread*, Survivor, 2002.

Ross, Susan, 'God's Embodiment and Women: Sacraments', in *Freeing Theology: The Essentials of Theology in Feminist Perspective*, ed. Catherine LaCugna, New York: HarperCollins, 1993, 185–210.

Rubin, Miri, *Corpus Christi: The Eucharist in Late Medieval Culture*, Cambridge: Cambridge University Press, 1991.

Scarry, Elaine, *The Body in Pain: The Making and Unmaking of the World*, New York: Oxford University Press, 1985.

Schillebeeckx, Edward, *Ministry: A Case for Change*, London: SCM Press, 1980.

Schroeder, H. J., *Disciplinary Decrees of the General Councils: Text, Translation and Commentary*, St Louis, MO: B. Herder, 1937.

Shoemaker, S. J., 'The Cult of the Virgin in the Fourth Century: A Fresh Look at Some Old and New Sources', in *The Origins of the Cult of the Virgin Mary*, ed. Chris Maunder, London: Burns & Oates Ltd, 2008, 71–88.

___ 'Epiphanius of Salamis, the Kollyridians, and the Early Dormition Narratives: The Cult of the Virgin in the Fourth Century' (in English), *Journal of Early Christian Studies* 16, no. 3, Fall 2008, 371–401.

Soskice, Janet, 'Trinity and "the Feminine Other"', *New Blackfriars* 75, no. 878, 1994, 2–17.

Steiner, George, *Real Presences: Is There Anything in What We Say?*, London and Boston, MA: Faber and Faber, 1989.

Steiner, Wendy, 'Silence', *London Review of Books* 11, no. 11, 1989, 10–11.

Tanner, Kathryn, *Jesus, Humanity and the Trinity: A Brief Systematic Theology*, Minneapolis, MN: Fortress Press, 2001.

Taylor, G. K., 'The Syriac Tradition', in *The First Christian Theologians*, ed. G. R. Evans, Oxford: Blackwell, 2004, 201–24.

Tonstad, Linn, *God and Difference: The Trinity, Sexuality, and the Transformation of Finitude*, New York and London: Routledge, 2016.

van der Kolk, Bessel, 'The Body Keeps the Score: Memory and the Evolving Psychobiology of Post Traumatic Stress', *Harvard Review of Psychiatry* 1, no. 5, 1994, 253–65.

van der Kolk, Bessel and Alexander McFarlane, 'The Black Hole of Trauma', in *Traumatic Stress*, ed. Bessel van der Kolk, Alexander McFarlane and Lars Weisaeth, New York: Guilford Press, 1996, 3–23.

Vloberg, Maurice, 'The Iconographic Types of the Virgin in Western Art', trans. Imogen Forster Associates, in *Mary: The Complete Resource*, ed. Sarah Jane Boss, Oxford: Oxford University Press, 2007, 547–85.

Ward, Graham, *Christ and Culture*, Oxford: Wiley-Blackwell, 2005.

Waterworth, J., *The Canons and Decrees of the Sacred and Oecumenical Council of Trent*, trans. J. Waterworth, London: Dolman, 1848.

Weinandy, Thomas G., 'Cyril and the Mystery of the Incarnation', in *The Theology of St Cyril of Alexandria: A Critical Appreciation*, ed. Thomas G. Weinandy and Daniel A. Keating, London and New York: T & T Clark, 2003, 23–54.

Wessel, Susan, *Cyril of Alexandria and the Nestorian Controversy: The Making of a Saint and of a Heretic*, Oxford Early Christian Studies, ed. Gillian Clark and Andrew Louth, Oxford: Oxford University Press, 2004.

Wile, Mary Lee, 'Surrogacy or Human DNA: What Happened When Mary Said Yes?', *Daughters of Sarah* 18, no. 4, 1992, 14–15.

Williams, Rowan, 'Epilogue', in *Praying for England: Priestly Presence in Contemporary Culture*, ed. Samuel Wells and Sarah Coakley, London and New York: Continuum, 2008, 171–82.

Wylie, Mary Sykes, 'The Limits of Talk: Bessel van der Kolk Wants to Transform the Treatment of Trauma', *Psychotherapy Networker* 28, no. 1, 2004, 1–11.

Young, Frances, '*Theotokos*: Mary and the Pattern of Fall and Redemption in the Theology of Cyril of Alexandria', in *The Theology of St Cyril of Alexandria: A Critical Appreciation*, ed. Thomas G. Weinandy and Daniel A. Keating, London and New York: T & T Clark, 2003, 55–74.

Index of Biblical References

Index of Names and Subjects